HISTORIOGRAPHY AND URBANIZATION

HISTORIOGRAPHY AND URBANIZATION

*Essays in American History
in Honor of*

W. STULL HOLT

Edited by Eric F. Goldman

BALTIMORE

THE JOHNS HOPKINS PRESS

1941

The men who studied under W. Stull Holt at the Johns Hopkins University will not forget the experience. He made research a quest for meaning, and gave to the quest a gallant and generous comradeship. These essays in historiography and urbanization, the fields of Professor Holt's special interest, have been prepared as an expression of respect and affection.

FOREWORD

Professor Holt directed graduate work in American history at Johns Hopkins from 1930 to 1940, when he became Chairman of the Department of History in the University of Washington. These essays have been written and edited by former students of Professor Holt. The publication of the volume was financed by a large number of other friends.

The editor, Eric F. Goldman, is Instructor in History in the Johns Hopkins University. Of the other contributors, St. Julien Ravenel Childs is Instructor in History in Brooklyn College; Bernard Mayo is Professor of History in the University of Virginia; Ollinger Crenshaw is Assistant Professor of History in Washington and Lee University; Albert K. Weinberg is a member of the Institute for Advanced Study, Princeton University; Charles Hirschfeld is State Editor for Maryland of the Historical Records Survey; Messrs. William Diamond, Donald E. Emerson and Alfred Goldberg are students in the School of Higher Studies at Johns Hopkins.

The Department's pleasure in this tribute to a former colleague is increased by the fact that it is a natural outgrowth of common interests and efforts during the past ten years.

KENT ROBERTS GREENFIELD,

Chairman, Department of History

The Johns Hopkins University
    March 1, 1941.

CONTENTS

CAVALIERS AND BURGHERS IN THE CAROLINA LOW COUNTRY

BY

St. Julien Ravenel Childs

In the past century when many scholars taught that the French Revolution had abruptly destroyed a flourishing feudalism, a concurrent interpretation of history represented the founders of all American colonies south of Pennsylvania, whether Spanish, French, or English, as cavaliers or country squires who with the aid of slaves had created in the New World a society closely patterned after the mediaeval feudal order. If these theories ever had value, it was because of a concept of feudalism that the twentieth century has rejected. West-European feudalism, in even the broadest meaning now given to the term, was unquestionably undermined by the growth of cities before the time of Columbus and it has become fairly obvious that so decadent an institution could not have transplanted itself intact to the new continents. Much as it may have meant to their grandfathers, the present generation see small significance in the resemblance of the mediaeval manor to the Southern plantation or Latin American *hacienda*. To an age preoccupied with the contest between communism and capitalism, it is plain that the manor was essentially communistic, the plantation and *hacienda* capitalistic. It is now a commonplace that but for the rise of urban (or bourgeois) capitalism in Europe, America would not have been discovered, much less colonized. Lest these facets of truth absorb more than their share of light, it may be well to turn the gem a little and recall that feudal Europe was capable of colonization

1

of a sort. Crusaders created in the Levant communities modeled on the feudal order of the West. Teutonic Knights in the North, Spanish Christians in the South, colonized as well as conquered. Colonization did not escape profound alteration by the forces that transformed the rural, feudal, and knightly Europe of the Crusades into the urban, bourgeois, capitalistic Europe of the Revolution, but it must be equally true that the colonization of America was not from the outset an exclusively urban achievement. Light on the relative strength of rural and urban forces in American colonization should be obtainable from a review of the history of any American colony or, better still, from a comparison of two or more colonies planted in the same area at different dates.

Two incidents in the white man's long struggle for a secure foothold on the western shore of the Atlantic between Cuba and Cape Hatteras afford an opportunity for such a comparison. The first incident is the recently rediscovered Spanish settlement of 1566 on the great harbor of Santa Elena, called Port Royal by the French and English, and now in South Carolina. There Spain maintained for ten years the *presidio* or chief post of her unbounded province of Florida, but she transferred the *presidio* to St. Augustine in 1576 and a decade later abandoned St. Elena except as a mission station.[1] The second incident is the much better known English settlement of Charles Town, planted on Ashley River in 1670 near the site of its descendant, the present city of Charleston. The English disobeyed their instructions to settle at Port Royal but the place they chose was only sixty miles further north

[1] Alexander S. Salley, *Parris Island* . . . (Bulletins of the Historical Commission of South Carolina, No. 8, 1926); Woodbury Lowery, *The Spanish Settlements within the present limits of the United States. Florida. 1562-1574* (New York, 1921), pp. 248, 352-353, 440; Herbert E. Bolton, ed., *Arredondo's historical proof of Spain's title to Georgia* (Berkeley, Calif., 1925), pp. 15, 335-336, 341-342.

and in the same sort of country.[2] The Indian tribes of the region were closely related and had changed little since the founding of Santa Elena.[3] Differences between the two colonies must be explained chiefly by changes which had taken place in Europe during the intervening century or, more accurately, by differences between the Spain of 1566 and the England of 1670. Even in the present moment when the world writhes in torments engendered by nationalism, it is not odious to compare the achievements of men of different nations if it be borne in mind that national character, the demagogue's stock in trade, is a thing so elusive and misleading that no honest scholar should attempt to imprison it in phrases, much less to offer it in explanation of any historical event.

The history of the two colonies presents many parallels. Both sprang from royal grants of feudal type conferring authority over the country on hereditary lords.[4] The colony in both cases owed its existence preeminently to one man—Santa Elena to the first *Adelantado* of Florida, Pedro Menéndez de Avilés, who had founded St. Augustine the preceding year, Charles Town to one of the eight original Lords Proprietors of Carolina, Sir Anthony Ashley Cooper, later Earl of Shaftesbury, who without leaving England essayed to manage Carolina affairs for himself and his colleagues.[5] Both Pedro

[2] *Collections of the South Carolina Historical Society* (cited as *SCHS Col*), V, 165-168, 178; Testimony of English prisoners at St. Augustine, October 2, 1671, in Library of Congress Transcripts from the Archives of the Indies at Seville (cited as LCT AGI), 58-1-26; Edward McCrady, *The History of South Carolina under the Proprietary Government, 1670-1719* (New York, 1897), pp. 114-115, 125-126.

[3] Lowery, pp. 58-74; Verner W. Crane, *The Southern Frontier, 1670-1732* (Durham, 1928), pp. 5-38.

[4] Eugenio Ruidíaz y Caravia, *La Florida su conquista y colonización por Pedro Menéndez de Avilés* (Madrid, 1893), II, 419-420; Lowery, pp. 142-143; *The Colonial Records of North Carolina*, I, 20-33, 102-114; McCrady, pp. 65-68.

[5] Lowery, pp. 158-160; McCrady, pp. 62, 94, 156-157; Crane, pp. 4-5, 118-120.

Menéndez and Ashley Cooper tried to derive private profit from their colonial enterprises, apparently without success.[6] Both availed themselves of credit facilities furnished by city bankers.[7] Both tried to plant true colonies, giving free transportation to the first families, extending them credit for supplies, and encouraging agriculture. Both desired their settlers not to scatter but to live compactly in villages or towns after the European fashion.[8] Both courted the friendship of the Indians and tried to prevent the settlers from selling them arms, trespassing on their lands, or carrying them off into slavery.[9] Both men died before the future of their colonies was assured, Menéndez in 1574 when Santa Elena was eight years old, Ashley Cooper in 1683 before Charles Town was thirteen.[10] The more important members of both colonies, holding official positions, usually praised the country and found means of prospering there.[11] The poorer settlers in both cases had trouble farming the strange land, suffered from want in the first winters, resented the Indian's pilfering ways, generally cursed the country, and often ran away.[12] As to moral character and general intelligence, nothing in the records indicates any great difference between the two groups of settlers.

Despite these and other similarities, there were differ-

[6] *Ibid.; Colonial Records of Spanish Florida* (cited as *Fla. Rec.*), I, 238-239, II, 2-3, 212-213.

[7] Ruidíaz, I, 53, 62, II, 95, 133, 159, 181, 192, 195, 517; *SCHS Col* V, 141, 152, 328-331.

[8] *Ibid.*, V, 143-152, 164-165, 311, 314-315, 402-403, 454-455, 466-468; Ruidíaz, II, 99, 199, 201; *Fla. Rec.* I, 82-101, 146-147, 158-159, 176-177, 180.

[9] Ruidíaz, II, 83, 99, 104; McCrady, pp. 106, 177, 201; Crane, pp. 137-139.

[10] Lowery, pp. 383-384; Louise F. Brown, *The First Earl of Shaftesbury* (New York, 1933), pp. 298, 301, 303.

[11] *Fla. Rec.* I, 139-145, 240-247, 249-251, II, 227, 279; *SCHS Col* V, 175, 188-189, 195, 197, 242-259.

[12] Lowery, pp. 225, 261, 352-353; St. Julien R. Childs, *Malaria and Colonization in the Carolina Low Country, 1526-1696* (Johns Hopkins

ences aplenty between the two colonies, and the differences show, as would be expected, that urban forces had much less influence on the earlier enterprise. The Spanish, like the Crusaders of old, began with a military occupation of the country. Not till their fort, garrisoned by from fifty to a hundred of the king's soldiers, had guarded the harbor of Santa Elena for three years did some fifty farmers arrive with their families from Spain and strictly economic activity begin.[13] The English expedition of 1670 included, besides a few women and children, less than a hundred men of military age and none of them were at the time supporting themselves by the profession of arms. They organized an unpaid militia and built a stockade but troubled to mount only a few of the guns which King Charles had given them. In 1680, when they moved Charles Town to the river's mouth, they did not fortify the new site. At Santa Elena, the soldiers were replaced from time to time, but scarcely any more civilian settlers came after the first group. At Charles Town, no soldier of the king was stationed until well on into the eighteenth century but the influx of civilians was almost continuous.[14] As standing armies in the sixteenth and seventeenth centuries were usually officered by scions of the feudal nobility and recruited from the peasantry, predominance of the military in a colony of that day indicates not only that its promoters adhered to mediaeval methods but, also, that rural ideas and customs had direct influence on the colonists.

The clergy of the state churches of Spain and England were likewise drawn largely from the rural classes. At Santa Elena the ecclesiastical element, if not as powerful as in the Crusades, was second only to the military. At

University Studies in Historical and Political Science, Series LVIII, no. 1, Baltimore, 1940), pp. 173-174.

[13] *Ibid.*, pp. 71-73; Lowery, pp. 248, 352-353.

[14] Childs, pp. 74-79, 117-118, 202-203.

Charles Town, it was practically non-existent. The Spanish made a serious effort after the fashion of mediaeval conquerors to convert the natives to European customs and beliefs. Lacking more orthodox missionaries, Menéndez in 1566 directed soldiers whom he quartered on the Indians to teach their hosts Christian manners and doctrines. Jesuit fathers began arriving in 1568, nearly a year before the farmers, but they had small liking for military coadjutors and withdrew abruptly in 1570 when the acting governor distributed a fresh batch of hungry soldiers among the tribal villages. They were temporarily replaced by Franciscans. After the departure of the garrison and settlers in 1586, there were no missionaries for some time, but eventually the Franciscans returned to their task. With occasional military aid, the friars held their ground for many years, teaching the Indians to lead a sedentary agricultural existence similar to that of European peasants.[15] From the expedition that founded Charles Town, ministers of religion were totally absent and none appeared there until about 1680. When they did come, they held no official position and secured no public support until about 1698.[16] There is no indication that they or any of the other settlers concerned themselves about the Indian's religion or way of life.

In relations with the Indians, the place filled by the soldier and missionary at Santa Elena was supplied at Charles Town by the trader. Before they chose a place to settle, the colonists of 1670 began barter with the natives, a fact which they recorded as a matter of course. The letters and reports from Santa Elena ignore the possibilities of this profitable activity. It was carried on secretly or under color of exchange of gifts and had almost no economic significance. For Charles Town, the Indian

[15] Ruidíaz, II, 155-156, 158, 301-308, 465-473; *Fla. Rec.* I, 143, 290, 331, II, 81, 162-169; Bolton, pp. 15-17, 21, 24-25, 342.
[16] McCrady, pp. 330-336.

trade became at once and long remained the principal industry. Incidentally it formed the basis of a system of alliances which protected the colony and at times enabled it to pursue a very aggressive policy.[17] Nor was this the only commerce in which Charles Town engaged. She was slow to find commodities for the markets of Europe and the North but began in 1670 to ship lumber to the English West Indies and soon added maize, peas, tobacco, salt pork, deer skins, and Indian slaves. Presently those ancient enemys of Spain, the buccaneers, whose depredations had brought ruin to Santa Elena, came to the new port to vend their spoil and found a welcome despite the prohibition of Proprietors and Crown.[18] In so far as the triumph of commerce over arms and religion may be a true index, the history of Santa Elena and Charles Town clearly foreshadows the victory of urban over rural forces in the colonization of America.

In agriculture, the contrast between the two colonies is less striking but scarcely less significant. The late arrival of civilian settlers explains the failure of the Spanish to begin serious cultivation of the soil until 1569 but even after that date they practiced only provision farming. Although the idea must have occurred to them, they recorded no attempt to find an agricultural product suitable for export even to the neighboring island of Cuba. The English began to experiment for a money crop so promptly and eagerly that their principal leader, Joseph West, himself no planter but a London merchant, had difficulty in persuading them to " provide for ye belly." In spite of many disappointments, the settlers persisted for over twenty-five years until at last success was achieved with rice, said to have been brought by pirates from Madagascar.[19]

[17] *SCHS Col* V, 165-168; Crane, pp. 6-7, 17-21, 139.
[18] Childs, pp. 136-138, 183, 195-198, 205-208, 229.
[19] Childs, *passim*; Alexander S. Salley, *The Introduction of Rice Culture*

One reason for the unadventurous character of farming at Santa Elena was that operations were restricted to the small island where stood the fort and the farmers' village. The soldiers farmed in their spare time, they married the farmers' daughters, and the sons of farmers enlisted for service in the garrison. Even the Spanish officials apparently did not attempt to establish *haciendas* in the surrounding country but dwelt with their wives and families in the fort. Indeed the island with its moated castle, cultivated plots, and flat roofed cottages plastered with lime must have resembled many a rural community of mediaeval Spain.[20] Charles Town wore no such aspect. As soon as the English ventured to leave the shelter of their stockade and start building houses, they began to scatter and go to live on their farms in defiance of Ashley Cooper's wishes. Those who stayed in the town planted crops in the streets and vacant lots. The town had a plan but each family built its dwelling and outhouses according to its own ideas so that as early as 1672 a Spaniard on a diplomatic mission from St. Augustine was startled by the irregularity.[21] A modern American would probably have had little difficulty in recognizing a frontier trading post.

Private titles to land, prized from the start by the settlers of Charles Town, apparently did not interest the colonists of Santa Elena. The *Adelantados* of Florida, unlike the Lords of Carolina, were not made proprietors of the soil. Nor did Menéndez encourage the importation of Negro slaves which Ashley Cooper rewarded with large bounties of land. A few Indian and other captives were forced to labor at Santa Elena but they were not used in

into South Carolina (Bulletin of the Historical Commission of South Carolina, no. 6, Columbia, 1919), *passim.*
[20] *Fla. Rec.* I, 144-185, 244-247, 282-283, II, 227; Bolton, p. 336.
[21] Deposition of Antonio Camuñas, July 12, 1672, LCT AGI 61-1-18; *SCHS Col* V, frontispiece, 361, 437-438, 441, 446.

private industry nor did slaves become a commodity in trade. The English expedition of 1670 included at least three Negroes belonging to the governor, and in spite of the failure to discover a money crop, other settlers from the West Indies brought in many more.[22] In other words, agriculture at Santa Elena was provision farming, aiming to make the community more nearly self-sufficient, carried on by peasant labor, and resting on what amounted to public ownership of land. Agriculture at Charles Town, after one hasty "common planting" of provisions in 1670, was capitalistic. Its aim was to produce a money crop. It was based on slave labor and private ownership of land.

Between the people who engaged in the two enterprises, there is a corresponding contrast. Menéndez and Ashley Cooper were both technically squires but the Englishman belonged to a small group of squires who were quite as much at home in the City of London as in the country and so had little in common with the majority of their class either in England or elsewhere. Pedro Menéndez was a squire of the common country variety, a cavalier. Impoverished by the rising prices of his time, he early saw in the service of his king the only possible road to fortune. He was a great black-bearded man, an able seaman, a courageous soldier, a resourceful leader, as ruthless to the enemy as he was loyal to family and friends. The authority of Crown and Church he accepted unquestioningly, even with enthusiasm. Ashley Cooper was a squire whose ancestors by inclosures and other forms of land grabbing, by shrewd commercial investments and prudent marriages with bourgeois heiresses had left him vast income-bearing rural estates as well as important interests in the City. Of slight frame, delicate health, keen mind, and limitless ambition, he preferred the contests of the counting house

[22] Childs, pp. 65-67, 70, 132-139, 183, 186, 195-198, 207-208, 237, 263-264.

and council chamber to those involving physical combat with men or nature. A professed Anglican with a patriotic hatred of Rome, he was hostile to the clergy, skeptical of their doctrine, reverential of astrologers, and credulous of horoscopes. Though scrupulously honest in financial dealings, public as well as private, the real Ashley Cooper had no more sense of political loyalty than the Achitophel of Dryden's satire. Pedro Menéndez sought in Florida besides rehabilitation of his family's fortunes, only the aggrandizement of the Spanish Church and State. Ashley Cooper framed for the autonomous province of Carolina a written constitution creating a deistic, timocratic republic such as he wished to see in England. There were to be no ecclesiastical privileges, and political privileges including titles of nobility were to be distributed in rough accordance with private ownership of land exempt, of course, from the payment of feudal aids and services or any other equivalent for economic rent.[23] The chasm that separated the minds of these two men was evidently far wider than the short century that lay between their times.

The lieutenants of Menéndez at Santa Elena were recruited largely among his numerous relatives and former companions in arms. The settlers he sent there were Spanish peasants. The majority of the soldiers, as already noted, were presumably of peasant stock. Shortly after the death of Menéndez, the Crown took over Florida, but it appointed as governor his nephew, Pedro Menéndez Marques, who had, he said, been born and bred in the navy and whose policies were substantially the same as his

---

[23] The first set of the Fundamental Constitutions of Carolina, containing 81 articles, was drawn July 21, 1669. The New York Public Library and the British Public Record Office have MS copies. The latter was printed in the Appendix to the thirty-third report of the Deputy Keeper of the Public Records. The second set, drawn March 1, 1669/70, contains 120 articles. The Proprietors printed it in pamphlet form (copy in John Carter Brown Library), and MS copies have been printed in *The Colonial Records of North Carolina*, I, 187-205, and *SCHS Col*, V, 93-117.

uncle's. Two civil officials, doubtless of bourgeois origin, were presently sent to assist him but their powers proved inadequate to restrain the resolute and resourceful governor.[24] The lieutenants of Ashley Cooper at Charles Town were almost without exception personally unknown to him, and his control over them dwindled as the colony grew. Sir Peter Colleton, the Lord Proprietor who succeeded Ashley Cooper in the management of Carolina affairs, was a West Indian nabob and London merchant, more interested in making money out of the colony than in ruling it. The balance of power swung steadily to the more well-to-do settlers from whose number local officials were chosen. Many of these came directly from England where they had usually been small merchants or tradesmen. Such was Joseph West, the level-headed Quaker who was governor off and on for more than ten years between 1670 and 1685.[25] Others had spent some time in older colonies, particularly Barbados where by 1670 large-scale sugar growing was squeezing out the lesser planters. For his services in interesting his neighbors in Carolina, John Yeamans of Barbados, the son of a Bristol brewer, received broad acres from the Lords Proprietors and a baronetcy from the Crown, but Ashley Cooper removed him from the governorship at Charles Town in 1674 for taking advantage of the settlers' necessities to buy their provisions cheap.[26] A colony founded under Ashley

[24] Ruidíaz, II, 178-179, 235, 245, 251, 291-292, 718; *Fla. Rec.* I, 17, 100-103, 127, 129, 131, 207, II, 3, 264-281, 303-307.
[25] Byrle J. Osborn, "Governor Joseph West," *The New York Genealogical and Biographical Record* (1934), LXV, 202-205, LXVI, 90; Henry A. M. Smith, "Joseph West, Landgrave and Governor," *The South Carolina Historical and Genealogical Magazine* (cited as *SCHGM*): (1918), XIX, 189-193; (1919), XX, 147-149.
[26] M. Alston Read, "Notes of some Colonial Governors of South Carolina and their Families," *ibid.* (1910), XI, 107-122; Henry A. M. Smith, "Sir John Yeamans, an Historical Error," *ibid.* (1918), XIX, 152-156.

Cooper's aegis naturally attracted Whigs and Noncon-
formists rather than Tory Anglicans. The Whig con-
spiracies that followed the defeat of the Exclusion Bill
were conducted under cover of schemes for the settlement
of Carolina, and the Tory reaction led some well-to-do
Whig merchants to migrate to Charles Town about 1682.
Among them were Daniel Axtell of London, son of the
regicide, and Benjamin Blake of Bridgewater, a younger
brother of the great Puritan admiral, Robert Blake.[27]
Some of the most successful planters had followed the
sea in their youth. West, Blake, and others had been naval
officers. Many more had been officers of merchantmen
or privateers. The only British nobleman known to have
visited Charles Town before 1700 was the Scottish Earl of
Cardross, a Whig, who with the financial support of a
Glasgow merchant brought a small group of his fellow
countrymen to settle at Port Royal in 1684. Most of them
were convicts. By arming his Indian allies to raid Spanish
missions for slaves, Cardross provoked retaliation from
St. Augustine, but before the Spanish struck in 1686, the
Earl had returned to Europe, disgruntled by Charles
Town's refusal to let him engross the southern Indian
trade.[28] The most prominent Tory to join the colony
during the century was Sir Nathaniel Johnson, Knight,
who resigned his post as governor of the Leeward Islands
on the fall of James II and retired to Carolina. He was
a mercer and former mayor of Newcastle-upon-Tyne, and
had sat for his borough at Westminster.[29] A very few of

[27] Alexander S. Salley, "Landgrave Daniel Axtell," *ibid.* (1905), VI,
174-175; McCrady, pp. 194, 269, 402; Great Britain, Public Record
Office, *Calendar of State Papers, Domestic, Reign of Charles II, 1678,*
pp. 290-291.

[28] Childs, pp. 221-223, 231, 235, 239-241, 259.

[29] W. H. D. Longstaffe, ed., *Memoirs of the Life of Mr. Ambrose
Barnes* (Publications of the Surtees Society, L, Durham, England, 1867),
p. 162; Great Britain, Public Record Office, *Calendar of State Papers,
Colonial Series, America and West Indies* (cited as *CSP AWI*), pp. 86-91.

the many French Huguenots who came to Charles Town before 1700 belonged to families recently ennobled, but socially and by occupation practically all were bourgeois.[30] Of the poorer settlers generally, the majority came as indentured servants. Apparently these were usually picked up where it was easiest to get them, that is on the streets of British ports, particularly London, or in Barbados where no public land remained for distribution. There is no evidence of peasants transplanted from rural villages in Europe like the settlers of Santa Elena. To Santa Elena, so far as the records show, no man went without having his transportation supplied either by the *Adelantado* or the crown. To Charles Town there was practically no free transportation after 1670 except for servants and slaves. The growth of the colony resulted chiefly from the coming of men who paid their own way and brought enough capital to set themselves up in trade if not to start a plantation. If successful, they sent for their families and imported servants and slaves. Occasionally an ex-servant saved enough money to imitate the example of his betters. Commercial talent or training was as indispensable at Charles Town as it had been worthless at Santa Elena. Not only was trade the chief industry of the English colony but its capitalistic farming and stock raising bore scant resemblance to anything in the experience of an English peasant or rustic squire. While the stumps of trees rotted slowly in the cleared land and his fields became free for the plow, the planter could learn at leisure the art of growing maize, sweet potatoes, cow peas, tobacco, indigo, and rice along with the jabbering black savages who had more to learn than he. What he had to know from the start was how to trade not only with skippers of colonial merchantmen or dealers in the port but also with wandering Indian tribes, how to sell and buy

---

[30] Act of Naturalization, March 10, 1696/7, in Thomas Cooper and D. J. McCord, eds., *The Statutes at Large of South Carolina*, II, 131-133.

not only things but men. Had Pedro Menéndez and his
followers understood that art and practiced it a century
before, it is safe to say that there would have been no
English colony at Charles Town in 1670. It was because
the founders of Charles Town were the sons not of country
squires but of urban business men that their colony lived
and grew.[31]

Many writers have contrasted the dependence of Spain's
American colonies on the central government with the
autonomy enjoyed by the colonies of England. Although
the picture is often overdrawn, it is clear that Santa Elena
was more directly created and controlled by the Spanish
Crown than Charles Town by the English. The fact itself
evidences the growth of urban influence on colonization.
Spanish merchants trading with America in 1566, such as
Pedro del Castillo, the merchant of Seville who was
Menéndez's banker, were in no position to demand a
share in the management of hazardous colonial enterprises.[32] They still leaned heavily on the Crown for protection not only against the buccaneers but also against
unsympathetic noblemen and ecclesiastics in colonial
offices. In England by 1670 the political decay of feudalism and the Church had progressed much further. The
chief merchants in the colonial trade had come to be great
capitalistic landlords like Ashley Cooper, who feared
royal absolutism and ecclesiastical intolerance more than
any private foe, foreign or domestic. Instead of relying on
assistance from Church and Crown like Menéndez, the
Lords Proprietors of Carolina secured the cooperation of
small capitalists in the settlement of Charles Town by
allowing them what amounted to free land, free trade,
freedom of religion, and a large measure of control over
the colonial government. The Lords Proprietors made

[31] McCrady, pp. 189, 315-318, 323, 343-352.
[32] On Castillo see Ruidíaz, I, 53, 62, II, 95, 133, 159, 181, 192, 195,
517.

some of these concessions slowly and grudgingly but the possessors of fluid capital would not go to the colony without them. As most of the possessors of fluid capital were townsmen, it is to urban influence that the autonomy of the colony must be attributed.

Yet between Santa Elena and Charles Town, the difference in autonomy was not so great as might be supposed, nor did it always operate to promote a greater degree of individual liberty in the English settlement. Communication between Santa Elena and Madrid was so slow that colonial officials could not in emergencies await the decision of higher authority, and even deliberate disobedience sometimes escaped unpunished because of cumbersome administrative machinery. For example, in 1570 the acting governor of Florida took half his troops back to Spain on his own initiative, alleging that there was not supplies enough in the Province to feed and clothe his men.[33] In 1576, Miranda, the second *Adelantado,* withdrew both garrison and settlers from Santa Elena in defiance of the known wishes of the Crown.[34] The official investigations which sometimes preceded and always followed acts like these afforded common soldiers and peasant settlers an opportunity of recording their grievances such as never came to the slaves, servants, and landless freemen who made a large majority of the colonists at Charles Town. The village at Santa Elena had the political organization of similar communities in Spain. All householders including widows and spinsters attended the public meeting and presumably participated in the choice of village officials. On at least one occasion, the Santa Elena meeting sent a petition to the King.[35] At Charles Town, a colonial parliament chosen by male freeholders could until 1690 discuss only matters proposed to it by a Grand Council selected partly by the Parliament and

[33] *Fla. Rec.* I, 292-321.   [34] *Ibid.,* I, 188-203.   [35] *Ibid.,* I, 147-187.

partly by the Proprietors but dominated in practice by a small group of well-to-do settlers.[36] Reading how in 1576 the women of Santa Elena expedited evacuation of the place by seizing the vacillating *Adelantado,* Miranda, and putting him forcibly aboard ship, or how these same women followed their men back to the post a year later in contumacy of the doughty Governor Marques, one wonders if the Spanish system were not in reality more democratic than the English.[37] Perhaps it was only more chivalric. However that may be, the lowliest settlers at Santa Elena evinced no more desire than their superiors to engage in trade or other capitalistic occupations. Widely as they disagreed on other topics, Crown, *Adelantados,* colonial officers, soldiers, clergy, and settlers seem not to have differed materially as to the purposes for which Santa Elena existed or the aims which its economy should pursue. Much the same agreement in regard to Charles Town seems to have obtained among the various human elements concerned in that settlement. If this be true, it explains the most striking differences between the two enterprises without reference to the degree of authority or freedom enjoyed by particular persons or groups in either colony. It becomes clear that Santa Elena failed because its people as well as its promoters were rural folk, born and bred in the traditions of declining feudalism; Charles Town succeeded because people and promoters alike were predominantly townsmen, uncomprehending of feudal concepts, saturated with the ideology of rising capitalism.

To find the place of Santa Elena and Charles Town in the history of West European colonization, it is necessary to look not only back to the Crusades but, also, forward to what is sometimes called the era of modern imperialism.

[36] Kathleen Singleton, " The Grand Council of South Carolina," *The Proceedings of the South Carolina Historical Association, 1934,* pp. 32-47.
[37] *Fla. Rec.* I, 198-203, 267-271.

In respect to colonial autonomy, to actual colonization by Europeans, and to individual economic enterprise among settlers, recent European expansion has obviously followed the pattern of Santa Elena more closely than that of Charles Town. As European society has continued to become steadily more urban, a question arises as to why European colonization, instead of developing along the lines it was apparently following in the seventeenth century, should have reverted to an earlier model. In the comparison of Santa Elena and Charles Town, a clue to this enigma may be found. All of the forces that combined in the English enterprise to differentiate it from the Spanish did not harmonize. Among the mediaeval ideas that influenced the history of Santa Elena were some that might have strengthened colonization of the type found at Charles Town, and some institutions conspicuous at Charles Town had an obvious capacity for leading colonization back to the model of Santa Elena. For example, the use of Negro and Indian slaves in private industry was logically inconsistent with Charles Town's relatively free institutions and dangerous to their future in European colonization. But slavery, perhaps because it was not deeply rooted in the historic economy of the mediaeval city, was destined to disappear before the era of modern imperialism. Present in the founding of Charles Town were other institutions more durable than slavery and more directly traceable to urban influence, but equally incompatible with economic individualism, colonial autonomy, and actual colonization by European settlers.

The Lords Proprietors of Carolina, though unincorporated, were a prototype of the great corporations that have dominated colonial activity in recent years. The Carolina charter combined the grant of political powers with economic privileges of unlimited scope. According to the letter of the charter, it would have been wholly legal for the grantees to monopolize the trade of their

province or to withold the land itself from actual settlers. To the Proprietors, such laws seemed natural and
right. Individually they derived their wealth largely from
monopolies. They were members of privileged corporations such as the Royal African Company,[38] and their
extensive lands, rural as well as urban, were no longer
held in a feudal tenure requiring substantial services or
payments to the Crown but privately owned in the same
sense that much earlier sharp mediaeval burghers in all
parts of Europe had acquired what amounted to individual ownership of the land on which their towns stood.
At Charles Town, the Proprietors tried to use their political power for economic ends. They strove to monopolize
the Indian trade to the exclusion of the settlers, and to
reserve for themselves large tracts of undeveloped land
within the settled area. Some of them attempted to
operate private plantations through paid agents.[39] It is
safe to assume that they would have exploited more land
themselves and held the rest out of use until they could
sell it to advantage, just as they would have cornered the
Indian trade and dictated to the colony in political matters, had it not been for the difficulty of communication,
an obstacle which time has removed from the path of their
successors.

Although some sixteenth-century Spanish colonial
schemes may have held the germ of an organization like
that of the Carolina Proprietors, nothing resembling it
can be detected in the settlement of Santa Elena. Pedro
Menéndez was not a wealthy man and he was not granted

[38] Six of the eight Proprietors were members of the old African Com-
pany in 1667, Elizabeth Donnan, ed., *Documents Illustrative of the
History of the Slave Trade to America* (Washington, 1930), I, 169-172.
When the Company was reorganized in 1672, Ashley Cooper became
deputy governor; Craven, Carteret, and Colleton became assistants. *CSP
AWI, 1669-1647*, pp. 410-411.

[39] Crane, pp. 4-5, 18-21; *SCHS Col* V, 127-129, 263-273, 297, 315-
318, 366, 438-447; Henry A. M. Smith, "The Colleton Family in South
Carolina," *SCHGM* (1900), I, 324-341.

the land of Florida. He sent his family there and expected
to live there. He had no partners, and his borrowings
from the capitalist, Pedro del Castillo, entailed no grant
of political powers. The *Adelantado* and his settlers
were as far from scheming to hold the land of Florida
out of use for a rise in value as Castillo was from planning a corporation to monopolize its trade.

Even in seventeenth-century Charles Town, the age
of monopoly still lay far in the future. Some of the more
prosperous settlers quickly formed partnerships with merchants in other colonies but they were even less able than
the Proprietors to gain exclusive control of any branch of
commerce. The Proprietors not only failed in their attempts at trade monopoly but they did not cooperate with
the Crown in its efforts to enforce the Navigation Laws.[40]
As for the land, the interest displayed by the well-to-do
settlers in the validity of their titles probably sprang more
from their desire to safeguard their improvements than
from the hope of selling unimproved land. Tracts held out
of use by Proprietors and a few other speculators increased
so slowly in value that they did relatively little harm. The
reality was that any freeman could obtain at nominal cost
as much land as he could use, and small benefit derived
from having more. Prosperity in the settlement depended
in the main on the productive employment of capital,
whether in trade or agriculture, and the investments of
would-be monopolists, including the Proprietors, generally resulted in loss. From their point of view the colony
was an utter failure. It survived their displeasure because
there was then in European towns an abundance of real
capitalists, not exigent of special privileges but willing
to take their chance where land and trade were free.

Yet if the various persons and groups concerned in the

[40] Great Britain, House of Lords, *Manuscripts*, New Series, II, 7, 21,
412, 440-441, 465-466.

settlement of Charles Town denied to one another the fruits of monopoly, they laid no axe to the root of the tree. The settlers apparently doubted no more than the Crown or the Proprietors the right of the state to grant unlimited private ownership of land and to create privileged corporations. Acceptance of these monopolistic concepts was significant for the future of colonization. When kings, bishops, and other relics of feudalism should finally have disappeared from practical politics, private promoters of colonial enterprises would again become able to cooperate with the state as cheerfuly as Pedro Menéndez with Philip II. When colonial traders should no longer venture to snap their fingers in the faces of customs officials, free trade would be a thing of the past and the successors of Ashley Cooper would find it easy to exploit their distant concessions without the interposition of such small merchants as Joseph West. When corporations should become powerful enough to enforce their legal privileges at any distance, land would become scarce everywhere and its owners able to exact as much for its use as the community could pay. The legal freedom which laborers even in colonies would by then have achieved would become in regions far from the seats of power a thing to arouse the pity of a well kept slave. With trade and land no more free in remote places than in metropolitan areas, capitalists, however small, would have no more incentive to emigrate than laborers, and actual colonization would have to give way to mere conquest. There would, indeed, be no more small capitalists to speak of in the West European world but only great monopolists, and the sons of burghers would become their hirelings. Yet privileged corporations and the freeing of landlords from obligations to society were not rural but urban ideas.

LEXINGTON: FRONTIER METROPOLIS

BY

Bernard Mayo

Just as California was the Promised Land for the distressed Okies of the 1930's, Kentucky was the Promised Land for the migrants of the 1790's. The Joad family and other dispossessed farmers, whose westward trek John Steinbeck has recorded in *Grapes of Wrath*, were quickly and terribly disillusioned when they reached their fancied Canaan. The migrants of the 1790's were far more fortunate, even though some of them upon their arrival, as Moses Austin recorded, were " exausted and worn down with distress and disappointment" and " Oblig'd to become the hewers of wood and Drawers of water."

In his journey from Virginia in December of 1796 Austin encountered

many Distress'd families . . . Travelling a Wilderness Through Ice and Snow passing large rivers and Creeks with out Shoe or Stocking, and barely as maney raggs as covers their Nakedness. . . . Ask these Pilgrims what they expect when they git to Kentuckey the Answer is Land. have you any. No, but I expect I can git it. have you any thing to pay for land. No. . . . can any thing be more Absurd than the Conduct of man, here is hundreds Travelling hundreds of Miles, they Know not for what Nor Whither, except its to Kentucky, passing land almost as good and easy obtain'd . . . but it will not do its not Kentuckey its not the Promis'd Land its not the goodly inheratence the Land of Milk and Honey. and when arriv'd at this Heaven in Idea what do they find? a goodly land I will allow but to them forbiden Land. . . ." [1]

[1] George P. Garrison, ed., " A Memorandum of M. Austin's Journey from . . . Virginia to . . . the Province of Louisiana . . . 1796-1797," *American Historical Review* (1900), V, 525-526.

21

Only a partial picture was painted by Austin. Pilgrims of all classes, afflicted with the " Kentucky fever," were going westward over Boone's Wilderness Road and down the winding Ohio to the rich Bluegrass region about Lexington, that fabulous land " where principalities are acquired and real Lords of Creation will arise." [2] Along with the Joads of the 1790's, quickened by the common hope of economic betterment, were business pioneers like Austin himself, speculators in land and trade, lawyers, yeoman farmers, and planters. Virginians predominated among these migrants to Kentucky, and a considerable number of them were of established reputation and fortune. One of this class wrote a description of his journey in 1796 which sharply contrasts with Austin's account of the same year. His description, and a bowing acquaintance with the man himself, help one to understand the social texture of the Bluegrass frontier and the rapidity with which its metropolis of Lexington evolved from a stockaded station to a center of industry and culture approximating and rivalling those of seaboard America.

This migrant of 1796 was Colonel David Meade, of Maycox plantation in Tidewater Virginia, a wealthy man despite reverses suffered during and after the Revolution. Educated at Harrow, in Tory England, yet an ardent Jeffersonian Republican, Meade held political views which served as an incitant of his " Kentucky fever." Samuel Hopkins, another propertied Republican who migrated to Kentucky, expressed a rather general feeling when he pictured Eastern America, under the " Mock Republicanism " of Washington's pro-British administration, as " Scuffling Shifting, wreathing and distorting itself to keep up the farsical appearance of Plenty & Greatness." In contrast, the " Rich New Country " of Kentucky, " endowing naturally its owners with ease & affluence as well as preserving

---

[2] John Taylor to ———, Richmond, June 23, 1790, Henry Clay MSS, Library of Congress.

them from the infection of prodigality & the poison of Aristocracy," gave promise of Republican freedom and contentment.[3]   Like Hopkins, and like the poor devils Austin passed on the Wilderness Road, David Meade saw Kentucky through rose-colored glasses.   More interesting, after his arrival and down to his death thirty years later, he continued to sing the praises of this goodly land and of its people.

Meade departed from the worn-out tobacco lands of Southside Virginia for the lush plains of central Kentucky in June of 1796.   He went overland through the mountains to Redstone on the Monongahela, floated down the Ohio to Limestone (Maysville), and then drove overland to Lexington.   With his coaches and " a chair," with three wagons loaded with household goods and twenty-one horses, he and his family and his slaves travelled comfortably, even luxuriously.

The passage from Winchester to our place of embarkation on the western waters [he reported] was much more easy than we expected—(I flatter myself) like all other evils of life either real or imaginary—the horrors of the Aleganys diminished on a near approach no howling Wolves—croaking Ravens—or growling Bears were heard . . . in the stead of those savage sounds— we were frequently cheered by the Plowmans whistle—the Waggoner cracking his whip—the Mower wheting his sythe . . . nor is this all that we have to say in favor of this much misrepresented region . . . we on the Aleganys [found] good Taverns.

After fourteen pleasantly uneventful days on the Ohio he landed at Limestone, Kentucky, on July Fourth.   In the excitement of the landfall one of his slaves " in a drunken frolic left his mistress without a driver," and some time was spent in retrieving this runaway slave and a runaway pointer bitch.   On July 7, 1796, the Meades

[3] Samuel Hopkins to John Breckinridge, March 29, 1794, Breckinridge MSS, Library of Congress.

3

were well within the Bluegrass.   After breakfasting at
Paris, in Bourbon County, " a very increasing Village—
and the best built of any I have seen in my travels," the
Colonel pushed on to Lexington with his carriages and
wagons and horses and slaves, arriving that day before
sunset " inveloped in a cloued of dust—all in good health
& good spirits—at this famed center of Kentucky." [4]

Unlike the penniless, horseless, and landless pilgrims
described by Austin, David Meade before migrating possessed 320 acres of first-rate land in Fayette County, nine
miles from Lexington.[5]   Upon his arrival he was able to
purchase 228 acres adjoining his tract, paying for this £4
an acre.   He was able to lodge his family in Lexington
until hired artisans had built an expensive, ingenious, and
tasteful house on his new Bluegrass plantation, which he
called " Chaumiere des Prairies."   In seven months from
his departure for the so-called " Wild Woods of Kentucky," the Colonel estimated that he had expended the
very large sum of £1,000.

It was money well spent, for Meade was delighted with
the luxuriant country and declared himself incapable of
painting it in colors sufficiently glowing.   He was delighted also with the many Virginians of family and kin-
dred tastes whom he found in Lexington and its vicinity—
men such as Buckner Thruston, a well-educated lawyer of
delicate sensibilities; Colonel Gabriel Madison, brother
of Bishop Madison of William and Mary College; and
Colonel George Thompson, whose plantation Meade declared was a worthy rival of the famous Westover of the
Byrds in the Old Dominion.   Meade's daughter Sally
during the first few days pined and sighed for the social

[4] David Meade to [John Driver?], Aug. 14, 1796, David Meade MSS,
in possession of Professor Robert Henning Webb of the University of
Virginia, kindly made available to me by Mrs. Helen Bullock, of the
University of Virginia, who is preparing a biography of Meade.

[5] In 1798 this section of Fayette became part of the new county of
Jessamine.

delights of the Tidewater, but only for a few days as the Colonel was glad to note. For Sally's "vapor soon exhaled and after a Ball or two—many Tea parties, and much flirtation—her Ladyship soon became as zealous a Lexingtonian as any in it." [6]

*　　*　　*

That Sally Meade's vapors could be so quickly dissipated was in itself evidence of the rapid strides Lexington had already made since 1782, when from the fort at Lexington the few Early Adventurers sent this piteous appeal to the Governor of Virginia:

> We can scarcely behold a spot of Earth but what reminds us of the fall of some fellow adventurer massacred by Savage hands. Our number of militia decreases . . . our officers and worthiest men fall a sacrifice. In short, sir, our settlement, hitherto formed at the Expence of Treasure & much Blood seems to decline, & if something is not speedily done, we doubt will wholly be depopulated.[7]

No longer were Lexingtonians a small band of Indian-fighters, in a few dirty cabins, striving desperately to sustain themselves in what was then truly a Dark and Bloody Ground. When the Meades arrived in 1796, Lexington, with a population approaching sixteen hundred, was the largest town in all Western America, larger than Pittsburgh at the head of the Ohio, and over three times as large as Cincinnati. It was the metropolis of the pioneers' "Land of the Western Waters." Yet it was altogether an inland town: the Kentucky River which ran down to the Ohio was some fifteen miles away. No heed was taken of the prediction made by General Victor Collot, a French visitor of 1796, that in time Lexington must yield

---

[6] Meade to Joseph Prentis, "Chaumiere des Prairies," Dec. 12, 1796; and to same, June 13, 1797, Meade MSS.

[7] *Calendar of Virginia State Papers* (11 vols., Richmond, 1875-1893), III, 301.

its supremacy to one of the river towns.[8] Located on the main overland arteries of trade and migration, and containing for its size an extraordinary number of enterprising promoters, Lexington was and confidently expected to remain the distributing and manufacturing, the political and cultural, center for Kentucky and for most of that vast region called " The Western World."

All visitors were astonished by " the immense amount of business " transacted in this booming wilderness metropolis, this " Philadelphia of Kentucky." [9] Migrants in a steady stream passed along Main Street, with its stores, taverns, stone courthouse, and Cheapside Market, and in passing bought supplies of all kinds. There was an incessant bartering. Kentucky's hemp, tobacco, and foodstuffs, for which Lexingtonians received specie downriver at Spanish New Orleans, were here exchanged for domestic articles and for the imported British goods and Parisian luxuries which land caravans brought in, via Limestone on the Ohio, from Baltimore and Philadelphia. At Andrew McCalla's, near the Stray Pen for wandering hogs and horses, one could exchange wheat and whiskey for " Just Imported French Medicines & Paints, copper stills, needles, wines, teas, and razors." At Lawson McCullough's Colonel Meade and Sally could pay in produce for " Ladies fashionable riding coats with vest and habit; Gents tight and loose coats, vests and small clothes, tight overalls and pantaloons with feet." About everything a Kentuckian or a passing migrant could desire was stocked by the Lexington merchants; everything from Lexington cloth and ironmongery to Dechard rifles and Hooper's female pills.[10]

---

[8] Victor Collot, *A Journey in North America* (Florence, 1924), p. 103.

[9] Lewis Condict, " Journal of a Trip to Kentucky in 1795," *Proceedings of the New Jersey Historical Society* (1919), n. s., IV, 120.

[10] *Kentucky Gazette*, Lexington, 1796-1797; and see Bernard Mayo, *Henry Clay, Spokesman of the New West* (Boston, 1937), pp. 54 ff., for a detailed account of Lexington and Kentucky, 1797-1812.

By the turn of the century Lexington had taken on many of the characteristics of a settled Eastern community. Horse-racing in the streets had been prohibited, along with the playing of Long Bullets, that popular frontier game in which a cannon ball was jerked about, sometimes to the injury of passers-by. This " Athens of the West" was the seat of infant Transylvania University, two newspapers, a public subscription library; of jockey clubs, churches, schools of fencing, French, and dancing. Debating clubs were active; dramas were given in the courthouse; Tom Paine's *Rights of Man* and Lord Chesterfield's *Letters* sold well; and young dandies in skin-tight pantaloons, escorting ladies in muslins with a yard-long trains, red morocco slippers, and turbans à la mode, could be seen sauntering along the plank sidewalks.

Buckskinned pioneers for miles around marvelled at the mansions and fine furniture of the Bluegrass gentry, and grumbled at the " rag money " and easy profits of Lexington's bank, the first in the West, by which the town's business pioneers overcame in part the handicaps of a primitive economy. In forest clearings and cross-road taverns many a tale was spun about that prince of merchant-manufacturers, Colonel Thomas Hart, who was making money hand over fist from his extensive wholesale and retail business; from his flatboats of produce sent down to Orleans via the Kentucky, Ohio and Mississippi; from the cordage and cotton-bagging and sail-duck made at his ropewalk and factory; from his smithy with four forges, his nailery, brickyard, and other enterprises. Colonel Hart, a " real Lord of Creation," admitted that his business pioneering was " a very pretty thing in this country," and invited his Eastern friends to join him at Lexington " in raking up Money and spending it with our friends." [11]

[11] Thomas Hart to William Blount, Feb. 15, 1795 (copy), Henry Clay MSS.

In 1802 Lexington's prosperity received a check when France and Britain by signing the Peace of Amiens deflated abnormal wartime markets. In the same year the Spaniards at New Orleans closed the Mississippi, the great outlet for the bumper crops of Western America. But good times soon returned, and in greater measure, with the purchase of Louisiana and the resumption of the great European war. Lexington's business and professional men steadily prospered also from the influx of settlers to "the fat and prolific vales of Kentucky," to "these immense and fertile regions" which seemed destined to be "the asylum common to all the inhabitants of the globe." [12] We in Kentucky, wrote Thomas Hart early in 1805, "have had a greater Emigration from Virginia and Carolinas than were experienced in two years before . . . our numbers will double before the next Census." [13]

Their numbers did double. Lexington's population in 1810 (and Kentucky's likewise) was four times that of 1790, and double that of 1800.[14] The home market increased, land values went up, and out from Lexington went more farmers' produce along with more cordage and sailcloth and other articles to supply the wants of the Lower South, of the European belligerents, and of neutral America's great merchant marine.

Some idea of the profitable activity by which Lexington maintained its supremacy over the towns of Western America, with the exception of the newly acquired port of New Orleans, may be derived from Fortescue Cuming's account of the frontier metropolis in 1807. Lexington,

[12] F. A. Michaux, *Travels to the Westward of the Allegheny Mountains, 1802* (Reuben Gold Thwaites, ed., *Early Western Travels 1748-1846*, III, Cleveland, 1904), p. 161.

[13] Hart to James Brown, Jan. 27, 1805, James Brown MSS, Library of Congress.

[14] Richard H. Collins, *History of Kentucky* (2 vols., Covington, Ky., 1878), II, 258-267, has convenient population charts of Kentucky, her towns and counties, 1790-1870.

then with a population of about 3,000, had four rope-
walks with sixty hands making 300 tons of cordage annually; a baling-cloth factory with thirty-eight hands turning out 36,000 yards; three nail factories producing 60
tons of nails; and six powder mills making 20,000 pounds
a year.   There were two cotton-spinning machines, an oil
mill, two copper and tin factories, ten blacksmith shops,
ten tailors with forty-seven hands, two breweries and
seven large distilleries.   Some $60,000 worth of leather
goods was made by the three tanyards, five currying shops,
and seven saddlers; $30,000 worth of hats by the five hat
factories with upwards of fifty hands; and $30,000 worth
of boots and shoes by the fifteen shoemakers and their
sixty hands.   Further, there were two publishing houses,
four silversmiths, two stocking-weavers and three blue-
dyers; one umbrella, one brush, one reed, four chair, and
two tobacco factories; and four cabinetmakers, whose
furniture in native walnut and cherry was " in as hand-
some a style as in any part of America."   Commercially,
Lexington's importance could be judged from its twenty-
two stores which annually retailed upwards of $300,000
worth of imported foreign merchandise.[15]

These industrial and commercial statistics are eloquent
when translated either in terms of the town's development, or the increasing Western market, or the long lines
of red and blue Conestoga wagons which at high freight
costs carried imported goods from the distant seaboard.
Translated in terms of Kentucky's early and unceasing
agitation for a protective tariff and for good roads to the
East, they suggest the background out of which came
Henry's Clay's " American System," a planned national
economy stressing tariff protection and internal improve-

---

[15] Fortescue Cuming, *Sketches of a Tour to the Western Country* . . .
(*Early Western Travels*, IV, Cleveland, 1904), pp. 185-188. See also
Thomas Ashe, *Travels in America Performed in 1806* . . . (3 vols.,
London, 1808), II, 152.

ments. Since the imported goods were almost exclusively British, and since Britain by her mastery of the seas controlled the prices and foreign marketing of Kentucky's exports, these figures have much meaning when viewed in terms of the general anti-British movement headed by Lexington's Henry Clay, spokesman of the New West and War Hawk leader of 1812.

Bluegrass Kentucky suffered from the general agrarian depression which preceded the War of 1812, and materially helped to precipitate that war. Yet the closing of foreign markets, the embargo and non-importation acts, and the war itself gave a great impetus to Lexington's manufacturing. Her business pioneers, however, were not content with this sort of temporary aid for their industries. Before, during, and after the war, such Lexingtonians as Congressman Clay, manufacturer Lewis Sanders, and the editors of the *Reporter* and the *Kentucky Gazette*, directed an aggressive campaign for a permanent protective system, for " permanent and heavy tariff duties." Lexingtonians toasted their hopes of " blowing the manufactures of Kentucky all over the Western World," and gave nine rousing cheers for " The plough, the spindle, and the loom—what the sword of the Revolution achieved, it remains for them to perpetuate—national independence." Constantly reiterated was the argument that as long as America remained dependent upon British imports independence was but a fiction—" only a NAME, as the wealth and industry of America must go to THEM for their manufactures." Lexington should pioneer " in this patriotic business. . . . Situated, as it were, in the centre of the Union, the spirit of patriotism will . . . like the circles on the surface of the water, extend to the remotest section." [16]

Lexington pioneered in the patriotic business, and with

---

[16] *Kentucky Gazette*, Jan. 21, 1809, July 8, 1806, July 11, 1809, Sept. 25, Dec. 25, 1810; Lexington *Reporter*, 1808-1812.

profit. Nothwithstanding the sharp decline in commodity prices, and the complaints about the scarcity of money, the little town's industries in eleven years, it was estimated in 1810, had increased forty-fold. Even with the great staple of hemp selling at the very low price of $4.00 a hundredweight, the value of hempen goods manufactured by Lexington's thirteen large rope-walks, five bagging and one duck factories was estimated in 1811 at $500,000. Flourishing on the same scale, reported John Melish, were the eight cotton, three woollen, and one oil-cloth factories, and some forty other diverse crafts and industries. There was even a labor shortage. Although most of the journey-man mechanics lived in their own houses, and all of them earned enough in a day to feed themselves for a week, skilled workers were constantly in demand, " the more so as the industrious journeymen very soon become masters." [17]

The social life of the little metropolis, which in 1810 had a population of 4,326, was in keeping with its eco-nomic and political leadership. The wide paved streets and some " six hundred houses mostly brick," the thirty stores and two book-shops with their swinging signs, the clean and commodious inns, the university and the three academies, the dancing assemblies and horse races and the theatre, where professional actors and even ballet-dancers amused middle-aged men who on this very spot a short time before had killed buffalo and Indians—all these gave point to a vistor's report of 1810: " I need hardly tell you that Lexington . . . has been, and yet is, the seat of wealth and refinement of the western coun-try." [18] More glowing than ever were Colonel David

[17] John Melish, *Travels Through the United States* . . . (2 vols., Philadelphia, 1815), II, 187-189.

[18] James McBride, " Journey to Lexington, Kentucky, 1810," *Quarterly Publication of the Historical and Philosophical Society of Ohio* (1910), V, 24.

Meade's reports of "the Lexington Country," in which there were now many plantations that rivalled his own Chaumiere in elegance. "The progress of the useful arts and all the refinements of civilized society advance even beyond the astonishing population," wrote Meade in 1808. "The town of Lexington and the District about it of at least fifty miles in diameter is in a state of improvement which places it about a Century forward of Virginia— and I shall be safe in predicting . . . that it will ever continue to enjoy its pre-eminence. . . ." [19]

*　　*　　*

Colonel Meade was not as good a prophet as General Victor Collot, for within a decade Lexington had lost its commercial and industrial preeminence. Supremacy in the West passed to the river towns, as Collot in 1796 had predicted. Aided by the revolution wrought by the steamboat, and the shift of emigration to the Northwest, Cincinnati by 1820 had grown to be twice the size of Lexington; by 1830 this Ohio River town was truly the "Queen City of the West," four times as large as Lexington, and the seventh largest in the Union.[20] Louisville, too, had gone rapidly forward. Lexingtonians had long looked with disdain upon the little settlement at the falls of the Ohio as a place of swamps and ponds and croaking frogs, of fever-ridden loafers and uncouth Kentuck boatmen, who described themselves as half-horse, half-alligator, tipped with snapping-turtle. Yet with the success of the steamboat as a practicable carrier of passengers and freight, Louisville had bounded forward, and in the 1820's overtook and passed her proud Bluegrass rival. For years to come Lexington retained her leadership in politics and in those intangible things which made her still the

[19] Meade to Joseph Prentis, Dec. 13, 1808, Meade MSS.

[20] Hezekiah Niles in April of 1816 estimated that in the five years since the census of 1810 Kentucky's population had increased 25 percent, Ohio's 80 percent, and Indiana's 400 percent. *Niles' Register*, X, 112.

" Athens of the West." Economically, however, she was shorn of her glory. Even within the state the former " Philadelphia of Kentucky " had become the commercial center of the Bluegrass region only.

Her economic decline came swiftly and unexpectedly. No Lexingtonian dreamed of such a fate during the War of 1812. The *Kentucky Gazette* on January 12, 1813, reported the sale of town lots " at the enormous price of $500 per foot." In the same year a visiting Boston Federalist was amazed to find " everything . . . brisk and profitable. The war, so far from depressing the people . . . is making the greater proportion of them rich. To this you may attribute a part of their patriotism, although to do them justice, they are the most patriotic people I have ever seen or heard of." [21] In 1814 Editor Hezekiah Niles of Baltimore, as strong an economic nationalist as Henry Clay, was happy to report that steam power was now applied to Lexington's factories, that two banks financed farmer and townsman, and that " every business has enlarged." Society was remarkably polished and polite, and town lots sold as high as those in Boston. " Strange things these in the ' backwoods!' " [22]

Lexington's industrial pioneering was a frequent theme with the Baltimore editor, who considered spindles and looms fully as important in winning America's second war for independence as Old Ironsides and Kentucky rifles. Already " the seat of a great commerce, and . . . many flourishing manufactures," this town, said Niles, " promises to be the great inland city of the western world." Six steam engines were now in operation: one for spinning cotton, one for a large woollen mill, one for making paper, two for grinding grain, and a sixth for various purposes. This last steam engine in itself illus-

[21] Letter from Lexington, Oct. 17, 1813, in Richmond *Enquirer*, Nov. 19, 1813.
[22] *Niles' Register*, VI, 249-250.

trated the pioneering spirit, for it was neither of the
Oliver Evans nor the Watt and Bolton type, but one
designed and erected by a Lexingtonian after plans of his
own. Everything inspired optimism as to the town's great
future.

> The farms in the neighborhood are well cultivated, and the
> farmers are generally rich and opulent, and many of them have
> coaches and carriages, made at Lexington [in the four large
> carriage shops], that cost one thousand dollars. Nothing seems
> wanting but artists of all classes, especially smiths, carpenters and
> joiners . . . cotton and wool machine makers. . . . It is with
> delight we notice the great prosperity and rapidly rising impor-
> tance of the future metropolis of the west. . . .[23]

When the *Enterprise* in 1815 made the first upstream
voyage by steamboat from New Orleans to Louisville,
and cut travelling time to less than half, Lexington might
well have seen the handwriting on the wall. Instead, the
town acclaimed this new and revolutionizing method of
transportation. " Less than a week from Kentucky to
New Orleans! " exclaimed the Lexington *Reporter* in
1817: the rapid run of the *Washington* has proven beyond
doubt the utility of stream navigation on western waters.
One can now hear preaching in Kentucky on Sunday and
on the following Sunday attend mass in New Orleans.[24]
The voyage upstream, " which in the ancient modes of
boating, used to be three times the length of a voyage
across the Atlantic, is now often performed in twelve
days." [25]   Wonderful age! " A new Steam Boat on our
Western Waters," said a Lexingtonian, " like a new State
in our confederacy, should be hailed as the unequivocal
symbol of the strength and greatness of our rising
Republic." [26]

[23] *Ibid.*, VII, 339-340.   [24] *Reporter*, May 21, 1817.
[25] Timothy Flint, *Recollections of the Last Ten Years* . . . (Boston,
1826), p. 78.
[26] Lexington *Western Monitor*, April 18, 1818.

Within five years of the *Enterprise's* upstream voyage no less than seventy-two steamboats were plying the Ohio-Mississippi route.[27]   New Orleans had been brought to Kentucky's doorstep, and West Indian fruits were now as plentiful in Lexington as in the Atlantic seaports. Yet little thought was given at first to the fact that the steamboat, with its lower freight rates, had also brought Lexington into sharper competition with the outside world; with the manufacturers of Britain, the East, and the river towns; and with the farmer-producers in such rapidly developing regions as Indiana, Illinois, and Missouri.

Encouraged by the tariff of 1816, Lexington was more confident than ever that her industries had " reached an eminence which ensures their permanent prosperity." In 1816 the new, large textile mills of Lewis Sanders and the Prentiss Company, each employing as many as 150 hands, were going full blast.[28]   These and other extensive manufactories " promise a continued growth of the town," said an enthusiastic visitor. At the same time he noted that Lexington's merchants were still importing and distributing " a prodigious quantity of European goods."[29] In 1817 the town's industries were at the peak of development. The list was impressive: twelve cotton mills, three woollen, three paper, and three steam grist mills; twelve mills for cotton-bagging and hempen yarn; as well as iron and brass foundries, gunpowder mills, and many other establishments. The total capitalization of Lexington's industries was estimated at over two and half millions of dollars.[30] With great pride the Lexington *Reporter* listed the rich resources of a town which within living memory had been " cradled in the most barbarous

---

[27] *Reporter*, Oct. 1, 1821.   [28] *Ibid.*, May 8, 1816.
[29] Samuel R. Brown, *The Western Gazeteer; or Emigrant's Directory* . . . (Auburn, N. Y., 1817), p. 93.
[30] Henry B. Fearon, *Sketches of America* . . . (London, 1818), pp. 248-249.

part of the revolutionary war." With a defiant gesture towards Cincinnati and Louisville, the *Reporter* declared that there was not a town " on the western waters but New Orleans which is entitled to claim preeminence over Lexington." [31]

Nevertheless, Lexington's rate of growth had slowed down perceptibly, while Cincinnati had leaped ahead and Louisville, as an English observer noted in this same year of 1817, was " daily becoming a most important town, being the connecting link between New Orleans and the whole western country." Louisville, he said, " must soon take the lead of Lexington in extent of population, as it has already done in the rapid rise of town property, the increase of which during the last four years is said to have been two hundred per cent." [32] With more and more steamboats cutting the time to and from New Orleans to less than half, and reducing freight rates correspondingly, Louisville steadily drained away Lexington's commerce and industry. Because of transportation costs from inland Lexington to the great river artery, farmers got much higher prices at Louisville for their produce, which was sent down river or was purchased by the new manufactories at the falls of the Ohio. Likewise, imported articles sold at lower prices at Louisville than at Lexington, which had to wagon the goods at high cost over the stony, flooded, " excessively disagreeable " road from Maysville (formerly Limestone) on the Ohio.[33]

The steamboat, at first hailed as a beneficent promoter, had introduced a transportation differential which was

[31] *Reporter*, May 14, 1817.

[32] Fearon, p. 245. See also, Brown, pp. 103-105.

[33] James Flint, *Letters from America* . . . (*Early Western Travels*, IX, Cleveland, 1904), pp. 128-131. Flint noted the abominable condition of this, the great road from Lexington through Maysville to Chillicothe and the East, and also that goods in 1818 were being carried from Maysville to Lexington at $1.00 per cwt., " somewhat lower than the usual rate."

decisive. Lexingtonians in erecting their wilderness metropolis had overcome the obstacles of Nature, Briton, and Indians. They had subdued the enemies of their pioneer bank and other institutions. And they thought they had overcome the disadvantages of their inland situation. But the steamboat was all-conquering. It was not to be overcome even if Lexington exerted to the full all those qualities of leadership which for over a generation had made " *Lexington dictation* " and " *Lexington influence* " respected and admired throughout the Western World.[34]

The downward spiral began in 1818, and gathered speed like a steamboat dashing down the Louisville Falls at high water. By 1820 there was very little left of the commerce and industry about which Lexington had proudly boasted in 1817. The forces which had been undermining her economic position became merged with those of a general nature which brought on the Panic of 1819, and the ensuing nation-wide depression. From 1818 on the town's newspapers portrayed the lamentable story of " hard times," " low prices," " drooping spirits," " languishing manufactures," the closing of the Sanders factory and others, the failure of commercial houses, unemployment, bankruptcies, emigrations *from* Kentucky, the evils of over-speculation and wild-cat banking.[35] Throughout Kentucky, it was reported, " nothing is seen but a boundless expanse of desolation. Wealth impoverished, enterprise checked, commerce at a stand, the currency depreciated . . ." [36] In vain did Lexingtonians inveigh against the importation of British " *Waterloo*

---

[34] *Kentucky Gazette*, Jan. 17, 1814.

[35] See the *Gazette, Reporter, Monitor*, 1818-1821, and the Lexington *Public Advertiser*, 1820-1821. A brief account is given by Theodore G. Gronert, " Early Trade in the Blue-Grass Region, 1810-1820," *Mississippi Valley Historical Review* (1918), V, 321-322.

[36] *Niles' Register*, XVII, 19.

stripes" and *" Wellington cords,"* and cheer Henry Clay's demands in Congress for internal improvements and higher tariff duties, and for an end to the un-American policy of " Do-nothing " and " Leave-things-to-themselves." In vain did Lexingtonians agitate for quicker and cheaper transportation to the Ohio, so as to meet the formidable rivalry of the river towns. In vain did they assure one another that their town had not passed its zenith; that good times would return, and with a little aid from government " Lexington will continue to be the greatest inland town in America. It will be a second Manchester." [37]

It was all of no avail. Nothing came of the agitation for improved highways: as late as 1829, Mr. Clay himself, with " the deepest mortification," publicly confessed that it had taken his family four days to travel, through mud and mire, the sixty-four miles from Maysville to Lexington, over the town's main highway to the Ohio.[38] Efforts at this time to improve the navigation of the Kentucky River likewise failed.[39] And it was the same story later on with the projected railroad from Lexington to the Ohio: not until 1852, the year of Clay's death, and after twenty-two years of agitation, did Lexington reach the river by rail. Neither did Clay's onslaught against the doctrine of laissez-faire bring relief during the depression that began in 1818, although the *Reporter* declared that from this detestable " Let Us Alone " policy a change " appears to be indispensably necessary to avert impending ruin both from our agricultural and manufacturing interests." [40] When the tariff bill of 1820 " was

[37] *Kentucky Gazette*, Oct. 30, 1818.

[38] Daniel Mallory, ed., *The Life and Speeches of the Hon. Henry Clay* (2 vols., 5th ed., N. Y., 1844), I, 584.

[39] Mary Verhoeff, *The Kentucky River Navigation* (Louisville, 1917), p. 24.

[40] *Reporter*, Aug. 9, 1820.

murdered by a majority of one vote " in the Senate, a Lexington editor bordered his pages in black and announced the bill's death in these words: " Mourn, oh, ye sons and daughters of Kentucky . . . put on sackcloth and ashes . . . You must still remain tributary to the workshops of Europe. Your factories must continue prostrate. Your agricultural productions must lie and rot on your hands." [41] The editor at this time might well have used black borders to symbolize the demise of Lexington as the frontier metropolis, for his town's economic leadership in the Western World had now been irretrievably lost.

*   *   *

Unlike the river towns, Lexington recovered very slowly from the Panic of 1819. When the storm finally abated, her rivals were far ahead, too far for Lexington ever to regain her former position. But she was still a prosperous town, and she was still the political and cultural metropolis of the West. Neither Louisville nor Cincinnati could deprive her of the political leadership embodied in her Henry Clay—although Louisville warred against the dominant Tammany Society, which had its headquarters in Lexington and blindly followed Henry Clay, " the great Tammany Chief." [42] In 1818, the year the town began to lose its economic leadership, Lexington began a remarkable cultural advance. In that year Horace Holley, through the instrumentality of Clay and other liberals in politics and religion, became the president of Transylvania University. Holley, a Unitarian, threw out the deadwood of Calvinistic orthodoxy, gathered about him a group of great scholars, and for a decade made Lexington

[41] *Public Advertiser*, May 17, 1820.
[42] Louisville *Public Advertiser*, Aug. 11, Sept. 8, 1818.

4

a formidable academic rival of Harvard and her title of
" Athens of the West " a glorious reality.[43]

The " restless, speculating " town of 1810 [44] now had
" the tone of a literary place . . . an air of ease and polite-
ness . . . of leisure and opulence that distinguishes it from
the busy bustle " of the river towns.[45] Both Cincinnati,
" Porkopolis on the Ohio," and Louisville were, in comparison, coarsely commercial, parvenu upstarts. Lexington was more than ever " the capital of fashion," [46] and
more than ever " a Paris in miniature." [47] It was a civilized oasis in the midst of a crude, sweaty, materialistic
Western World. In this region of Mike Finks and Daniel
Boones and Colonel Sellerses one found here such leaven-
ing influences as a well-patronized theatre; an Atheneum,
which combined a natural history museum with a well-
supplied reading room for scholars and publicists; a
Lexington school of painting, headed by the well-patronized native son and able portrait-painter, Mathew Jouett;
a remarkably good *Western Review* monthly, with articles,
poems, and stories by the gifted Transylvania group,
which included the distinguished scientist, Constantine
Rafinesque.[48] Lexington, the Western World's cultural
center, was then " vocal

> With the eloquence of youthful Orators,
> Kentucky's glorious sons—her future Clays."

---

[43] See Niels Henry Sonne, *Liberal Kentucky, 1780-1828* (New York,
1939), pp. 135 ff.

[44] George Ord, *Sketch of the Life of Alexander Wilson* (Philadelphia,
1828), p. cxlvii.

[45] Timothy Flint, pp. 67-68.

[46] James Flint, p. 137.

[47] Fearon, p. 238.

[48] James Flint, pp. 137-138; *Western Monitor*, April 18, 1818 (letter
on " The Fine Arts in Kentucky "); and the best mirror of cultural
Lexington at the time, the four volumes of *The Western Review . . .
devoted to Literature and Science*, which William Gibbes Hunt edited
and published from August, 1819, through July, 1821.

Further, Lexington remained the metropolis of the rich and gracious Bluegrass, glory enough for any town. Clustered about the former wilderness metropolis were prosperous farms and some fifty or sixty large plantations renowned for their hospitality and good living, their blooded horses and imported cattle; situated in the midst of orchards and sheltered by fine groves of forest and sugar-maple trees; commanding fertile acres of hemp and tobacco and rolling bluegrass meadows. Henry Clay's Ashland was the best known, but surely the most interesting was Colonel David Meade's Chaumiere. This republican aristocrat who had migrated from Virginia in 1796 was now an old gentleman. He dressed in the small clothes, white stockings, and square coat with great cuffs fashionable in his youth; and he had the manners of a grandee. He was " entirely a man of leisure . . . never using his fortune but in adorning his place and entertaining his friends and strangers." Dinner, at four, was always ready for visitors who might chance to call. Such was the case when Mr. Horace Holley visited Colonel Meade in May of 1818, and afterwards drew this picture of a charming Bluegrass estate: [49]

Twenty of us went out to day, without warning, and were entertained luxuriously on the viands of the country. Our drink consisted of beer, toddy, and water. Wine, being imported and expensive, he never gives; nor does he allow cigars to be smoked in his presence. His house consists of a cluster of rustic cottages, in front of which spreads a beautiful, sloping lawn, as smooth as velvet. From this diverge, in various directions, and forming vistas terminated by picturesque objects, groves and walks extending over some acres. Seats, Chinese temples, verdant banks, and alcoves are interspersed at convenient distances. The lake, over which presides a Grecian temple, that you may imagine to be the

[49] Horace Holley to [Mrs. Holley], May 27, 1818, quoted in Charles Caldwell, *Discourse on . . . the Rev. Horace Holley . . .* (Boston, 1828), pp. 153-154.

residence of the water nymphs, has in it a small island, which communicates with the shore by a white bridge of one arch. The whole is surrounded by a low rustic fence of stone, surmounted and almost hidden by honeysuckle and roses, now in full flower, and which we gathered in abundance to adorn the ladies. Everything is laid out for walking and pleasure. His farm he rents, and does nothing for profit. The whole is in rustic taste. You enter from the road, through a gate between rude and massive columns, a field without pretension, wind a considerable distance through a noble park to an inner gate, the capitals to whose pillars are unique, being formed of the roots of trees, carved by nature. Then the rich scene of cultivation, of verdure and flower-capped hedges, bursts upon you. There is no establishment like this in our country. Instead of a description, I might give you its name, ' *Chaumière du Prairies.*'

Here in Colonel Meade's Lexington Country was the heart of Kentucky—" Old Kentucky," as the people now affectionately said, although but a few years back they had looked up to Virginia as a mother. The Bluegrass town was still the real metropolis of a Kentucky now " proudly exalted as the common mother of the western states," whose migrating sons had already stamped " the character of this state . . . her modes of thinking and action " upon the great empire stretching " from the falls of St. Anthony to the gulph of Mexico, and from the Allegany hills to the Rocky Mountains." [50] And it was Lexington and the Bluegrass that these distant sons had in mind when they boasted of " Old Kentuck," of her unexcelled whiskey, horses, maple-sugar, and fair women, and taught their children to recite in tribute to these products of the Lexington Country—

> The first is strong, the second are fleet,
> The third and fourth are exceedingly sweet,
> And all are uncommonly hard to beat.

---

[50] Timothy Flint, p. 73.

URBAN AND RURAL VOTING IN THE
ELECTION OF 1860

Ollinger Crenshaw

A considerable literature has been devoted by historians
to the critical presidential election of 1860. Various
aspects of the subject, such as slavery in the territories, the
economic demands of free state capitalists and farmers,
and the influence of the foreign born, have been exten-
sively treated in learned articles. Two distinguished students of the period, James Ford Rhodes and Edward
Channing, have assigned many pages in their comprehensive works to the election of 1860, and Emerson D.
Fite has written an entire book on it. Yet no analysis of
this much-studied presidential election with reference to
the political reactions of urban and rural voters has been
made.[1]

It will be the main purpose of this paper to present the
mere mathematical aspects of the urban-rural vote as a
beginning of a more complete investigation of the
subject.

Although by 1860 urban development had not reached
the quickening pace of the years following, by this date
nearly one in every six Americans lived in communities
of 8,000 or more, and numerous large cities existed. New
York City, exclusive of Brooklyn, was one of the ranking

[1] James Ford Rhodes, *History of the United States from the Compromise of 1850* (8 vols., New York, 1893-1919), II, 440-502, and
Edward Channing, *A History of the United States* (6 vols., New York,
1905-1925), VI, 227-254, entirely omit the subject. Emerson D. Fite,
The Presidential Campaign of 1860 (New York, 1911), says (p. 233):
"Of the large cities, New York went against Lincoln for fusion by
30,000, Philadelphia for Lincoln by 1,000, and St. Louis for Lincoln by
700."

cities of the western world, and Philadelphia exceeded Berlin in population.[2] These and other American cities were not only characterized by large populations, but also by a cultural and economic atmosphere which was peculiar to an urban environment. Many factors produced this urban atmosphere. Among them may be enumerated facility of communication and transportation, newspaper and periodical presses, theatres, colleges, universities and professional schools, cultivation of the arts and literature, cosmopolitan racial groups, factories, banks, and commercial houses.

Pending a more exact definition of the term " city," arbitrary minima of population will be adopted as defining, for present purposes, the elusive word. In the more urbanized sections of America, the Northeastern states, higher population minima will be employed than in areas such as the South and West, where urban agglomerations were fewer and of smaller size.[3] A word of explanation may be offered concerning the cities of the old South. By far the larger number of great cities were located in the North and West, but in 1860 three of the nation's most important cities, New Orleans, Baltimore, and St. Louis, were in slave states. The South has correctly been considered as predominantly rural, but scholars have recently begun a more intensive study of the smaller cities of that region, and their findings indicate that a more or less urban milieu existed in such cities as Nashville and Memphis as well as in New Orleans.[4] A careful scholar has demon-

[2] A. M. Schlesinger, "The City in American History," *Mississippi Valley Historical Review* (1940), XXVII, 43-66.

[3] New England and the Middle Atlantic states 20,000 minimum; Northwest and Pacific Coast states 15,000; slave states 12,000. It may be noted that urbanization did not—and does not—respect legal boundary lines, whether state or city, and urban districts comprising a cluster of adjoining cities will be considered as units, as for example, the Boston and New York districts.

[4] See summary of papers of M. Swearingen, F. Gavin Davenport, and

strated that there were surprisingly large numbers of foreign born in the cities of the old South. Not only was this true of New Orleans, but Charleston, Memphis, Mobile, and Savannah each had foreign born residents ranging from over 15% to more than 30% of the population.[5]

The presidential election of 1860 has been adequately discussed elsewhere, and it will be impossible here to describe fully the conduct, issues, and candidates of that campaign.[6] Rarely in the history of American politics had there been a more complex situation. Four serious aspirants were nominated for the presidency, three of them with more or less well defined platforms, and each backed by a considerable and articulate following. The disruption of the Charleston and Baltimore conventions ultimately resulted in two Democratic candidates, Senator Stephen A. Douglas of Illinois and John C. Breckinridge of Kentucky, vice president of the United States. Douglas was supported by the Northern faction of the party, and in the campaign advocated his Popular Sovereignty doctrine and personally appealed for a continuation of the Union. Breckinridge, though himself a moderate, ran on a platform which demanded Southern equality and Congressional protection for slaveholders in the territories. He was supported by such extremists as William L. Yancey of Alabama, and other fire-eaters. Each claimed to be the " regular " party nominee, and much ill feeling was engendered between the hostile factions.

G. M. Capers, Jr., *Mississippi Valley Historical Review* (1939), XXVI, 222-224.

[5] Ella Lonn, *Foreigners in the Confederacy* (Chapel Hill, 1940), 1-32; Appendix I, 481, gives table of foreigners in Southern cities.

[6] Rhodes, II, 440-502; Emerson D. Fite, *The Presidential Campaign of 1860*; Dwight L. Dumond, *The Secession Movement 1860-1861* (New York, 1931), pp. 35-112. For map of the election, see Charles O. Paullin, *Atlas of the Historical Geography of the United States* (Baltimore, 1932), plate 105.

The Republican party, making its second bid for the presidency, nominated Abraham Lincoln, and promised a homestead law, a Pacific railroad, and, in language ambiguous but understood in the proper quarters, a protective tariff. The platform opposed the extension of slavery. Although the party's position on this issue was officially toned down from earlier idealism, the circulation of Sumner's speech, " The Barbarism of Slavery," and Helper's *Impending Crisis* as campaign documents, the speeches of Carl Schurz and the extreme attitude of " Long John " Wentworth's Chicago *Democrat,* disquieted conservatives and tended to discount the moderation of candidate and platform.[7]

A fourth group, composed of old line Whigs and conservatives generally, who found it impossible to join with the " sectional " parties, formed the Constitutional Union party, and nominated John Bell of Tennessee. This party professed to believe that the country was weary of the slavery question, and promulgated the unrevealing slogan, " The Constitution, the Union, and the Laws." Supporters of Bell could thus take different attitudes towards slavery in different sections. The primary aim of this group was to defeat Lincoln by throwing the election into the House of Representatives, where it would be possible to elect a conservative.

In the free states the election was largely a contest between Lincoln and Douglas, while in the slave states it was between Breckinridge and Bell. In the South, which

[7] A vote for Lincoln in the free states may or may not have been for an aggressive policy against the South, and certainly it was not a vote for war. Some of Lincoln's adversaries in the North declared that his election would precipitate a revolution at the South and bring about war, which the Republicans dismissed as Southern rodomontade. But a vote against Lincoln in the North was a vote to keep out of power the man and the party most feared and execrated at the South. For an interesting explanation of what a vote for Breckinridge meant in Connecticut, see Channing, VI, 251.

was a unit in support of the " peculiar institution," Lincoln received a scattering vote in the border states, but in the lower South not a single Republican elector appeared. The operation of Popular Sovereignty in the late fifties had rendered Douglas unpopular in the South, which believed him to be hostile to slavery. The main issue in the slave states revolved around the proposition of immediate resistance or delay and cooperation in the event of Lincoln's election. Generally speaking, the adherents of Breckinridge in the far South favored the former course, while the supporters of Bell, concentrated in the upper South, urged the latter. There was no irreconcilable difference between the positions of Douglas and Bell, and votes cast for them in the South should properly be considered as of a moderate and Unionist character.[8]

[8] Some historians have contended that the mass of Bell-Douglas voters did not subscribe to the strong Unionism of the candidates. Dumond, *Secession Movement, 1860-1861,* p. 111, note 45. The Richmond *Examiner,* November 16, 1860, is also cited to prove this point. *Ibid.,* 124, note 17. Yet it hardly seems just to allow a paper which had been bitterly critical of the Bell-Douglas forces before the election to interpret the motives of their rank and file shortly afterwards. The Richmond *Whig* would be a more accurate interpreter of the Bell-Douglas parties, at least in the upper South. It is not contended here that there were not individuals and newspapers in the Bell-Douglas ranks who were covert secessionists, for it has ever been difficult to attain complete unity in a political party. It is recognized that the Georgia Bell-Douglas press was not unqualified in its Unionism. See Augusta *Daily Chronicle and Sentinel's* vacillation, August 26, October 13, 1860. The Atlanta *Southern Confederacy* was an extremist supporter of Douglas. Memphis *Daily Avalanche,* August 17, 1860. Men like Benjamin H. Hill of Georgia and Thomas H. Watts of Alabama were prominent Bell advocates who were ready to secede if Lincoln won the election. Watts to Daniel Sayre, September 21, 1860, Montgomery *Daily Mail,* September 26, 1860; Hill wrote, October 13, 1860, that he feared the Union was lost. He would not accept *any* man elected to the presidency. Savannah *Daily Republican,* October 19, 1860. But the evidence on the other side is mountainous and widespread. The repeated expressions of devotion to the Union by Bell-Douglas orators, platform resolutions, and presses make it difficult to dismiss as " lip service " their intense loyalty to the Union. In New Orleans, the *Daily Picayune,* October 21, 1860, objected to the " dead sea of political uni-

It was plain to practical men that the divided opposition to Lincoln would insure his election, and efforts were made to reduce the anti-Lincoln elements to a single ticket. But there was much friction among these elements, and Douglas, the leading candidate in the free states, was unsympathetic towards the fusion movement. In the few states where fusion was achieved the net result was the deduction of only three electoral votes from the Republican column. Several states held their gubernatorial elections early in October, a month in advance of the presidential election which was held in all states, except South

formity which the Breckinridge crowd seeks to secure under the cry of a United South." The same paper sharply criticized Southern politicians as " loud prophets of coming woe " in the midst of a section " blooming with prosperity." *Ibid.*, October 3, 1860. As late as November 1, 1860, it protested against the secession movement as " one of dictation and proscription." The New Orleans *Bee*, July 27, 1860, reviewed sectional clashes and found the South had triumphed nine out of ten times. The Vicksburg *Daily Whig*, October 19, 1860, denounced secession doctrine. See also speech of W. A. Lake at Natchez, who declared, " The election of no one, in conformity with the Constitution, is ground for disunion." *Natchez Daily Courier*, September 13, 1860. See also speech of Jere Clemens, at Huntsville, Alabama, vigorously denying secession. Louisville *Journal* in St. Louis *Daily Missouri Republican*, September 28, 1860. Tuscumbia *North Alabamian*, July 13, 1860, opposed secession. S. D. Cabaniss wrote Governor A. B. Moore of Alabama describing sentiment of Bell-Douglas men in the Tennessee valley region, which he thought was stanchly Unionist. Cabaniss to Moore, October 29, 1860. MS, Alabama Department of History and Archives, Montgomery. The strong Douglas paper, the *Mobile Daily Register*, January 21, 1860, opposed the Alabama legislature's famous secessionist resolutions. The Mobile *Daily Advertiser*, October 9, 1860, dared Breckinridge to answer the " Norfolk questions." The Bell and Douglas papers in Memphis were emphatic Unionists. Memphis *Morning Bulletin*, November 7, 1860, said of the Bell-Douglas majority in that city: " Her language is so emphatic that there can be no mistake about her devotion to Union and loyalty." Memphis *Daily Appeal*, October 17, 1860. Significant in this connection were the repeated attacks by the Breckinridge press on Bell-Douglas men as " submissionists." Northern men were being led to believe that in case of Republican success " a host of Bell and Douglas men would whip them [Southerners] into submission." Nashville *Union and American*, November 1, 1860. See also Mobile *Tribune* in Mobile *Daily Advertiser*, September 23, 1860.

Carolina, on November 6, 1860. The October states were closely observed, especially Indiana and Pennsylvania, as affording an indication of the probable outcome of the presidential contest. When the Republicans carried these states, Lincoln's success was confidently predicted, and the final result bore out this prophecy, as he carried almost all the electoral votes of the free states, polling 54% of the popular vote there. But of the total national popular vote, Lincoln received less than 40%, and the Southern Democrat, Breckinridge, polled less than 45% of the total cast in the slave states.[9]

During the progress of the canvass, there were indications that contemporaries, North and South, were aware of urban-rural differences. Shipowners and manufacturers of New England, merchants and mechanics of New York, manufacturers and mining interests of New Jersey and Pennsylvania, it was contended, ". . . all draw no small portion of their daily wages and profits from the stream that rises in the cotton fields of the South." [10] A correspondent writing from Boston, although over-estimating Douglas' rural strength in New England, predicted accurately that " . . . Bell will find his chief strength in the cities and large towns of the eastern tier." [11] The New York *Express* declared shortly before election day that Lincoln's conservatism was stressed by those " Black " Republican organs ". . . whose role . . . is to play the ' conservative ' tune in the great commercial cities, where

[9] Electoral vote: Lincoln 180, Breckinridge 72, Bell 39, Douglas 12. *The Tribune Almanac and Political Register for 1861* (New York, 1861), p. 34. Popular vote: Lincoln 1,866,452 (39.87%), Douglas 1,375-157 (29.37%), Breckinridge 847,953 (18.11%), Bell 590,631 (12.65%). *Tribune Almanac and Political Register for 1865* in *Tribune Almanac 1838-1868* (2 vols., New York, 1868), II, 68. State totals may be found in *The Tribune Almanac and Political Register for 1862* (New York, 1862), p. 64.

[10] *New York Herald*, July 26, 1860.

[11] *Ibid.*, September 2, 1860.

abolitionism is most at a discount." [12] Special appeals were made to New York City's interests in support of the anti-Lincoln ticket. At a meeting in Cooper Institute, September 17, Joshua J. Henry of the firm of Henry, Smith and Townsend, "engaged largely in Southern trade," made an appeal to merchants, mechanics, traders, workingmen of all classes to vote for the fusion.[13] On the same occasion, Mayor Fernando Wood, of New York City, expressed concern for commerce, though also for manufacturing and agriculture—"its handmaiden." He thought that the issue of slavery in the territories was trivial beside the important issue, "our continued commercial prosperity." If the Republicans won, Wood contended, the existing social and political system into which nationality and property were interwoven, would be weakened.[14] Rhodes long ago called attention to the alarm of New York capitalists at the prospect of Lincoln's election, and to the large campaign fund they were reported to have raised.[15]

Bennett's New York *Herald* described New York as the metropolis of this Union, the ". . . heart of all these vast interests, the soul of trade, industry, and thought." The voice of New York must be heard in the crisis, if the city would "worthily wear the metropolitan crown." A monster Union demonstration was urged for the psychological effect it would have on the nation.[16] Two-thirds

[12] Quoted in Montgomery *Daily Mail*, November 1, 1860.

[13] New York's domination of the cotton export trade was established early in the nation's history, and by 1860 cotton still ranked first in the city's exports. Robert G. Albion, *The Rise of New York Port* (New York, 1939), pp. 95-121.

[14] *New York Times*, September 18, 1860.

[15] Rhodes, II, 499-500. Samuel J. Tilden, a New York lawyer close to railroad and investment interests, deeply desired the defeat of Lincoln, and collected funds for fusion, which his biographer believes have been exaggerated. Alexander C. Flick, *Samuel Jones Tilden, A Study in Political Sagacity* (New York, 1939), pp. 124-125.

[16] *New York Herald*, August 22, 1860.

of the city's legal voters, including merchants and manufacturers, were anti-Lincoln, the *Herald* believed.[17] Abram Hewitt, son-in-law of Peter Cooper, the famous iron manufacturer and philanthropist, wrote just before election that he wished personally to go into the manufacturing cities of New Jersey to warn against Republican victory, which would destroy industry there.[18] Stephen A. Douglas' speech at Jones' Wood alluded to New York City as not sectional but "continental and metropolitan." The "great monetary heart of the American continent" required the maintenance of the Union.[19] At Bangor, Maine, Douglas indicated his deep interest in the fostering of American business interests.[20] In his Harrisburg address, Douglas favored tariff protection, and various anti-Lincoln men were also for the tariff.[21] Senator William Bigler of Pennsylvania asked the merchants of Philadelphia to reject Lincoln, and proclaimed himself a tariff man.[22] The Republicans made an identical appeal to industrial and commercial interests in the cities. Horace Greeley, long an ardent protectionist, urged old Whigs to support Lincoln if they wanted a government which would "encourage commerce."[23]

In the South there was a lively appreciation of the urban-rural problem. Throughout the South complaints were voiced in the Breckinridge press of the hostility or

[17] *Ibid.*, August 24, 1860.

[18] Allan Nevins, *Abram S. Hewitt With Some Account of Peter Cooper* (New York, 1935), pp. 187-188.

[19] *New York Times*, September 13, 1860.

[20] *Ibid.*, August 18, 1860.

[21] *New York Herald*, September 8, 1860; Silas Seymour, a protective tariff man, supported Douglas. *New York Times*, July 17, 1860.

[22] Washington *National Intelligencer*, October 9, 1860.

[23] At a rally where Greeley spoke, resolutions were adopted urging Lincoln's election on the ground that it would "insure renewed and most needed attention to the great industrial and commercial interests of the city, too long made the sport of faction and the plaything of reckless ambition." *New York Times*, July 17, 1860.

lukewarmness of the cities towards their candidate and Southern rights. The Montgomery *Mail* had lost patronage in the towns because of its ardent championship of the South.[24] The New Orleans *Delta* put the matter bluntly: " It is a notorious fact, that the two classes stand arrayed against each other in nearly all the political contests of the day. Three fourths of the planters are of one party, and an equal proportion of the merchants are the opposite." [25] Still another observer lamented the decline of the martial spirit among the people of New Orleans, and explained this condition by the aversion which commercial people were said to entertain for war.[26] The Mobile *Mercury* advised its rural friends that the city of Mobile had grieved that journal.[27] The Memphis *Avalanche* sarcastically observed that there were " patriots " even in the city of Memphis, an allusion to the dearth of Breckinridge sentiment there.[28]

The Bell press replied in kind. The New Orleans *Bee* severely indicted the Southern chivalry, which would rather arm to do battle with the North than patiently to plan for Southern economic and educational development, a process which might consume years.[29] A desolate picture of New Orleans was painted if " revolution " came, and the Bell campaign stressed the importance to the city's economic life of the preservation of the Union. Ships would rot at the levee, real estate values and cotton prices would decline sharply, and bankruptcy and ruin would befall the city. " Let our rich men bestir themselves," was the watchword of those who foresaw the danger.[30]

---

[24] Montgomery *Daily Mail*, October 6, 1860.
[25] New Orleans *Daily Delta*, October 2, 1860.
[26] New Orleans *Daily Crescent*, April 6, 1860.
[27] Quoted in New Orleans *Daily Picayune*, October 27, 1860.
[28] Memphis *Daily Avalanche*, November 1, 1860.
[29] Quoted in New Orleans *Daily Delta*, October 24, 1860.
[30] *New Orleans Commercial Bulletin*, September 1, 21, 22, 1860.

Bell men might describe such a dire fate for the port of New Orleans, but a diametrically opposite conclusion was reached by the Charleston *Mercury,* which contended that merchants and mechanics of Southern cities would gain by a dissolution of the Union. Southern ports would prosper following the establishment of direct trade with Europe, long a dream of Southern nationalists.[31] Not only would this benefit the agricultural interests, but the city of Charleston would rival Boston and New York in commercial importance.[32] While such argument may have impressed Charleston and perhaps Savannah, it was received coldly by the Memphis *Appeal*, which conceded that Charleston would profit vastly, but at the expense of such cities as Louisville, Memphis, and St. Louis.[33]

At the end of September, the New York *Herald* correspondent wrote from the South that there was intense excitement in isolated areas caused by the alleged activities of abolitionist incendiaries, and that the agricultural population was " rife " for revolution.[34] A few days later another article to the same paper discussed the violent hostility to Lincoln among the Mississippi planters, reported by the writer after visiting the cotton, rice, and sugar plantations,

the great and overpowering agricultural influences of these latitudes. . . . Cities and towns in the South do not express the feeling of the agricultural population. Traders and merchants are not farmers nor planters, nor do they altogether sympathize with each other. While the merchants in the cities desire peace and Union, the planters demand protection in the Union, or independence, under their own self-reliance out of it.[35]

[31] Quoted in *New York Herald*, November 4, 1860. For earlier efforts to establish direct trade between Charleston and Europe, see Robert G. Albion, *Square-Riggers on Schedule* (Princeton, 1938), p. 76.

[32] Rhodes, III, 121.

[33] Memphis *Daily Appeal*, October 5, 1860.

[34] *New York Herald*, September 27, 1860.

[35] *Ibid.*, October 6, 1860.

A summary of the *Herald* correspondent's tour reflected a most pessimistic attitude but "even yet," he wrote, some in the South opposed dissolution and revolution. Among them were capitalists, bankers, large real estate owners in cities, and leading merchants. A bank president in Augusta, Georgia, was quoted as having called the secession movement "folly and absurdity." But such men were careful to emphasize that if Lincoln invaded Southern rights, all would come to the aid of their section. In other words, the conservative elements were for peace "now," and dissolution as a last resort.[36]

Such were some of the pre-election comments on, and analyses of, urban-rural trends in North and South. But political prediction has ever been a hazardous pursuit, and the best method by which to test the accuracy of the urban-rural hypothesis is to examine the presidential election returns of 1860.

In the New England states, which went solidly Republican, the Lincoln vote, with one important exception and several lesser deviations, was distinctly heavier in the rural areas than in the cities. Vermont, entirely rural, was the banner Republican state of the Union, giving Lincoln 76% of the total vote cast. Likewise Maine and Connecticut cast a somewhat heavier Republican rural vote than did the cities of Portland, New Haven and Hartford. The exceptions to this trend were in New Hampshire and Rhode Island, where Lincoln's majorities in the cities of Manchester and Providence were proportionately heavier than in the rural portions of the two states. But it was in the Boston metropolitan area, with a population of more than a quarter of a million, that the sharpest divergence between urban and rural prefer-

[36] *Ibid.*, October 16, 1860. Louis M. Hacker considers the Southern cities as part of the planting system. Louis M. Hacker, *The Triumph of American Capitalism* (New York, 1940), p. 291.

ence may be observed. The city of Boston proper gave Lincoln only 48%, and in the Cambridge-Roxbury-Charlestown-Chelsea suburban district the proportion was about the same. On the other hand, the rural vote of Massachusetts went Republican by 66%. Thus the city of Boston, so often execrated by Southerners as the home of abolition, was notably less enthusiastic for Lincoln than were rural New Englanders.[37]

Urbanization had developed in the Middle Atlantic region to a greater degree than in any part of America. The area comprising New York City, Brooklyn, and Jersey City had in 1860 a population much in excess of a million inhabitants, and had established primacy among American urban districts.[38] Although Lincoln won the important electoral vote of New York state, he did so against the will of the great urban masses. A Bell-Douglas-Breckinridge fusion ticket received 65% of the New York City returns, and 58% in Brooklyn, while in upstate rural New York Lincoln amassed 58% as against 42% for fusion.[39]

[37] See Appendix, Table I, " New England."

[38] A contemporary pointed with pride to the fact that within five miles of City Hall was a population over 1,200,000. New York's greatness as a commercial city was noted, and it was said that the prosperity of inland cities was tied to the great city. But also it was observed that manufacturing was becoming of " great magnitude." New York *Evening Post* in Washington *National Intelligencer*, September 22, 1860. Indeed, New York county was the leading manufacturing county in the United States. In 1860 the facts there were: number of establishments 4,375, capital invested $61,212,757, cost of raw material $90,177,038, people employed 65,483 males and 24,721 females, annual cost of labor $2,705,922, annual value of products $159,107,369. *Manufactures of the United States in 1860 . . . Compiled from the Original Returns of the Eighth Census* (Washington, 1865), p. 411. To which may be added the figures for Kings county (Brooklyn): number of establishments 1032, capital invested $12,320,876, cost of raw material $19,040,316, people employed 11,571 males and 1,187 females, annual cost of labor $4,462,633, annual value of products $34,241,520. *Ibid.*, p. 374.

[39] For explanation of the New York fusion, see D. S. Alexander, *Political History of the State of New York* (4 vols., New York, 1906), II, 324-33; and S. D. Brummer, *Political History of New York State*

Although Lincoln carried the upstate cities of Buffalo, Rochester, Syracuse, Albany, and Utica, the voters of those smaller cities were not for him quite as strongly as their rural neighbors, and Troy went against him.

Nearby, the Jersey City returns were in accord with those of New York City, and though the New Jersey country precincts were also against Lincoln, the Republican ticket was measurably stronger in the districts outside Jersey City and Newark. America's second largest city, Philadelphia, was carried by Lincoln with a slight majority, but the city was far weaker in Lincoln sentiment than rural Pennsylvania. Lincoln had only 50.7% of the great city, but won a decisive 57% outside the urban precincts. On the other hand, in the Pittsburgh-Allegheny sector, Lincoln's vote soared far above even his rural figure, reaching 66% in Pittsburgh, and 74% in Allegheny. Pittsburgh had " peculiar institutions," the iron and steel manufacturing establishments, which were eager for protective tariffs.[40]   The smaller city of Reading gave Lincoln 55%.[41]

While the heaviest urban concentration existed in the Northeast, there were in 1860 five other American cities which boasted populations of more than 100,000, two of which were in the old Northwest. Cincinnati, the largest city west of the Appalachians, went for Lincoln by a plurality, but cast only 46% of its total vote for him. Rural Ohio, on the other hand, voted Republican by 53%. Columbus rejected Lincoln in favor of Douglas, who polled 50% there. But the impression must not be gained that all urban Ohio was cool to Lincoln, who was given majorities

During the Period of the Civil War (*Columbia University Studies in History, Economics, and Public Law*, XXXIX, no. 2, New York, 1911), pp. 103, 70-98.

[40] M. R. Eiselen, *The Rise of Protectionism in Pennsylvania* (Philadelphia, 1932), pp. 255-263.

[41] See Appendix, Table II, " Middle Atlantic States."

in Cleveland and in Dayton. The former was one of the strongest Republican cities of the Northwest, casting 58% for that party, a larger proportion than Lincoln obtained in rural Ohio.[42]

An urban-rural situation comparable to that of northern Ohio may be noted in Indiana, where the rural voters gave Lincoln a bare majority of 50.8%. The city of Indianapolis clinched his hold on the state by casting 61% for the Republicans. And in Illinois a similar condition existed. The city of Chicago, second largest in the old Northwest, assured a Republican electoral victory by an emphatic majority of 59%. Rural Illinois returned an even narrower majority for that party than did rural Indiana, giving Lincoln 50.19%.[43] However, in the only other cities of the region, Detroit and Milwaukee, the Republicans were weaker than in Chicago, the former voting for Lincoln by 52%, while Douglas carried Milwaukee with 55%. In rural Michigan and Wisconsin the Republicans received 57%. The frontier states of Minnesota and Iowa were without cities in 1860; each was carried by Lincoln, who obtained 63% and 55% respectively in the two states. On the Pacific coast the only city was San Francisco, where the Republican ticket ran far better than in rural California. The election was a hard fought three-way contest in that state, the electoral vote of which went to Lincoln by a small plurality. It was the better showing of the Republicans in the city which enabled them to carry the state. Lincoln had 47.5% in San Francisco, and only 31% in the rural vote. Douglas led the poll in the country, and

---

[42] See Appendix, Table III, "Northwest and Pacific Coast."

[43] There was a difference between the rural voters of the northern and southern portions of the states of Ohio, Indiana, and Illinois. In Illinois, for example, Douglas carried the 9th Congressional district, far downstate, by 80%. A. C. Cole, *The Era of the Civil War 1848-1870* (Springfield, 1919), p. 200. Lexington *Kentucky Statesman*, November 27, 1860.

Breckinridge ran stronger there than he did in the city. Oregon, wholly rural, went for Lincoln by a close plurality over Breckinridge.[44]

Three of the great cities of the nation were situated in the slave states, where the election turned on a contest between Breckinridge and Bell, with Douglas an occasional factor. The city of Baltimore, where Southern feeling flared up in 1861, gave Breckinridge relatively more votes than did rural Maryland, which placed Bell first, although no candidate had a majority in either city or country. In Delaware, which was carried by Breckinridge, the rural voters were far more pronounced in support of him than was the city of Wilmington. Lincoln was second to Breckinridge in the city but last in rural areas, although nowhere in this state did any candidate receive a majority.[45]

A Breckinridge rural trend was clear in Virginia, and a marked preference for Bell and Douglas characterized every city in the state. Richmond and Norfolk gave them 73%, Petersburg 87%, Alexandria, 63%, and Wheeling, 55%—where, in contrast with every other Virginia city, Lincoln received 21%. Breckinridge fail to poll as high as 40% in a single Virginia city, but he was far more popular in the rural precincts, in which he was consistently the leading candidate, and with whose votes he was able to press Bell in the totals. It seems plain that the city vote enabled Bell to win Virginia's electoral vote. North Carolina, a state of villages in 1860, went for Breckinridge by a small majority.

In Kentucky a situation similar to that in Virginia existed. The city of Louisville, the largest in the state, overwhelmed Breckinridge by giving Bell-Douglas the impressive total of 87%. Rural Kentucky also preferred Bell, but Breckinridge was more than three times stronger

[44] Appendix, Table III.
[45] See Appendix, Table IV, " The Upper South."

there than in the city. It may be noted that Douglas'
rural strength was far less than in Louisville. The urban
districts across the Ohio River from Cincinnati, Covington and Newport, Kentucky, were also emphatic in reject-
ing Breckinridge, and gave Lincoln the only appreciable
vote he received in Kentucky. The other border slave state,
Missouri, furnished a further example of urban-rural dis-
agreement. Lincoln carried the city of St. Louis, whose
Germans were a solid Republican phalanx, but only with
a 40% plurality. Bell and Douglas received 57% between
them in the city, and significant was the almost complete
lack of support for Breckinridge, who was the choice of
only 2.4% of the city electorate. But in rural Missouri
the picture was very different. Outside St. Louis, Bell and
Douglas ran well, the former making a much stronger
race than in St. Louis, While Douglas was slightly
stronger in the city. The greatest contrast was in the
Breckinridge rural showing, which was ten times greater
than his city proportion, and in Lincoln's small rural total
of 5.6%. The fact that he was moderately strong in both
St. Louis and the outstate gave Douglas the electoral vote
of Missouri.

Tennessee's two cities, Memphis and Nashville, exhibited the urban-rural clash in their preference for Bell
and Douglas. Memphis gave a tremendous share to them,
89%, with the remainder for Breckinridge. Nashville
voted heavily for John Bell, a resident of the city, and if
the weak Douglas vote be added, went against Breckinridge by 66%. Rural Tennessee gave Bell only a scant
margin over Breckinridge, 47.5% to 46%. The Bell-
Douglas rural total of 55% was less than in either city.

Farther South, the great city of New Orleans returned a
smashing 76% for Bell and Douglas, but rural Louisiana
reversed the city by giving Breckinridge a small outright
majority of 50.3%. Patently it was the rural strength of
Breckinridge which gave him the state's electoral vote.

At Mobile, Alabama's only city, the situation was comparable to that of New Orleans. Douglas carried the city by a plurality, and his vote, together with Bell's, accounted for over 71% of the city's total. But as in Louisiana, the precincts outside Mobile gave Breckinridge 55%, and the electoral vote of Alabama.[46]

The urban-rural division was not so clear in Georgia, where the city of Savannah differed from Mobile and New Orleans in giving Breckinridge the substantial majority of 67%. Augusta, however, was not in accord with Savannah; there Douglas won a plurality, followed by Bell and Breckinridge. The Bell-Douglas total in Augusta exceeded 81%. Rural Georgia gave Breckinridge 49%. The state of South Carolina had not, in 1860, yet made the concession to democracy of adopting popular election in the choice of presidential electors. Charleston has been usually considered the stronghold of secession, and to have been in the van of the movement for Southern nationalism.[47] The argument that the ports of Charleston, Norfolk, Savannah, Mobile and others would be freed from thralldom to Northern ports, apparently was not everywhere heeded, judged by the rejection of Breckinridge in Norfolk, Mobile, and New Orleans.[48]

Certain questions of interest to the historian arise from the foregoing statistical recital.

To what extent did urban political behavior differ from rural? So far as the old Northwest and Pacific coast regions were concerned, the urban-rural results appear to be negative, in that the cities and rural districts differed among themselves and no trend is discernible. But in the most highly urbanized sections of America, New England and the Middle Atlantic states, there was, with some exceptions, a cleavage between city and country. Especi-

[46] See Appendix, Table V, " The Lower South."
[47] Rhodes, III, 123-125.
[48] Appendix, Table V, " The Lower South."

ally was this true with reference to the largest cities of the Northeast. In the slave states all the cities of the border and upper South, save one, and all the cities of the lower South, except Savannah (and probably Charleston), preferred the moderate candidates Bell and Douglas to Breckinridge, the candidate who was represented as an extremist. The rural South nearly everywhere gave either majorities or impressive pluralities to Breckinridge.

The returns from Southern cities were noted hopefully by the Boston *Traveller,* which asserted: " The voting in the principal Southern cities was of a wholesome character. The vote of New Orleans shows that the disunionists can have but little hope of obtaining the control of the lower Mississippi, without which a Southern Confederacy would be worthless." [49] While this prediction proved to be excessively optimistic, the Southern cities, judged by their vote in the election, might have served as nuclei of moderation in the months when peace and war were in the balance.[50] But it was the great Northern cities which by their vote in 1860 tempt the student to speculate whether, if there had been more urbanization, more great cities dependent upon pecuniary relationships—and thus sensitive to tremors and fearful of cataclysms—there would have been an American Civil War.[51] In the month following the election, the New York *World* asserted:

[49] Boston *Daily Evening Traveller,* November 8, 1860, which appended a table of the vote of the more important Southern cities.

[50] Historians have been challenged to investigate the relationship of Southern cities to the secession movement. The fact that New Orleans chose 20 secessionists and but 4 Unionists to the state convention has been cited as proof that cities gave " powerful support " to secession. A. M. Schlesinger in the *Mississippi Valley Historical Review,* XXVII, 56. Although the secession conventions are beyond the scope of this study, it may be suggested that fast-moving events in 1860-1861 may have altered sentiment in the towns which voted for Bell-Douglas.

[51] A recent scholar has pointed out that urban dwellers wished to compromise in 1860-1861. J. G. Randall, " The Civil War Restudied," *Journal of Southern History* (1940), VI, 453. For workingmen's favor-

The strength of the Republican party lies in the rural districts. In rural communities the moral element has more influence in politics than it has in towns, where the quick succession of events and ideas keeps the mind more alert, and does not allow that immobility of mental attitude which is favorable to a persistent contemplation of fixed principles. The slower perceptions of the agricultural mind do not enable it readily to keep up with the rapid pace of movements in revolutionary times.[52]

Did the monetary dependence of dwellers in large cities tend to make them favorable to adjustment and compromise, and, on the other hand, were those who lived in the country more intransigent and favorable to positive action?

On the eve of the Civil War, Congressman Reuben Davis of Mississippi declared his belief that the basic cause of the sectional conflict was an aggressive attack by a combination of interests that we should now describe as Northern capitalism. Ostensibly directed against slavery, it was actually an assault on agriculture—" the primary pursuit of man." The moral issue of slavery was raised merely to screen this attack of " incorporated avarice." With this view Jefferson Davis, a more eminent Mississippian, agreed.[53] Long ignored by historians who could write of the Civil War only in terms of slavery, this thesis has in recent years found wide acceptance among scholars.[54]

able attitude toward peace and compromise, see John R. Commons *et al.*, *History of Labour in the United States* (2 vols., New York, 1921), pp. 10-12.

[52] New York *World*, quoted in Rhodes, III, 165-166, note 4.

[53] *Appendix to the Congressional Globe . . . of the First Session Thirty-Sixth Congress*, pp. 384-387; Charles A. and Mary R. Beard, *The Rise of American Civilization* (2 vols., New York, 1927), II, 3-6. That some with covert economic motives were working to arouse the North to hostility against the South on the moral question of slavery has recently been further demonstrated. George Winston Smith, " Generative Forces of Union Propaganda: A Study in Civil War Pressure Groups." MS, doctoral dissertation, University of Wisconsin, 1939.

[54] For examples, see Frank L. Owsley's essay, " The Irrepressible Con-

Examination of the urban-rural figures of the election of 1860 throws some light on this industrial-agricultural interpretation. It becomes clear that the great urban agglomerations of the Northeast did not, on the whole, vote for Lincoln. If a vote for Lincoln is to be interpreted as a vote for a radical solution of the conflict between North and South, and if the cities are assumed to represent the combination of interests which Davis saw arrayed against agriculture, then the cities of the Northeast, at least, did not cast a vote for Lincoln of such proportions as to follow the Davis formula.[55] The difficulty is that the equation of the cities of the Northeast with the interests of industrial capitalism cannot be made with assurance. To obtain a truer correlation of economic interests with political action further analysis is needed.

flict" in Twelve Southerners, *I'll Take My Stand* (New York, 1930), pp. 61-91; and Louis M. Hacker, *The Triumph of American Capitalism*, p. 339. Prof. A. M. Schlesinger suggests that ". . . the widening breach between South and North rested in considerable part on differences between rural and urban ways of life." *Mississippi Valley Historical Review*, XXVII, 55.

[55] Recently scholars have been reminded that there was perhaps more reason for economic interests to favor peace and conciliation in this crisis than war. James G. Randall, "The Blundering Generation," *ibid.*, pp. 3-28.

APPENDIX

Population figures are from *Census of 1860* (Washsington, 1864), pp. 200-206. Urban election returns are from *The Tribune Almanac and Political Register for 1861* (New York, 1861), and from contemporary city newspapers. For clarity, urban and rural returns have been translated into percentages. The rural vote has been ascertained by deducting the votes of the cities listed below from the state totals.

TABLE I

New England

	Population	Linc.	Doug.	Bell	Breck.
Portland	26,341	58	36	3	3
Rural Maine		62	29	2	6
Manchester	20,107	63	35	1	1
Rural New Hampshire.		57	39.4	.6	3
Vermont (rural)......		76	19	4	1
Boston	177,840	48	23	25	4
Cambridge	26,060	50.06	24	23	2
Roxbury	25,137	46	30	20	4
Charlestown	25,065	34	30	24	12
Chelsea..............	13,395	See Boston			
Lowell	36,827	64	23	10	3
Worcester	24,960	65	26	8	.2
New Bedford	22,300	74	12	8	6
Salem	22,252	64	13	21	2
Rural Massachusetts ...		66	20	11	3
Providence	50,666	65	35 *		
Rural Rhode Island		60	40		
New Haven	39,267	49	21	4	26
Hartford	29,152	53	22.2	2	22.4
Rural Connecticut		55	21	4	20

* Fusion of Douglas-Bell

TABLE II

Middle Atlantic States

	Pop.	Linc.	Fusion (Breck., Bell, Douglas)	Doug.	Bell
New York City	805,658	35	65		
Brooklyn	266,661	44	56		
Buffalo	81,129	53	47		
Albany	62,367	44	56		
Rochester	48,204	56	44		
Troy	39,235	45	55		
Syracuse	28,119	57	43		
Utica	22,259	51	49		
Rural New York........		58	42		
Jersey City & Hoboken..	38,888	42	58		
Newark	71,941	46	54		
Rural New Jersey.......		49	51		
Philadelphia	565,529	50.7	28	12	9
Pittsburgh	49,217	66	25	6	2.5
Allegheny	28,702	74	21.5	.5	3.8
Reading	23,162	55	40	2	3
Rural Pennsylvania		57	40	1.5	1.3

TABLE III

Northwest and Pacific Coast

	Pop.	Linc.	Douglas	Bell	Breck.
Cincinnati	161,044	46	41	12	1
Cleveland	43,417	58	38	.7	3
Columbus	18,554	47	50	1	1
Dayton	20,081	52	45	2	1
Rural Ohio		53	42	2	3
Indianapolis	18,611	61	34	3	2
Rural Indiana		50.8	42.6	2	4.5
Chicago	109,260	59	39	.6	.5
Rural Illinois		50.19	47.5	1.4	.7
Detroit	45,619	52	46	1.3	.7
Rural Michigan		57	42	.5	.2
Milwaukee	45,246	44	55	.4	.4
Rural Wisconsin		57	42	.07	.5
Minnesota (rural)....		63	34	.2	2
Iowa-rural		55	43	.8	1.3
San Francisco	56,802	47.5	28	6.5	18
Rural California		31	33	5.6	30.4
Oregon-rural		36.5	27.4	1.3	34.7

TABLE IV

The Upper South

	Pop.	Breck.	Bell	Doug.	Bell-Doug.	Linc.
Wilmington ...	21,258	33	25	12	37	28
Rural Delaware.		48	24	5	29	23
Baltimore	212,418	49.6	42	5	47	3
Rural Maryland.		44	47	7	54	2
Louisville	68,058	11.5	51.5	35.5	87	1.2
Covington	16,471	10.6	41.8	37.6	79	9.8
Newport	10,046	55.6	33.5	38	71	23.5
Rural Kentucky.		38	45	16	60	.5
St. Louis	160,773	2.4	19.5	37.4	57	40.7
Rural Missouri.		21.4	37.6	35	72.6	5.6
Richmond	37,910	27	56	17	73	
Norfolk.......	14,620	27	59	14	73	
Portsmouth	9,462	38	46	15	61	.2
Petersburg.....	18,266	12	53	34	87	
Alexandria	12,654	37	55	8	63	.1
Wheeling	14,083	23	33	22	55	21
Rural Virginia .		46	44	9	53	1
North Carolina (rural)		50.4	46	2.8	49	
Memphis	22,623	11	45	44	89	
Nashville	16,988	34	59	6.5	66	
Rural Tennessee		46	47.5	6.4	54	

TABLE V

The Lower South

	Pop.	Breck.	Bell	Doug.	Bell-Doug.	Linc.
Savannah	22,292	67	21	12	33	
Augusta	12,493	18.6	35	46	81	
Rural Georgia..		49	41	10	51	
Mobile	29,258	28.6	33.5	37.8	71	
Rural Alabama.		55	31	14	45	
Florida (rural).		59	38	2.5	41	
Mississippi (rural)		59	36	5	41	
New Orleans...	168,675	24	47.5	28	76	
Rural Louisiana.		50.3	38	11	49	
Arkansas (rural)		53	37	10	47	
Texas (rural)..		75.5	..	..	24.5 Fus.	
Charleston	40,522					
South Carolina..	No popular election					

ON THE DANGERS OF AN URBAN INTER-
PRETATION OF HISTORY

BY

WILLIAM DIAMOND

" There seems likely to be an urban reinterpretation of our history," Frederick Jackson Turner predicted near the end of his career.[1] Certainly the past decade has witnessed a great increase of interest in the city among students of American history. A vast number of books devoted to the history of individual cities and to the whole process of urbanization has been published. The American Historical Association has recently devoted several sessions to various aspects of urbanization. Finally, Arthur M. Schlesinger, who first used the growth of cities as a synthesizing principle around which to write part of the history of the United States, has submitted a plan for a " reconsideration of American history from the urban point of view." [2] In view of this increasing interest and of the tendency towards the use of an urban interpretation, it may be useful to reexamine the meaning of the term " city," the way in which the concept has grown among the sociologists who have studied the phenomenon, and its usefulness and validity as a synthetic principle.

Sociological interest in the city began in America towards the end of the nineteenth century. Throughout the century, in popular and scholarly literature alike, may be found evidence of a growing awareness of the city and of

[1] Letter to Arthur M. Schlesinger, Madison, Wis., in Schlesinger, " The City in American History," *Mississippi Valley Historical Review* (1940), XXVII, 43.

[2] *Ibid.*

its dissimilarity from and antagonism to the countryside. Even the historians, with their notoriously narrow approach to history, could not fail to note the towns and to include in their writings a few brief comments concerning them. During the last quarter of the century they began to exhibit a greater interest in the contrast of city and country, though even then they rarely went beyond a statistical enumeration of urban facts, an occasional interpolation of anecdotes of social life, and a brief discussion of the municipal problems and corruption which accompanied the emergence of an urban civilization. Of the men who wrote of America on a grand scale, only Edward Channing pointed to growing urban society as having a culture filled with significance for American history.[3] Even less frequent were the historical writers who, like Ellen Churchill Semple or Frederick Jackson Turner, concerned themselves with the conditions prerequisite to the rise of cities and to the significance of their geographic location.[4] But while the historians were writing the stories of cities primarily in terms of statistics and anecdotal antiquarianism, another group of scholars and writers were coming to the front, devoting much of their attention to the life of the city, well aware of the contrast of city and country, and interested in making the city a better place in which to live. This new point of view came in the eighties and nineties with the municipal reform movements and the development of sociology as an autonomous science. From this view was to develop urban sociology, with which much of this essay is concerned

[3] Edward Channing, *A History of the United States* (6 vols., New York, 1905-1925), V, Ch. III, " The Urban Migration."
[4] See, for instance, Ellen Churchill Semple, *American History and its Geographic Conditions* (Boston, 1903) ; Frederick Jackson Turner, *Rise of the New West, 1819-1829* (New York, 1906), pp. 96, 98-99, and " The Significance of the Mississippi Valley in American History," in *The Frontier in American History* (New York, 1920), pp. 194-96.

because it is primarily the sociologist who studies " the groups, institutions, customs, traditions, attitudes, and relations which characterize the city as a type of human aggregation." [5]

Several factors contributed to bring about the simultaneous birth of the municipal reform movement and of urban sociology at this time.[6] Both developed during the period when American cities were growing with astonishing rapidity and began to dominate the nation economically and politically. Industrialization and urbanization contributed to the development of various problems whose intensity seemed to vary in proportion with the size of the city—slums, public health, bossism, and political corruption especially struck everyone who visited a big city and impressed themselves upon the minds of students and travellers alike as signs of urban degeneration. They provided ocular evidence for the dictum of Thomas Jefferson that cities are cancers on the body politic. James Bryce impressed his public with the judgment that municipal government was the one conspicuous failure of American democracy. Just as cities were seen to corrupt those who lived within them, so they appeared to enslave the non-urban inhabitants of the nation; for in the cities were centered the new power of finance, the management of railroads, and the manufacture of machinery which were

[5] Stuart A. Queen and Lewis Francis Thomas, *The City: A Study of Urbanism in the United States* (New York, 1939), p. 15.

[6] For discussions of the rise of urban sociology, see Nels Anderson, " The Trend of Urban Sociology," in George A. Lundberg, Read Bain, Nels Anderson, *et al., Trends in American Sociology* (New York, 1929); Carle C. Zimmerman, " The Trend of Rural Sociology," *ibid.*; Floyd N. House, *The Development of Sociology* (New York, 1936), Ch. XXIX. The sketch which follows is meant merely to give an indication of the scope and range of urban sociology. There is no intention of giving a full bibliography, of giving more than a sample of trends in urban study. Nor is it possible within the range of this essay to discuss popular literature on the city, which itself has a long history and is a subject for the historian of social thought, or scholarly literature in other disciplines.

revolutionizing agriculture, subjecting it to omnipotent capitalism. Upon the cities was therefore focused the hate of the rural majority of America, and at the same time to the cities flocked millions of farmers and small-towners attracted by economic opportunity, intellectual preeminence, urban social advantage, and the general " lure of the city."

At the same time, American universities were undergoing a renaissance. The universities were being freed at last from the yoke of theology, and a new generation of scholars, trained in the scientific seminars of Europe, was coming to the front. The universities of Europe, and especially of Germany, had never lost the civic tradition; and during the second half of the nineteenth century the attention of historical and political scholars was focused on the problems connected with the origins of towns and cities. American students therefore returned to the United States with greater awareness of urban life. Moreover, they had seen the beginnings of German and English municipal socialism in action, and they frequently came back with an enthusiasm for municipal ownership of public utilities as the chief cure for urban ills.

The first stage in the development of urban sociology lasted until the first decade of the twentieth century—a period when most of the writing on the city was characterized by the zeal and idealism of the reformer, whether it came from evangelical sociologists, or from " humanitarian statisticians," or from leaders of the settlement house movement. As Nels Anderson has put it, " we cannot separate the beginnings of urban sociology from the perennial battle to wipe out the slum." [7] The new study was " the rationalization of philanthropy and social reform." [8] Whether they saw the city as a blot on the

[7] Anderson, " The Trend of Urban Sociology," in *Trends in American Sociology,* p. 270.

[8] House, *The Development of Sociology,* the title of his chapter on the subject.

American escutcheon or as "the hope of democracy," writers on the city were unanimously impressed by the urban "problem," and they described it in terms of reform and in the style of the muckraker. They generally believed utility companies and franchises were the source of urban difficulties. More often than not, there was a strong strain of ethical idealism in their thought. Almost unanimously they prescribed political reform, or education of the masses, or propaganda for the public ownership of utilities as the urban cure-all. They were militant applied sociologists. Typical of various elements in this group of writers are Josiah Strong, D. F. Wilcox, Lincoln Steffens, Richard T. Ely, and Frederic C. Howe. To these should be added Charles Zueblin, who was, in a sense, a transitional figure.

Strong, in *The Twentieth Century City,* expressed his conviction that the problem of the city was essentially an ethical one. "The sudden expansion of the city marks a profound change in civilization, the results of which will grow more and more obvious; and nowhere probably will this change be so significant as in our own country, where the twentieth century city will be decisive of national destiny." [9] For in the city social ideals undergo drastic change, and the old morality is forgotten. The "social dynamite" that produced the city was machine technology, the application of machinery to agriculture, and railroad transportation. But the only cure for the growing ills of urban society is twentieth-century Christianity; for a nation ruled by cities is a nation ruled by materialism, and in such a nation free institutions must perish. Through the teachings of Jesus, a public conscience must be developed. Then will the city become "the symbol of *heaven*—heaven on earth—the Kingdom fully come." [10]

[9] *The Twentieth Century City* (New York, 1898), p. 32.
[10] *Ibid.,* pp. 180-81. In *The New Era or The Coming Kingdom* (New

6

Like Strong, Wilcox, in *The American City: A Problem in Democracy*, declared that " the influence of cities upon the national life is quite out of proportion to their population. For the city is the distributing centre of intelligence as well as of goods." It "tends to impose its ethical and social ideals upon the whole people." " Democracy . . . has been badly damaged by its contact with city conditions." " Shall the city be permitted to destroy democracy and thereby undermine our national institutions? " he asked. " Shall the city be permitted to absorb the brains and wealth of the nation and consume them wastefully? " [11] After devoting chapters to the problems of the city street, of the control of public utilities, of civic education, municipal insurance, popular and official responsibility, Wilcox suggested remedies, but all were "ultimately dependent upon the transformation of our

York, 1893), Strong cites a few passages from Tennyson's Locksley Hall Sixty Years After, which includes such gems as:

Is it well that while we range with Science, glorying the Time,
City children soak and blacken soul and sense in city slime?

There among the glooming alleys Progress halts on palsied feet,
Crime and hunger cast our maidens by the thousands on the street.
(p. 193)

See also Strong: *Our Country: Its Possible Future and Its Present Crisis* (New York, 1885) ; " Problems of the Twentieth Century City," *North American Review* (1897), CLXV, 343-49; *The Challenge of the City* (New York, 1907). See also Walter Rauschenbusch: *Christianity and the Social Crisis* (New York, 1907) ; " The State of the Church in the Social Movement," *American Journal of Sociology* (1897), III, 18-30. " The larger our cities grow the less hold does religion seem to have over the multitude of men and the general life. . . . For one thing, the people of our great cities are cut off from nature and from nature's God. All that they see and touch was made by man. To men in Chicago the heavens do not declare the glory of God, for they are covered with smoke. . . ." (pp. 29-30). See also L. Abbott, *Christianity and Social Problems* (Boston, 1896). Though the emphasis was at first on evangelism alone, this was soon supplemented with " charity, neighborhood work and social legislation." Anderson, " The Trend of Urban Sociology," in *Trends in American Sociology*, p. 267.

[11] New York, 1904, pp. 14, 21, 22.

ethical standards." [12]   Like Strong, Wilcox believed an ethical reawakening would solve the problems created by the economic and social facts which channeled city life. He believed in the efficacy of a "combined civic intelligence and civic conscience so far removed from the spirit now dominating municipal politics that it may be said to involve a radical change in human nature or in the conditions under which human nature finds expression." [13] Again in *Great Cities in America. Their Problems and Their Government*, Wilcox discussed the problems of six metropolises—each in terms of political corruption. The panacea was to be public ownership, and all who opposed it did so only because they thought government corrupt and inefficient.[14]

In *The Shame of the Cities* Lincoln Steffens took his readers through several great American cities revealing the political and social decay which lay beneath the surface.[15]   Steffens may be cited as representative of the whole group of muckrakers who, from the early nineties, tried to point out the inequalities in capitalist society. His was a literature of exposure.   He presented "cold facts," the result of painstaking observation; but he presented them in such a way as to arouse sympathy and indignation.

The shame of the shameless cities was pointed to by others like Steffens—by such men as Jacob Riis and Hutchins Hapgood, S. S. McClure and George Kibbe Turner, novelists Paul Leicester Ford and Alfred Henry

---

[12] *Ibid.*, p. 402.   [13] *Ibid.*, p. 20.

[14] New York, 1910. For a similar approach to the city, see Frank Parsons, *The City for the People; or, The Municipalization of the City Government and of Local Franchises* (Philadelphia, 1900). "The most pressing problem of the age is the problem of monopoly," and public ownership was the cure. (p. 14) "In education lies the final hope, for at bottom it is a new intelligence and a new ideal, that must be relied on to mould the real to a more perfect form." (p. 13)

[15] New York, 1904. The volume was originally published as individual essays in *McClure's Magazine*.

Lewis.[16] These men wrote; others wrote and acted. "Working with the intellectual tools forged for them by Henry George, a group of old-fashioned Americans, Jeffersonians in their tastes and predilections, marched forth in the nineties and the early years of this century to face down the hosts of predatory privilege" as it appeared in cities.[17] "Golden Rule" Jones and Tom Johnson, Brand Whitlock and Newton D. Baker, above all Frederic C. Howe, saw the city, despite graft and slums, as " the hope of democracy."

Howe's study of municipal problems, entitled *The City. The Hope of Democracy*, promised a new approach to the city. This book, he wrote,

is an attempt at the Economic Interpretation of the City. It holds that the corruption, the indifference, the incompetence of the official and the apathy of the citizen, the disparity of wealth, the poverty, vice, crime, and disease, are due to causes economic and industrial. They are traceable to our Institutions rather than to the depravity of human nature. Their correction is not a matter of education or of the penal code. It is a matter of industrial democracy. The incidental conditions are personal and ethical. Whether we adopt the personal or the economic interpretation will determine our attitude towards the problems of modern city life.[18]

[16] See the discussion of the contents of these writings in the chapter on " The Shameless Cities," in C. C. Regier, *The Era of the Muckrakers* (Chapel Hill, 1932), and the very full bibliography of muckraking in the same volume. See also " The Shame of the Cities " and " The Search for Democracy" in Louis Filler, *Crusaders for American Liberalism* (New York, 1939). The results of the factory system, slums, poverty, transience, the mission and settlement work such as Hull House and South End House were all the subject of a voluminous literature. See, for instance, the work of Jane Addams, such as *The Spirit of Youth and the City Streets* (New York, 1914); or of Robert A. Woods, such as *The City Wilderness* (Boston, 1898).

[17] John Chamberlain, *Farewell to Reform* (New York, 1932), pp. 56-57.

[18] New York, 1905, pp. vii-viii.

Howe's approach to the city seems far different from that of Josiah Strong, yet in reality the two men did not differ so greatly. Like the other municipal reformers, like Steffens and Whitlock, Howe had never learned, in John Chamberlain's words (and Howe himself admitted it later), "to pursue the truth to its ultimate lair—at bottom he was a moralist, not a realist or a scientist." Democracy was to be saved by the "best minds," like those of Richard T. Ely and Woodrow Wilson, whose lectures at the Johns Hopkins University helped rouse in him the desire to reform the city.[19]

Ely had done his graduate work in Germany and had returned to America to join the ranks of the municipal reformers. In *The Coming City* he pointed out the approaching preeminence of the city and demanded a program of reform in city government, an application of business principles to government. If religion would take municipal reform under its wing, Ely saw a bright future for the city. "If I forget thee, O Chicago, O New York, O St. Louis," he cried, "let my right hand forget her cunning."[20] It was Ely's discussions of urban problems that helped persuade young Albion W. Small to go to the Johns Hopkins University. Many years later Professor Small said of Ely's writings:

The argument was relatively novel on this side of the Atlantic, and not only in Baltimore but all over the country it was provocative of wholesome discussion. I was on the whole inclined to accept in the main Professor Ely's views about municipal control of public services, but at the same time it seemed to me that the case had been built so far too much upon mere opinion, and that

[19] Chamberlain, *Farewell to Reform*, p. 79. See also Frederic C. Howe: "The City as a Socializing Agency," *AJS* (1912), XVII, 590-601; *The Modern City and Its Problems* (New York, 1915); *The Confessions of a Reformer* (New York, 1925).

[20] New York, 1902, p. 73.

a foundation should be constructed for it by penetrating into the essentials of urban life, and demonstrating the vital character of municipal activities as modes of human effort in general.[21]

Small helped start the Chicago school on its scientific urban studies.

Like Ely, Charles Zueblin was an academic man. He has been credited with the founding of the school of urban sociology at the University of Chicago, although William I. Thomas and Charles R. Henderson did much to turn Chicago's sociological interest to the study of conditions in that city.[22] In his *American Municipal Progress*, Zueblin emphasized the social activities of cities and attempted to develop a rough sociology of municipal communities.[23] In *A Decade of Civic Development*, he discussed the state of urban America at the turn of the century.[24] His book was probably the first used for courses in urban sociology. At any rate, the availability of his *American Municipal Progress* " and a number of other interesting but less comprehensive books dealing with city problems " provided some of the impetus for the appearance of " courses in urban sociology, problems of city life, and the like." [25]

Under the leadership of Henderson, Small, Thomas, and Zueblin, the department of sociology at the University of Chicago was organized in the 1890's and from then dates the beginning of the scientific study of urban sociology. Innumerable studies of various aspects of the

[21] Albion W. Small, "Fifty Years of Sociology in the United States (1865-1915)," *AJS* (1916), XXI, 734, 768.

[22] Lewis Mumford, *The Culture of Cities* (New York, 1938), p. 500; Louis Wirth, "The Urban Society and Civilization," *AJS* (1940), XLV, 746; Jesse Bernard, "The History and Prospects of Sociology in the United States," in *Trends in American Sociology*, pp. 25-26.

[23] *American Municipal Progress. Chapters in Municipal Sociology* (New York, 1902).

[24] Chicago, 1905.

[25] House, *The Development of Sociology*, p. 294.

urban environment began to appear. But it was at Columbia, not Chicago, that the first landmark in the scientific stage of the study of American cities was set up. In 1899 Adna F. Weber published *The Growth of Cities in the Nineteenth Century.*[26] It was a thorough statistical analysis of American and European cities, a study of their population and economic activities, of their growth and development, and of rural-urban migration.

Meanwhile the Chicago school, impressed by the hustle and bustle of a great city, was turning its attention to the systematic study of Chicago. It was a common belief of the time, advocated by Herbert Baxter Adams among others, that "the city offers a laboratory of social and political life in which the problems of society can be more effectively studied" than anywhere else.[27] No aspect of Chicago's environment was neglected. The way was pointed, Louis Wirth has suggested, by the publication of the *Catechism for Social Observation* by Charles Richmond Henderson and *An Introduction to the Study of Society* by Small and George Vincent, both in 1894.[28] A host of dissertations began to appear which were "modelled after the pioneer studies of American communities begun at Johns Hopkins University" under Adams, but which differed from them in being "based upon firsthand observations of life rather than the perusal of books."[29] Courses in municipal problems or municipal sociology appeared in college curricula all over the coun-

[26] Columbia University Studies in History, Economics, and Public Law, XI, New York, 1899.

[27] John Martin Vincent, "Herbert B. Adams," in Howard W. Odum, ed., *American Masters of Social Science. An Approach to the Study of Social Sciences Through a Neglected Field of Biography* (New York, 1927), p. 118.

[28] Wirth, "The Urban Society and Civilization," *AJS* (1940), XLV, 745-46. This article concerns primarily the work done in urban sociology at the University of Chicago from the beginning to the present.

[29] *Ibid.*, p. 746.

try.[30] Though urban sociology has never become a clear-cut, distinct branch of study, its outlines were separating out of the parent subject early in the century.

Coincident with the rise of the academic schools of urban sociology, a new instrument for the study of urban communities was developed—the social survey. This was one of the products of the revelations of the muckrakers, an attempt by scholars and municipal and philanthropic organizations to make more systematic, more objective the investigations of city life made by the journalists of exposure. The goal of the investigations was practical reform. In 1909, the Pittsburgh Survey was begun, the first of a long series of similar surveys of American cities which are less important to the historian for concrete results in social reform than as invaluable source material concerning American life. Like Charles Booth's monumental *Life and Labor of the People in London*, the Pittsburgh Survey suggested new approaches and new techniques in social study. Not only the city as a whole, but such aspects of urban society as religion or the slum, were subjected to the searching investigations of the social survey.[31]

With the growing use of the social survey and the increasing interest in urban sociology in the universities, more people devoted their attention to the study of various aspects of urban life. The names of Robert E. Park, Ernest

[30] See Frank L. Tolman, "The Study of Sociology in Institutions of Learning in the United States," *AJS* (1902), VII, 797-838; (1902-03), VIII, 85-121, 251-72, 531-38; L. L. Bernard, "Some Historical and Recent Trends of Sociology in the United States," *Southwestern Political and Social Science Quarterly* (1928), IX, 264-93; Harmon O. DeGraff, "The Teaching of Urban Sociology," *Social Forces* (1926), V, 248-54.

[31] See Niles Carpenter, "Social Surveys," *Encyclopedia of the Social Sciences*, XIV, 162-65. For a useful history and bibliography of the social survey, see Allen Eaton and Shelby M. Harrison, *A Bibliography of Social Surveys. Reports of Fact-Finding Studies Made as a Basis for Social Action; Arranged by Subjects and Localities. Reports to January 1, 1928* (New York, 1930).

W. Burgess, R. D. McKenzie, William F. Ogburn, and Louis Wirth, among others, are inseparably associated with the study of urbanism in America. In 1915, Park published his challenging essay on "The City: Suggestions for the Investigation of Human Behavior in the City Environment." [32] It was a discussion of problems to be investigated, a set of hypotheses concerning the nature of the urban environment and urban behavior. The essay, though it suggested subjects primarily for the social survey and the student of sociology, is important for the historian as well, since it pointed the questions he must ask of the city at every stage of its development. Under the impetus of Park, Burgess, and McKenzie developed a study called urban ecology, of loosely defined limits, concerned with "the relations between men and their natural environments." Its advocates have taken over the terminology of plant and animal ecology to the study of natural areas within the city, the spatial distribution of people and institutions, ecological organization and succession, and symbiosis. The result is a vast literature of precise and detailed works on population succession and concentration, on the physical organization and growth of the city and its region, and on urban areas and personalities—such studies as Wirth's *The Ghetto*, Thrasher's *The Gang*, Zorbaugh's *The Gold Coast and Slum*, and Anderson's *The Hobo*. Debate has raged around the concept of urban ecology. Indeed the ecologists themselves generally reject the strict environmental determinism implicit in the concept and the work they do is usually descriptive in character.[33]

[32] *AJS* (1915), XX, 577-612.

[33] For a discussion of the meanings of ecology and of how it has been used, as well as for a comprehensive bibliography of the subject, see James A. Quinn, "Topical Summary of Current Literature on Human Ecology," *AJS* (1940), XLVI, 191-226. His bibliography of 347 items illustrates the range of ecological literature, from housing and mental diseases to natural areas and migration. See also R. D. McKenzie, "The Ecological Approach to the Study of the Human Community," *AJS*

Despite the vast growing literature on cities, there was no formal urban sociology until the late twenties. In 1925 appeared *The City*, a volume of essays designed to provide a frame of reference for studies on the nature of urbanism and on urban life.[34]   All offer suggestions to the historian, but the most important for the historian of the American city are undoubtedly the first, Park's 1915 essay on " The City," and the last, Louis Wirth's detailed selective " Bibliography of the Urban Community."   Not quite so provocative, but more indicative of the character of the overwhelming bulk of urban sociological research in America, was a second volume of essays, *The Urban Community*, made up of papers read before the 1925 meeting of the American Sociological Society.[35]   This, like the preceding volume, was meant to be " an introduction to an urban sociology," a " prospectus of the present state and promise of sociological research " on the city. The assumption implicit in most of these studies is that the city is a living organism; it is, therefore, studied in terms of human ecology.   The first textbook in urban sociology, by Nels Anderson and Eduard C. Lindeman, appeared in 1928, and since then various systematic treatments of urbanism have been published.[36]

(1924), XXX, 287-301, and " The Field and Problems of Demography, Human Geography, and Human Ecology," in L. L. Bernard, ed., *The Fields and Methods of Sociology* (New York, 1934), pp. 52-66; C. A. Dawson, " The Sources and Methods of Human Ecology," *ibid.*, pp. 286-302.

[34] By Park, Burgess, and McKenzie, with a Bibliography by Wirth (Chicago, 1925).

[35] E. W. Burgess, ed. (Chicago, 1926).

[36] Anderson and Lindeman, *Urban Sociology: An Introduction to the Study of Urban Communities* (New York, 1928). See for instance, Scott E. W. Bedford, *Readings in Urban Sociology* (New York, 1927), valuable for its bibliography; Maurice R. Davie, *Problems of City Life. A Study in Urban Sociology* (New York, 1932); Pitrim Sorokin and C. C. Zimmerman, *Principles of Rural-Urban Sociology* (New York, 1931), important primarily for the huge quantities of material it contains, not for its formulation of an urban-rural sociology; Niles Carpenter, *The*

On the initiative of Professor Park, Charles E. Merriam, and others, the Local Community Research Committee of the University of Chicago was organized in 1923. The result was to make Chicago the most thoroughly studied city in the United States. The numberless studies of political, economic, and social life were frequently semi-historical in nature, presented a wealth of material concerning contemporary Chicago, and therefore suggested conclusions concerning the nature of urban growth throughout America. In 1929 a review of the work of the Committee was published which discussed many of its activities and provided a useful bibliography of all the work undertaken under its sponsorship.[37]

The group of scholars associated with this work has since expanded its definition of the urban community to

Sociology of City Life (New York, 1932); Noel P. Gist and L. A. Halbert, *Urban Society* (New York, 1933); Howard Woolston, *Metropolis. A Study of Urban Communities* (New York, 1938); Stuart A. Queen and L. F. Thomas, *The City: A Study of Urbanism in the United States* (New York, 1939); Lewis Mumford, *The Culture of Cities* (New York, 1938); National Resources Committee, *Our Cities. Their Role in the National Economy* (Washington, 1937). The short sketch in the survey of *Our Cities*, the first national study of cities on a scale comparable to that of Theodore Roosevelt's Country Life Commission in 1909, presents, in brief scope, the underlying forces in the process of urbanization, the characteristics of urban populations, and the problems of cities. The emphasis is on present urban problems, but the study notes the development of those problems through the past and their importance in inducing the attitudes and institutions which characterize urban populations. A summary of the special studies undertaken by the Urbanism Committee of the NRC appears in *Our Cities*, p. 71. Historians of the American city have the advantage of the information on various aspects of urban life collected for many years by agencies of the federal government. Unfortunately that material has many and serious gaps and deficiencies. For a summary and discussion of what is available, see the section on "Federal Reporting of Urban Information," in the NRC's report on *Urban Government* (Washington, 1939).

[37] T. V. Smith and Leonard D. White, *Chicago: An Experiment in Social Science Research* (Chicago, 1929). For a more recent description of the work being done on the metropolitan region of Chicago, see *AJS* (1936), XLII, 563-65.

include the entire metropolitan area of the city. This change in the focus of urban studies—common to students of the city all over the country—came in response to the fact that as new and faster means of communication and transportation developed, the style of urban growth began to change. Instead of continuously accelerating concentration, a counter-trend towards decentralization and suburbanization had set in. Population began to spill out of the municipality. The result was great sprawling conurbations of people and " the emergence of metropolitan districts instead of individual cities as the actual areas of urban life." [38]   The legal " city " was a unit which no longer corresponded to a real situation. Its students had therefore to concern themselves with the metropolitan area, which had no respect for political boundaries. As a consequence of this realization came such studies as Merriam's *The Government of The Metropolitan Region of Chicago*, Max R. White's *Water Supply Organization in the Chicago Region*, and Albert Lepawsky's *The Judicial System of Metropolitan Chicago*.[39] Transportation and communication had been sped up to the point, as Professor Lepawsky put it, " where the daily movement of people and of goods and the judicial conflicts arising from this movement are no longer restricted by political boundaries or jurisdictional lines." [40]

Various methods have been used to delimit the metropolitan area or the city region. The United States Census has defined " metropolitan districts " in terms of " continuous density "; all those parts of the urban environs having a certain density are considered part of the metro-

---

[38] NRC, *Our Cities* (Washington, 1937), pp. 10-11. This is a digest of the full report cited previously.

[39] Charles E. Merriam, Spencer D. Parratt, and Albert Lepawsky (Chicago, 1933); Max R. White, *Water Supply Organization* (Chicago, 1934); Lepawsky, *The Judicial System of Metropolitan Chicago* (Chicago, 1932).

[40] *Ibid.*, p. 9.

politan district of the city.[41]   A definition larger in extent but based on economic and social conditions has expanded the region to include " the area within which there is a large daily movement of population to and from the center for work, trade, amusement or other purposes." [42] Many criteria have been used for actually delimiting such a district—including various definitions of the trading area of a city.[43]   Roughly upon such a scheme as this the Chicago Region has been defined.   " It was adopted as the basis of study after a number of factors, including retail trading, commutation, telephone service, and free delivery zones, showed the fifty-mile district to be the approximate area of daily activity around the metropolis of Chicago." [44]

One of the more interesting definitions—a definition associated with one of the functions performed by the city in every culture—has been suggested by Professor Park.

People go to the city, as the farmer goes to town, not merely to market their products or their talents, as the case may be, but to meet people and to get the news. As the ultimate source of a common culture is, in a manner of speaking, common talk, the

[41] United States Bureau of the Census, *Metropolitan Districts. Population and Area* (Washington, 1932), p. 5. See the note on the same page concerning the efforts of the United States Chamber of Commerce to define a metropolitan region.

[42] Thomas H. Reed, " Metropolitan Areas," *Encyclopedia of the Social Sciences*, X, 397. See the bibliography following the article.

[43] In 1927 the United States Bureau of Foreign and Domestic Commerce published an atlas in which the nation was divided into metropolitan trading regions based on wholesale grocery trading. See United States Department of Commerce, *Atlas of Wholesale Grocery Territories* (Domestic Commerce Series, No. 7, Washington, 1927). The trade area of a city has been defined as " the surrounding geographical territory economically tributary to a city and for which such city provides the chief market and financial center." John W. Pole, Comptroller of the Currency, quoted in R. D. McKenzie, *The Metropolitan Community* (New York, 1933), p. 84.

[44] Lepawsky, *The Judicial System of Metropolitan Chicago*, p. x.

market place, wherever it is, has been, and still remains, a cultural center for the territory tributary to it.

The trade and culture areas of a city therefore coincide, Professor Park maintains, and this area may be measured by newspaper circulation. The circulation of metropolitan dailies likewise measures " the extent and degree of dependence of the suburbs upon the metropolis, and of the metropolis upon the larger region which it dominates." The " area of urban influence " may be measured in terms of the " gradients of declining newspaper circulation." [45] In the region dominated by a particular paper, " the trade routes, agencies of communication, news, and objects of attention come to focus in the metropolis. Metropolitan patterns of behavior are successively modified with increased distance from the center of dominance." [46]

Associated to some extent with the study of metropolitan regions is the rapidly growing literature of regionalism. Stemming from a revived interest in human geography, from the planning movement, and from the administrative problems of urban areas, the study of regions is generally associated in America with the names of Howard W. Odum, Harry E. Moore, and Rupert B. Vance.[47] It is related to the whole body of literature on

[45] " Urbanization as Measured by Newspaper Circulation," *AJS* (1929), XXXV, 62. See also Seldon Cowles Menefee, " Newspaper Circulation and Urban Regions," *Sociology and Social Research* (1936), XXI, 63-66; Park and Charles Newcomb, "Newspaper Circulation and Metropolitan Regions," in McKenzie, *The Metropolitan Community*, Ch. VIII.

[46] Dawson, " The Sources and Methods of Human Ecology," in *The Fields and Methods of Sociology*, p. 296.

[47] See the series of articles on regionalism by Shelby M. Harrison, Rupert B. Vance, William E. Cole, L. L. Bernard, Paul S. Taylor, and Louis Wirth in *Publications of the American Sociological Society* (1935), XXIX, 81-115, especially that of Vance, " Implications of the Concepts ' Region ' and ' Regional Planning.' " See Howard W. Odum, *Southern Regions of the United States* (Chapel Hill, 1936), for a discussion of regionalism and of the urbanization of the South; Odum and Harry E. Moore, *American Regionalism* (New York, 1938) ; Vance, *Human Geography of the South. A Study in Regional Resources and Human Adequacy*

city and regional planning, which blossomed in the 'twenties and 'thirties and is perhaps best summed up in Lewis Mumford's comprehensive and brilliant, if occasionally erratic and unintelligible study, *The Culture of Cities*.[48] *The Regional Survey of New York and Its Environs*, which has been called the " most complete discussion of urban growth and its control," and the work of the National Resources Committee are models of the technique of city and regional planning.[49]

A step further in the determination of urban regions is involved in the study of metropolitan economy. The concept of metropolitan economy is associated with N. S. B. Gras who has pointed the way in the study of the great American cities as nuclear centers, as the economic nerve centers of huge hinterlands.[50] Various cities, through control of markets and finance and through the development of manufactures and of transportation and communication facilities, have become the " symbols " for the economic organization of huge subsidiary territories, the cores of

(Chapel Hill, 1932), like Odum's volume, includes material on the rise of cities in the South and discussion of the differences between southern and northern towns; Benton MacKaye, *The New Exploration; A Philosophy of Regional Planning* (New York, 1928).

[48] Mumford's book is one of the most stimulating and suggestive studies of urbanism published in America. It contains an excellent critical bibliography of the most important works in English, French, and German on the nature of urban life, the history of towns and cities, city planning, and regionalism.

[49] *The Regional Survey of New York and Its Environs* (8 vols., New York, 1927-31), especially Volume I, R. M. Haig and R. C. McCrea, *Major Economic Factors in Metropolitan Growth and Arrangement*. See Henry Wright's important " Report on a Plan for the State of New York," in New York State, Housing and Regional Planning Commission, *Final Report* (Albany, 1926). NCR, *Regional Factors in National Planning* (Washington, 1926); *Regional Planning. Part I—Pacific Northwest, Part II—St. Louis Region, Part III—New England* (Washington, 1936).

[50] See N. S. B. Gras: " The Development of Metropolitan Economy in Europe and America," *American Historical Review* (1922), XXVII, 695-708; *An Introduction to Economic History* (New York, 1922); " The Rise of the Metropolitan Community," *Pub. Amer. Soc. Soc.* (1926), XX, 155-63.

great economic structures, rather than independent entities. For instance, Mildred L. Hartsough's analysis of *The Twin Cities as a Metropolitan Market: A Regional Study of the Economic Development of Minneapolis and St. Paul* is a discussion of those cities as the center of a great economic region.[51] This kind of region, however, is based on economic organization; it is the area of economic dominance.

These studies may be considered a part of the vast literature on ecology. Summed up in Professor Park's article, and to a lesser extent in the work of Professor Gras, is not only a definition of the metropolitan region, but a statement as well of the ecological concepts of dominance and the gradients by which dominance is measured. The concept of dominance has been applied not only to the metropolitan region, but also to world economic organization focused in cities, by Professors Gras and McKenzie, for instance, and to local areas, such as the dominance of the downtown areas of modern cities, by Professor Burgess.[52] Such studies suggest a biological analogy.

The differentiation of areas, the distribution of institutional units [Professor Dawson says] and their complex integration take place with reference to the center of dominance somewhat after the manner in which a higher organism has its parts coordinated and controlled by means of the specialized and central cerebral cortex.[53]

[51] Minneapolis, 1925. On the nature and technique of urban financial organization and of urban economic control of the hinterland, see such studies as George Walter Woodworth, *The Detroit Money Market* (Ann Arbor, 1932) and Henrietta Larson, *The Wheat Market and the Farmer of Minnesota* (New York, 1926).

[52] See, for instance, McKenzie, "The Concept of Dominance and World Organization," *AJS* (1927), XXXIII, 28-42, and Burgess, "The Determination of Gradients in the Growth of a City," *Pub. Amer. Soc. Soc.* (1927), XXI, 178-84.

[53] Dawson, "The Sources and Methods of Human Ecology," in *The Fields and Methods of Sociology*, p. 295.

The development of *The Metropolitan Community*, as well as its place in historical perspective, has been ably described by Professor McKenzie in a volume which concentrates, however, on its present nature and problems.[54] The volume discusses the factors making for concentration of people, the economic and social structure of the metropolitan community, and the institutional changes that accompanied its growth. For Professor McKenzie, the economic unity of these metropolitan regions depends upon the functional integration of territorially differentiated and specialized parts. Such an economic relationship is but the latest development in the history of the American city—a product of the bus and the automobile which permitted a tightening up of the immediate hinterland of the city. McKenzie associates the history of American settlement and urbanization with the techniques of transportation, and sketches for each period the rise and growth of urban communities, their function and significance, and the story of interurban conflict. The emphasis is, of course, on the metropolitan organization of twentieth-century America.[55]

James A. Quinn, discussing urban sociology, has pointed out some of the methods used by the sociologist in studying city life.[56] Professor Quinn's classification includes: the historical and geographical method, whereby the location and growth of cities are investigated (thus Weber and Gras) ; historical and community case studies, includ-

---

[54] This is one of the monographs that came from the President's Research Committee on Social Trends. The report of the Committee was published as *Recent Social Trends in the United States* (2 vols., New York, 1933). This, as well as the other volumes enlarged from the report, contains valuable material on American cities.

[55] McKenzie, *The Metropolitan Community, passim.*

[56] Niles Carpenter, T. Earl Sullenger, and James A. Quinn, "The Sources and Methods of Urban Sociology," in *The Fields and Methods of Sociology*, pp. 328-45. See also the chapters on community, ecology, urban and rural sociology.

7

ing the social survey and the study of segregated culture areas in the city (thus the Lynds, Zorbaugh, and Reckless) ; [57] analysis of personal case histories (thus Wirth, Shaw, Thomas, and Cavan) ; [58] statistical method, stemming from the work of Franklin H. Giddings at Columbia, which has too frequently resulted in one of the great weaknesses of American sociology, in what Mumford rightfully calls " the injudicious use of irrelevant statistics" (thus the Census, Ogburn, Park, Burgess, and others on gradients within and without the city) ; [59] the use of maps for the study of land utilization, parks, business, recreation, and for the distribution of various economic and social data; [60] ecological organization. The new work of the Census in preparing population data by permanent census tracts " is now laying the basis for future studies of population distribution, composition and movement within large cities." Professor Quinn's classification is admittedly not exhaustive, yet it suggests to the historian of the American city the many kinds of material placed at his disposal by the urban sociologist.

Another such methodological technique, even more important for the historian, is the concept of culture, adopted by the sociologist from the work of the cultural anthro-

[57] Robert S. and Helen M. Lynd, *Middletown* (New York, 1929), and *Middletown in Transition; A Study in Cultural Conflicts* (New York, 1937), two volumes which use the methods of cultural anthropology and which are of great importance for the study of contemporary urban life; Walter R. Reckless, *Vice in Chicago* (Chicago, 1933), a study of the spatial distribution of vice and of its relation to urban conditions.

[58] Clifford R. Shaw, *The Jack Roller* (Chicago, 1930), and *The Natural History of a Delinquent Career* (Chicago, 1938) ; W. I. Thomas, *The Unadjusted Girl* (Boston, 1923), and the famous volumes by Thomas and Florian Znaniecki, *The Polish Peasant in Europe and America* (5 vols., Chicago, 1918-20) ; Ruth S. Cavan, *Suicide* (Chicago, 1928).

[59] House, *The Development of Sociology*, pp. 367 ff.; Mumford, *The Culture of Cities,* p. 501; William F. Ogburn, *Social Characteristics of Cities* (Chicago, 1937).

[60] See *Region of Chicago Base Map* (Chicago, 1926) and such studies of urban land utilization as Richard M. Hurd, *Principles of City Land Values* (4th ed., New York, 1924).

pologist. The concept of culture was applied to the history of the city by Ralph Turner, at the 1939 meeting of the American Historical Association, in a provocative paper on " The Industrial City: Center of Cultural Change." Dr. Turner described the three classes of social factors— the paradox of competitive economy, the implications of machine technology, and the consequences of urban association—which are concentrated in the industrial city and make up the experience of city people. The day-to-day unconscious working of these factors has channeled the activities of urban dwellers along new lines, has changed their patterns of thought and behavior, has provided the basis for a new culture. In the industrial milieu, new institutions appeared to serve the felt needs of a new society; old institutions fought for survival, adapting themselves to the new conditions, or falling by the wayside.[61] The development of the cultural pattern of the American industrial city has similarly been very briefly sketched by Leon S. Marshall in a study of " The English and American Industrial City of the Nineteenth Century." [62]

This brief sketch of the development of sociological interest in the American city should make evident the fact that the historian of the American city has already at his disposal a wealth of literature on almost every phase of urban development. Unfortunately the great bulk of that material, since it has been produced by the sociologist, relates to the recent history of the American city; for the crowning provincialism of American urban sociology, as Lewis Mumford says, is its preoccupation with the contemporary metropolitan community.[63] Never-

[61] This paper is to be published this winter. The material used here comes from a copy of the MS which the author generously loaned me.

[62] Western Pennsylvania Historical Magazine (1937), XX, 169-80.

[63] The Culture of Cities, p. 501. See also Maurice R. Davie, " The Field and Problems of Urban Sociology," in The Fields and Methods of Sociology, p. 103, who points out that urban sociology " must gather

theless, not much of modern urban life has been neglected, though little effort has been devoted to the development of a comprehensive theory of urbanism.[64] The literature of the city is filled with material on the economic and technological pre-conditions of urban growth; the relation of geography to the city;[65] the nature and quantity of rural-urban migration;[66] the demography of the city;[67]

more data on the history of cities and make more social historical studies of problems like city government, crime, recreation, etc. Most of its data are ultra-modern and cross-sectional."

[64] Some appreciation of the volume and nature of urban studies may be secured from the two bibliographies already mentioned, and even more from an examination of the articles, book reviews, and bibliographies of the *American Journal of Sociology* (Chicago, 1895–) and other sociological journals or journals in special fields. A recent and exceedingly interesting attempt to formulate a theory of urbanism is Louis Wirth, "Urbanism as a Way of Life," *AJS* (1938), XLIV, 1-24.

[65] See, for instance, M. Aurousseau, "Recent Contributions to Urban Geography: A Review," *Geographical Review* (1924), XIV, 444-55.

[66] Since the city has acquired a large part of its population from rural migrants, the quantity and quality of, as well as the reasons for, rural-urban migration is of great importance for the study of the city. Although writers of popular literature wrote of the effects of migration throughout the nineteenth century, it was not until the World War that academic interest began to focus on this flow of population that has probably been as important as, if not more important than, the westward movement. The War and the immigration laws of 1921 and 1924 cut down the number of Europeans coming to America just at the time that American industry was increasing its demand for labor; the result was increased internal migration. During the twenties, too, the declining birth rate centered attention on rural-urban differentials. The depression, finally, and its effect on farmers especially, increased interest in internal migration and accelerated the flow of literature on its quantity and quality. Few issues of the sociological reviews since then lack an article on selective migration. The best introduction to the literature, and the study on which this paragraph is based, is Dorothy Swaine Thomas, *Research Memorandum on Migration Differentials* (Social Science Research Council, Bulletin No. 43, New York, 1938), which is especially valuable for its lengthy critical bibliography of studies on rural-urban migration with summaries of their conclusions. See also Vance, *Research Memorandum on Population Redistribution Within the United States* (Social Science Research Council, Bulletin No. 42, New York, 1938), and Carter Goodrich, *et al.*, *Migration and Economic Opportunity; The Report of the Study of Population Redistribution* (Philadelphia, 1936).

[67] See NRC, *The Problems of a Changing Population* (Washington,

the social relationships of people living in the city; the breakdown of the integrity of the family; individualization; marriage and divorce; mental diseases of city people; the urban church; suicide; urban problems, from traffic to prostitution, from Americanization to zoning; the attempts to meet these problems; government and education in the city; city politics; [68] the city as a focal point of cultural activity; the conflict of urban and rural populations; the " effects " of city growth on the countryside.

The overwhelming bulk of urban bibliography is concerned with aspects of city life, yet the city is an integrated whole, each aspect of which is functionally associated with every other. Classified differently, the material offered to the historian by the sociologist runs from examinations of *Small Town Stuff* and of the culture of *Middletown* to studies of the life of the metropolitan area and of highly specialized suburban communities.[69] It is the history of the total city which the historian wishes to distil from the frequently formless, fluid mass of material available to him. Though formless, the material offers suggestions for writing a history of cities far from the sentimentality, antiquarianism, and chamber of commerce advertising that have characterized most local history.

1938) and *Population Statistics. 3. Urban Data* (Washington, 1937), which discuss not only the population of cities but also the conditions that make agglomerations possible and the effects of that agglomeration.

[68] On the government, administration, and politics of cities there is also a tremendous amount of literature, sprinkled with the observations and treatises of such acute students as Bryce, Goodnow, and Beard. To say more than that the literature exists is, unfortunately, beyond the scope of this paper, for the history of municipal government and politics is itself a fascinating story.

[69] See, for instance, Herbert Blumenthal, *Small Town Stuff* (Chicago, 1932); H. P. Douglas, *The Suburban Trend* (New York, 1925); G. A. Lundberg, M. Komarovsky, M. A. McInery, *Leisure. A Suburban Study* (New York, 1934); Graham R. Taylor, *Satellite Cities, A Study of Industrial Suburbs* (New York, 1915).

There is nothing comparable in America to such monumental studies of European cities as those of Davidsohn
and Poëte. Yet the rise of interest in cities during the
past decade offers promise for the future, and already
there have appeared several valuable histories of American cities. It seems that most of these studies stem from
the growing interest in economic and social history, are
not closely related to the thought and efforts of urban
sociology, and do not attempt to integrate all aspects of
the history of the city. Several such histories of individual cities are worth noting as examples. Constance M.
Green's biography of *Holyoke* is a history of a product
of the industrial revolution.[70] Thomas J. Wertenbaker's
Norfolk: Historic Southern Port emphasizes the first two
centuries of the story and tries to tie it in with the movement of national history.[71] Gerald M. Capers, Jr., in
the *Biography of a River Town: Memphis; Its Heroic
Age*, relates his history of the Tennessee town to both
sectional growth and national development.[72] G. R.
Leighton's miniatures of *Five Cities: The Story of Their
Youth and Old Age* are only slightly marred by his occasional over-emphasis on a few individuals.[73] Several
valuable studies of New York have recently appeared:
Sidney I. Pomerantz, *New York: An American City, 1783-
1803*;[74] Robert G. Albion, *The Rise of New York Port,
1815-1860*;[75] Ralph Foster Weld, *Brooklyn Village, 1816-
1834*.[76] Bessie L. Pierce's *A History of Chicago*, not yet
completed, is a synthesis of all aspects of the life of a
great American city.[77]

This growing interest in the history of cities has pro-

[70] *Holyoke, Massachusetts: A Case History of the Industrial Revolution
in America* (New Haven, 1939).

[71] Durham, 1931.   [72] Chapel Hill, 1939.   [73] New York, 1939.

[74] Columbia University Studies in History, Economics, and Public Law,
No. 442, New York, 1938.

[75] New York, 1939.

[76] New York, 1938.   [77] 2 vols., New York, 1937—.

duced two notable efforts to write the story of all urban culture in America, though both cover only a specified period of American history. In *The Rise of The City 1878-1898*, Professor Schlesinger attempted to write the history of all America in that period by focusing his attention on cities, by relating everything to the growth of cities.[78] The bulk of the volume is devoted to certain aspects of urban life, but no comprehensive, integrated picture of the culture of cities emerges. In the foreword, Dixon Ryan Fox sounded a keynote for the book, when he said that the city is " the new social force " in American history.

In the ever-widening reach of its influence the author finds the key to an understanding of the most multifarious developments. . . . Aside from the part played by urban leadership in building a new structure of industry and trade . . . the city is envisaged as the dominant force of all those impulses and movements which made for a finer, more humane civilization.[79]

Professor Schlesinger himself wrote that in " America in the eighties urbanization for the first time became a controlling factor in national life." [80] " Underlying all the varied developments that made up American life was the momentous shift of the center of national equilibrium from the countryside to the city." [81]

An excellent survey of the first century of urban life in America is Carl Bridenbaugh's *Cities in the Wilderness*.[82] Professor Bridenbaugh presents the five largest towns, Boston, Newport, New York, Philadelphia, and Charles

---

[78] New York, 1933.
[79] Schlesinger, *The Rise of the City*, p. xiv.
[80] *Ibid.*, p. 79.
[81] *Ibid.*, p. 435.
[82] Bridenbaugh, *Cities in the Wilderness. The First Century of Urban Life in America 1625-1742* (New York, 1938). Parts of Mumford's *The Culture of Cities* concern the history of urban culture in America and are stimulating reading, as all of Mumford is.

Town, as urban America, and tells the story of the changing physical appearance, the economic development, the growth of urban problems and the efforts to meet them, and social life, as a phase of general European economic history under the conditions of the American environment. The result is a skillfully done picture of urban life, perhaps overburdened at times with minute detail, but detail always to illustrate a general proposition.

The increasing attention devoted to cities has reached a new stage in the thought of Professor Schlesinger whose recent article on " The City in American History " seems to point the way to what Turner called an " urban reinterpretation " of American history. What lay below the surface in *The Rise of the City* became explicit and is deliberately stated in this recent essay.

" The true point of view in the history of this nation is not the Atlantic Coast," declared Frederick Jackson Turner in his famous paper of 1893, " it is the Great West." Professor Turner had formed his ideas in an atmosphere of profound agrarian unrest; and an announcement of the superintendent of the census in 1890 that the frontier line could no longer be traced impelled him to the conclusion that " the first period in American history " had closed. His brilliant essay necessitated a fundamental reappraisal of the springs of national development. Today, however, it seems clear that in his zeal to correct older views he overlooked the antithetical form of social organization which, coeval with the frontier, has played a significant and ever-enlarging part in American life. Turner himself wrote in a private letter in 1925, though with evident misgiving, " There seems likely to be an urban reinterpretation of our history."

A reconsideration of American history from the urban point of view need not lead to the distortion which Professor Turner feared. It should direct attention to a much neglected influence and, by so doing, help to illumine the historian's central problem: the persistent interplay of town and country in the evolution of American civilization. Recent historical writings reveal an increasing interest of scholars in the role of the city. It seems desirable, if only in broad outline, to develop certain of the larger implications of these studies and to indicate some of the further possibilities of the general subject for scholarly investigation.[83]

And out of the thread of urbanization Professor Schlesinger, in swift, broad strokes, weaves the whole fabric of American history. The essay, in short, may be an answer to the prayer of one of the critics of his earlier volume: that historians " do with the city what Turner and his students did with the frontier . . . use it as a means of explaining the problems and the pace of American life in the post-frontier period of American history." [84]

In Professor Schlesinger's essay are to be found two separate and distinct ideas. There is, in the first place, an appeal to students of American history to devote more attention to the history of cities, and it may indeed be that Professor Schlesinger meant primarily to call for such emphasis. With this there can be no quarrel. An ever-increasing number of people have come to live in cities; the city has been in this country, as in all cultures, a focal point and disseminating source of varied activity. The American city, therefore, richly deserves to have its history written.

It may be, however, that Professor Schlesinger meant to suggest not only the study of cities but also the use of the " city " as a causal factor in American history. Certainly that inference might be drawn from the introductory statement, from the treatment in the body of the essay itself, and from such statements as " cities . . . exerted an important influence on the struggle for manhood suffrage, the effort to abolish war, and the antislavery cause," or cities " sought to carve out economic dependencies and

[83] " The City in American History," *Mississippi Valley Historical Review* (1940), XXVII, 43.
[84] Review of *The Rise of the City* by Albert Lepawsky, *AJS* (1933), XXXIX, 253.

spheres of influence in the more distant country," or
" southern secession was a revolt against the urban imperialism of Yankeedom," or " the city forged ahead,
imposing its economic fiat on the rest of the nation," or
" the urban dynamic . . . was the governing force." [85]

If the city or urbanization is to be used in a causal sense,
then it is desirable to define those two terms. Anyone
examining the literature on the city can hardly escape
the disheartening conclusion that the " city " has been
defined in many and varied ways. In his " Bibliography
of the Urban Community," Professor Wirth pointed out
that the " differences in standpoint and method in the
various sciences show graphically in the definitions which
each formulates of the same object." [86] The bibliographer,
he continues, " has neither chart nor compass to guide
him in his search, for the sociologist himself is not yet
certain of the meaning of the concept ' city ' and of the
relationship of his science to the phenomenon." [87] Thus
the geographers see the city as a part of the landscape;
many historians, as an autonomous political unit; statisticians and most others, as a human aggregate of a certain size or density; economists, as an economic unit, a
form of society " typical of a certain stage in economic
development." A legal definition of the city as " an
incorporated community " is obviously inadequate, for
legal characteristics differ in various parts of the nation,
and the growth of the metropolitan community has out-
moded if not destroyed legal boundaries.[88] Using a statistical definition, Professor Bedford finds a city when cer-

[85] Schlesinger, in the *MVHR*, XXVII, 52, 50, 56, 61, 57.
[86] Wirth, " Bibliography of the Urban Community," in Park, *The City*,
p. 165.
[87] *Ibid.*, p. 161.
[88] Maurice R. Davie, " The Field and Problems of Urban Sociology,"
in *The Fields and Methods of Sociology*, pp. 98-99. This essay has an
interesting discussion of the meaning (or, better, lack of meaning) of
" city " and " urbanization." Much of its material is used here.

tain specifically urban problems appear and uses 100,000 as his line of demarcation.[89]   But it has been pointed out that a " problem . . . may be so defined that it is present in some degree in every city.",[90]   Thus Professor Bridenbaugh discusses the urban problems of five colonial towns at times when they would barely have qualified under the Census definition of a city.   Recently, Professor Wirth has attempted a " sociologically significant definition " of the city, one which will " select those elements of urbanism which mark it as a distinctive mode of human group life," and he has defined the city " as a relatively large, dense, and permanent settlement of socially heterogeneous individuals."   From these independent variables and their conjunction, Professor Wirth says, flow all peculiarly urban characteristics.[91]

Many students present a compound definition of a " city " by enumerating various urban characteristics.   Thus Lewis Mumford defines a city as

a related collection of primary groups and purposive associations: the first, like family and neighborhood, are common to all communities, while the second are especially characteristic of city life.   These varied groups support themselves through economic organizations that are likewise of a more or less corporate, or at least publicly regulated, character; they are all housed in permanent structures, within a relatively limited area.   The essential physical means of a city's existence are the fixed site, the durable shelter, the permanent facilities for assembly, interchange, and storage; the essential social means are the social division of labor, which serves not merely the economic life but the cultural processes.[92]

Such compound definitions, which seek characteristics of

[89] *Readings in Urban Sociology*, p. vii.
[90] Davie, " The Field and Problems of Urban Sociology," in *The Fields and Methods of Sociology*, p. 99.
[91] " Urbanism as a Way of Life," *AJS* (1933), XLIV, 4, 8.
[92] Mumford, *The Culture of Cities*, p. 480.

cities distinguishing them from the countryside, appear in
every systematic treatise on urban sociology. A close examination of these distinguishing characteristics, however,
discloses the fact that they are generally based on one distinction. Thus the definition offered by Sorokin and
Zimmerman in their *Principles of Rural-Urban Sociology*

is at bottom based upon a single trait, that of occupation, or
more broadly, economic organization. Their principle criterion of
rural society or population is occupational, the collection and
cultivation of plants and animals. The urban world is engaged
in manufacturing and mechanical pursuits, in trade, commerce,
and the professions, in short, in non-agricultural occupations.
The rural world is based primarily on an agricultural economy,
the urban on an industrial and commercial. From this basis there
develop those characteristics whereby size of community, density
and heterogeneity of population, differentiation and stratification,
mobility and interactions are correlated positively with urbanism.[93]

Adna F. Weber pointed out that this economic distinction
between town and country was recognized by law in
medieval times, when charters were given to wall-enclosed
populations granting the privilege of engaging in commercial and industrial activities.[94] Maurice R. Davie, discussing the meaning of " city," places the basis of urban
culture upon the commercial and industrial activities which
" tend by their very nature to lead to a concentration of
population; which produces great complexity of social
relations and calls for a highly evolved type of social
organization. These are the basic characteristics of urban
civilization." [95] Robert M. MacIver's analysis of the difference between the urban and the rural environments is

[93] Davie, " The Field and Problems of Urban Sociology," in *The Fields
and Methods of Sociology*, p. 100.
[94] Weber, *The Growth of Cities in the Nineteenth Century*, pp. 6 ff.
[95] Davie, " The Field and Problems of Urban Sociology," in *The Fields
and Methods of Sociology*, p. 101.

similarly based in the final analysis on differences in economic activity. Differences flow from the fact that the countryman extracts his livelihood from the soil; he lives in an intimate, immediate contact with the land and nature which is unknown to the city dweller, who derives his living from wages earned in an infinity of specialized occupations.[96]

No matter what definition of city is used, " urbanization " is generally applied to the process whereby an " urban trait " becomes increasingly characteristic of a population. Thus if size is the basis of a " city," society is urbanized as aggregations increase in size and number; if the city is defined by the presence of certain problems, a community becomes urbanized in proportion as those problems grow in intensity. Professor Wirth calls urbanization " the development and extensions " of the " complex of traits which makes up the characteristic mode of life in cities." [97] To Professor Park, urbanization is not alone the growth of great populations and the movement of people to the cities; it is also " a wider extension of industry, commerce, and of personal and social relations which have grown up with and are characteristic of great cities." [98] Professor McKenzie writes of " urbanization in a cultural . . . sense." [99] To another, urbanization is the process whereby " cities dominate greater and greater areas of hinterland populations, due especially to the multiplication of the kinds of cultural goods and the

[96] MacIver, *Society. Its Structure and Changes* (New York, 1931).

[97] " Urbanism as a Way of Life," *AJS* (1938), XLIV, 7, 5.

[98] " Urbanization as Measured by Newspaper Circulation," *AJS* (1929), XXXV, 69. " Specialization, the division of labor, more elaborate organization, and more effective direction and control is now taking place in agriculture, just as it formerly took place in the highly organized industries. These changes, with all that they involve, are what we properly describe as urbanization."

[99] *The Metropolitan Community*, p. 25.

appearance of new agencies of distribution."[100] Urbanization in this case does not refer to the rise of cities, but to their influence over the countryside; and that influence is essentially the result of economic activity.

The uncertainty regarding a precise definition of the concepts under consideration has been neatly summed up by Professor Wirth, who says that " despite the preponderant significance of the city in our civilization . . . our knowledge of the nature of urbanism and the process of urbanization is meager."[101]

Which of the many meanings of " city " and " urban " Professor Schlesinger prefers is not certain, for nowhere in his essay is there an explicit definition of terms. From the context it seems that at various times different things were in the author's mind when he spoke of cities. For instance, if the city is to be considered causally relevant to the struggle over the Kansas-Nebraska act or to the widening breach between North and South in general, as Professor Schlesinger suggests, and if one is to speak of the city " imposing its economic fiat," then the city is apparently being thought of in terms of economic activity.[102] When the appearance and intensification of such problems as housing are related to the city, it is apparently being identified with a dense aggregation of people.[103] In references to " the currents of civilization flowing through the northern cities " or to cities as " nerve centers for creative cultural achievement," Professor Schlesinger seems to be thinking of the city as a nuclear center which, for various reasons, provides certain services for a wider hinterland and which, through its multiple

[100] J. M. Gillette, "Urban Influence and Selection," in *Pub. Amer. Soc. Soc.* (1929), XXIII, 1.
[101] "Urbanism as a Way of Life," *AJS* (1938), XLIV, 3.
[102] Schlesinger in the *MVHR*, XXVII, 50-51, 55-56, 61.
[103] *Ibid.*, p. 45.

agencies of contact, is closely connected with other such centers.[104]

To be sure the city is all of these things. But more detailed analysis will break the concept down into its components and give to each its full significance. Each of the elements may have consequences of its own, and it would only becloud the analysis to identify the city with each of them. In using the city as a causal factor to explain certain culture traits or certain events in American history, students may usefully distinguish between the city and its parts. For example, investigations of political behavior have shown that analyses in terms of economic classes give higher correlations than do analyses in terms of urban and rural interests. William F. Ogburn and Delvin Peterson have investigated the political behavior of the population of Oregon during several elections. Instead of merely comparing rural Oregon with Portland, they divided Portland's population into three groups which they believed corresponded with upper, middle, and lower classes, and they compared these groups with each other and with rural Oregon. Ogburn and Peterson found that the three urban classes differed greatly, rural voting generally corresponding very closely with that of the middle urban class.[105] The results of the polls of the American Institute of Public Opinion have shown time and again that " urban " is but an average, that when it is divided into various groups a broad range of opinion appears, that for political attitudes at least, economic level is probably more significant as a classification of American society than is urban or rural residence.[106]

[104] *Ibid.*, p. 55.

[105] Ogburn and Petersen, " Political Thought of Social Classes," *Political Science Quarterly* (1916), XXXI, 300-17.

[106] See, for instance, Edward G. Benson and Paul Perry, " Analysis of Democratic-Republican Strength by Population Groups," *The Public Opinion Quarterly* (1940), IV, 467-68; " The Gallup Poll," Baltimore

The differentiation of classes made in modern political analysis has also been successfully applied in historical investigations and has served to reveal more precisely what is meant in many cases by " cities." Professor Schlesinger, in " The City in American History," asserts that Boston's preeminence in the revolutionary movement " may well have been due to the fact that, having recently fallen behind Philadelphia and New York as an emporium, she was resolved at any cost to stay the throttling hand of the British government." [107] As Professor Schlesinger's well-known volume on *The Colonial Merchants and the American Revolution 1763-1776* has shown, it was primarily upon the colonial merchant that " the throttling hand of the British government " fell; " the merchants of the commercial provinces were the instigators of the first discontents in the colonies." [108] In the essay itself, Professor Schlesinger points out that the " business classes rallied promptly to the defense of their interests and, heedless of the possible political consequences, enlisted the support of the artisan and mechanic groups." [109] Certainly a clearer picture of Boston's revolutionary activity emerges if the situation is described in terms of interests, such as Professor Schlesinger himself suggests.

Because of the danger of substituting a vaguely defined whole for a more precisely defined part, one may similarly challenge Professor Schlesinger's suggestion that " historians might well give greater attention to the question of the extent to which southern secession was a revolt against the urban imperialism of Yankeedom. . . . It is significant that one of the early acts of the Confederate

Sun, Sept. 27, 1940; Stuart F. Rice, *Quantitative Methods in Politics* (New York, 1928), pp. 170-72.

[107] Schlesinger in the *MVHR*, XXVII, 46.

[108] *The Colonial Merchants and the American Revolution* (Columbia University Studies in History, Economics, and Public Law, No. 78, New York, 1918), p. 591.

[109] Schlesinger in the *MVHR*, XXVII, 46.

and state authorities was to outlaw the accumulated indebtedness of many millions owing to northern merchants, bankers, and manufacturers." [110] The second sentence makes it clear that by "urban imperialism" is meant the imperialism of a certain urban class, the "merchants, bankers, and manufacturers." This was more precisely stated by the Beards in their *Rise of American Civilization*, when they suggested that the war arose from a clash of opposing economic interests. Certainly American political history is the story of the conflict and reconciliation of interests.[111] But it is doubtful whether the antagonists can be most fruitfully classified as urban and rural, for the interests of some people in the city differ from those of other urban groups as well as from those of the country population.

The fact that urban and rural populations are not homogeneous is also of importance for non-political questions. The terms "urban" and "rural" certainly cover a multitude of interests. This is the burden of Professor MacIver's statement that "the city, especially the large city, is not only a whole environment for all its inhabitants but also a series of extremely different environments for the groups within it." [112] Much of the work

---

[110] *Ibid.*, p. 55.

[111] The introduction of petitions for tariff protection in the first Congress "foreshadowed a conflict of interest in the new government between city and country, which led directly to the formation of the first national parties. . . . From that day to this the chief business of American politics has been to reconcile these interests in the service of the national welfare." *Ibid.*, p. 48.

[112] For example, Professor MacIver says, "If we take vital statistics alone, we find remarkable differences in birth-rates and death-rates in conditions favorable to health or to disease, for different groups and districts. A great metropolis, like London or New York, will exhibit for localized groups within it extremes of healthiness and unhealthiness, no less than of wealth and poverty, surpassing those found elsewhere in the whole countries to which they belong. The city is the home of opposites, and in these respects it is misleading to take the average figures for city and country respectively, to treat as unities for the purpose of comparison the less homogeneous and the more homogeneous." *Society*, p. 360.

8

done by urban ecologists has been predicated upon the existence of many environments within the city. The National Resources Committee recognized this fact as basic to its investigations. Town and country, it pointed out,

each cover a wide range of different and conflicting interests. A rural dweller may be a farm laborer, a tenant, a small owner of acres, clear or encumbered, or the possessor of a great estate. There are also holders of great blocks of mortgages upon farm lands. The city dweller may be a worker, white collar or not, a small business man, a large business man, or an industrial giant. In this sense, the interests of farmers as farmers are not always the same any more than the interests of city dwellers are always the same.[113]

The differences between various groups within the urban and the rural environments may be much greater and therefore more important than the differences between the total urban and total rural environments. The statements cited above suggest that it may be practically irrelevant to the study of American history to know that in 1890 the average wealth of families in the rural districts did not exceed $3,250 while the average wealth of city families surpassed $9,000.[114] They imply that the terms

[113] *Our Cities*, p. v.

[114] C. B. Spahr, *An Essay on the Present Distribution of Wealth in the United States* (New York, 1896), pp. 46-49, cited in Schlesinger, *The Rise of the City*, p. 77. Professor Schlesinger cites Spahr's statement that "When American political parties shall again divide upon issues vitally affecting the distribution of wealth, the clearly marked line of division will not be between East and West, but between city and country."
    Perhaps the great interest in studying urban-rural conflict in American history is a manifestation of the overwhelming interest of American historians in sectionalism. As a matter of fact, it is now frequently said that urban America constitutes a new section in continuous opposition to rural America. Thus Professor Bridenbaugh, examining seventeenth century America, and defining a "section" as a "social and psychological" rather than as a purely geographical entity, finds three sections: "the rural, agricultural society of the country-side; the restless, advancing

urban and rural are averages which may have less significance than the individual data or classes of data of which they are an average.

There is some evidence to support such a contention. For instance, birth rates have been declining in the United States for many years, and since cities have lower rates than the countryside, the decline is frequently ascribed to urbanization. A close examination of Census statistics has revealed the fact (which is indeed a popular commonplace) that " fertility declines rapidly as the level of living rises in all regions of the United States " and this " even when the counties are classified by density of population, in order to differentiate rural and urban areas." [115] Studies made by the Milbank Memorial Fund indicate not only that birth rates vary with occupational classes, but also that " differences in birth rates by occupational classes have been of long standing duration." Though rural women are more fertile than urban, there are marked differences within each group.[116] The importance of this intra-urban difference is evident from the fact that birth rates vary " from year to year with prosperity and depression." [117] Such studies suggest that birth rates may be more highly correlated with occupation groups and social classes than with urbanism.

society of the frontier; and the urban commercial society of the larger seaports." With other "village communities," they emerged in the eighteenth century " as a social and economic ' section '." (*Cities in the Wilderness*, p. 467.) Even the Turnerians support such a view. They have attempted to transfer the concept of the frontier to new and different conditions. Thus Percy H. Boynton, in *The Rediscovery of the Frontier* (Chicago, 1931), pp. 22-24, suggests that Frederick L. Paxson has seen the conflict of West against East blurred into or replaced by the conflict of rural against urban; " the farmer still prolongs the life of the pioneer."

[115] NRC, *The Problems of a Changing Population*, pp. 136, 137.

[116] *Ibid.*, p. 142. See the entire chapter on " Social Conditions Affecting Birth Rates," prepared by Clyde V. Kiser.

[117] *Ibid.*, p. 23. See also the evidence presented by William F. Ogburn

Furthermore certain culture traits may not be products of a city or even of aspects of city life but rather of change in an environment. It is essential to distinguish between the characteristics of adjusted city dwellers and of rural migrants to urban centers who are in the process of adjustment. This has been frequently pointed out, by Professor MacIver for instance, and by Professors Davie and Carpenter.[118] Thus Professor Davie notes that agnosticism and skepticism are positively correlated with cities. But, he asks, are they products of modern society which have so far gained headway in the city? Or are they the result of maladjustment to the city environment and will they therefore disappear? Or is the prevailing conception of religion, like those of government, marriage, and the family, the product of rural life and hence destined to disappear under urban condition? [119] The same questions may be asked concerning divorce, crime, or mental breakdown, so frequently associated with cities. As Professor Carpenter puts it, " *phenomena which at the moment seem to be characteristics of urban civilization* may rather represent *transitional aspects of a population's adaptation to urbanism or the initial stages in the evolution and diffusion of new culture traits.*" [120] The distinction between effects of urbanism, of adjustment to urbanism, and of cultural change common to city and country alike is especially important for the student of American history, for the American city grew with astounding rapidity, drawing huge portions of its population from the countryside and from rural Europe.

and Clark Tibbitts, "Birth Rates and Social Classes," *Social Forces* (1929), VIII, 1-10.

[118] See MacIver, *Society*, p. 361.

[119] Davie, "The Field and Problems of Urban Sociology," in *The Fields and Methods of Sociology*, p. 106.

[120] *The Sociology of City Life*, pp. 248, 217-18. Davie cites the same paragraph quoted here.

Since American cities grew during a period of rapid technical advance, when city and country were drawing more tightly together, many of the characteristics of urban life may have been but manifestations of cultural changes that were affecting the countryside too, but more slowly. This is illustrated by a recent study of the changes in the nature of recreation in rural America. The fact that " the common denominator of these changes is a growing similarity to the recreational life of the city," led the author of the study to inquire into the possible causal relationship between the growth of cities and the increasing similarity. He found that some of the new recreational activities were the results of diffusion from the city, some came as a result of rural adaptation to city life, as when city products reached out into a rural market. Most important, however, was the fact "that certain forces that have been felt only in cities for many years past are now beginning to be felt in the country with the result that changes are occurring in rural life similar to those that developed long ago in urban life." [121] Among such forces is, of course, the introduction of machine technology with a resulting multiplication of social contacts, a greater ability to buy products, and a decreased dependence on the family and community alone for recreation.

The danger of not distinguishing between the results of urban life and those of cultural change common to both city and country, like the other difficulties involved in an urban interpretation of American history, was summed up by Professor Wirth when he warned against confusing urbanism with capitalism and industrialism.[122] Unless the concept " city " is carefully analyzed, students, in their enthusiasm for a fresh and attractive reinterpre-

---

[121] Edward Wilkerson Montgomery, *The Urbanization of Rural Education* (Chicago, 1936).
[122] " Urbanism as a Way of Life," *AJS* (1938), XLIV, 7.

tation of American history, may make of the "city" another "frontier" and fall into the difficulties inherent in Turner's "hazy and shifting concept," which have been pointed out with increasing frequency and sharpness.[123] Students of urbanization, reading phrases like "the contrast between urban and frontier conceptions of democracy," cannot but be disturbed at the way in which the "frontier" became a bottleneck of American historiography.[124]

---

[123] See, for instance, George Wilson Pierson, "The Frontier and Frontiersmen of Turner's Essays. A Scrutiny of the Foundations of the Middle Western Tradition," *The Pennsylvania Magazine of History and Biography* (1940), LXIV, 449-78; Murray Kane, "Some Considerations of the Frontier Concept of Frederick Jackson Turner," *MVHR* (1940), XXVII, 379-400.

[124] Quoted phrase from Schlesinger in the *MVHR*, XXVIII, 53.

WASHINGTON'S "GREAT RULE" IN ITS HISTORICAL EVOLUTION

BY

Albert K. Weinberg [1]

A basic assumption of the historiography of American foreign relations is that national policy toward the formation of political connections has been determined preeminently if not almost exclusively by one "Great Rule"—the testament of Washington in his Farewell Address. This assumption is true only if qualified by a paradox. The great rule was created not in the Farewell Address alone but in all subsequent American history as well. The maxim ascribed to Washington alone is, in the deepest sense, the joint product of Washington and the American people.

The creators of the great rule comprise all who paid the counsel of the Valedictory thoughtful deference. That to which they paid deference was not a principle of obvious meaning but one that called for and encouraged interpretation. The resultant exegesis, which enlisted the best thought of innumerable individuals, was creative in a twofold sense. In the first place, the interpreters sought to clarify Washington's actual intent. In so doing they ascribed to him ideas which he cannot be known with certainty to have had since his words are in certain respects ambiguous. In the second place, the exponents of the great rule attempted to determine, not its meaning in terms of Washington's own intent, but its logical im-

---

[1] This essay is part of a study which is being completed through a grant-in-aid from the American Philosophical Society.

109

plication in terms of issues which were outside his framework of discourse. Thus they derived from the Farewell Address a basic rule much broader than Washington set forth, policies of reserve which he had not specified, and protective corollaries which he could not have envisaged. Such inferences may or may not be warranted but at best they are warranted by logical elaboration rather than by historical reconstruction.

The great rule which figured as directive of the American people is the sum total of all the aspects of meaning which Washington's counsel has presented to posterity. Some of these aspects may be reality and others may be illusion, but whether they are the one or the other is purely a matter of tenuous hypothesis. Outside of a relatively small proportion of the issues to which the rule has been applied, there is no indisputable logic of inference by which one can say what Washington really meant or what his words necessarily implied. This consideration seems sufficiently evident from the striking lack of consensus among a host of interpreters all of whom felt certain that they were right. In heated debates throughout American history opposite positions with regard to Washington's meaning were taken by individuals of equal perspicuity. It is true, to be sure, that the controversy has raged much less among historians than among the statesmen and other leaders of national opinion whose ideas were occasioned by practical and immediate issues of foreign policy. But the professional historiographers exhibit no less variety of opinion, even if somewhat less dogmatism, than do those without scholarly equipment. The divergences among individual interpreters did not, indeed, prevent certain interpretations from proving decisive for national policy in a specific age. But, corresponding to the conflict of opinion among those of the same age, there was an equal disparity between the views characteristic of different ages from Washington's time to the present. In all periods the dominant interpretation of the great rule exhibits such a striking correlation with the contemporaneous interests or desires of the American people that pure exegetical logic scarcely seems to have been of dominant influence. At any rate, in each set of conflicting hypotheses the Farewell Address could have inspired only the one correct view and only a fraction of the arguments by which it was sustained. The sum of the matter is that what purported to be exegesis was really a process of creative evolution.

This, however, is merely to say that one must view the Farewell Address just as scholars have come to view the three classics comparable to it in influence upon American history—the Declaration of Independence, the American Constitution, and the Monroe Doctrine. The view with regard to these is that their signification constantly changed in accordance with time and need—a fact which, indeed, is seen as largely explanatory of their enduring influence. Calhoun and Lincoln each had his conviction as to what the Declaration's postulate of human equality meant, but precisely what it signified to the signers, if they knew themselves, is something which prudent historians now scarcely venture to say. So too it is today a truism that the American Constitution comprises, in addition to the few original pages, a vast body of judicial interpretations and political practices which only by legal fiction can be subsumed authoritatively under the intentions of the statesmen of 1789. Further, it is now axiomatic that the Monroe Doctrine and the message of 1823 are not one and the same, that the Doctrine as contemporaneously understood includes so-called corollaries which were contributed by Monroe's successors. In general the historian of ideas has come to realize that the concepts used in most normative generalizations are so vague that their boundaries fluctuate relatively to the shifting language, logic, and interests of the time. Thus ideological testaments are not stable in content but pass from generation to generation with the same diminution or expansion, the same deterioration or improvement, that mark the career of a legacy of material wealth.

But the transmutations of Washington's great testament, if not overlooked, tend to be deprecated as distortions. Thus there are many who, facing the great variety of interpretations, seek to "reclaim the Address from this turmoil of confusion by telling us what Washington actually said. . . ."[2] Unfortunately only what Washington actually said can be told us with certainty, not its implication for issues that he did not raise. This fact is ignored by those who hold with Henry Cabot Lodge, less inhibited in praise of the dead than of the living, that the American people have turned in all times to the Farewell Address in the knowledge that "there was no room for error in following its counsel."[3] At least there is room for error in choosing between Lodge's interpretation of Washington and Wilson's, or between Lodge's pro-League version in 1916 and Lodge's anti-League version in 1919. There are some, however, who find error enough in the Valedictory itself. One of these was Richard Olney, who, believing that popular historiography had glorified the Washington rule beyond all reason, maintained that it was "necessarily unfortunate and injurious . . . that a maxim stripped by time and events of its original virtue should continue current in the community under the guise of a living rule of action."[4] But the maxim *was* a living rule of action and

[2] Robert Ellis Jones, "Washington's Farewell Address and Its Applications," *Forum* (Sept., 1899), XXVIII, 13.

[3] Henry Cabot Lodge, *George Washington* (2 vols., Boston, 1896), II, 245.

[4] Richard Olney, "International Isolation of the United States," *Atlantic Monthly* (May, 1898), LXXXI, 582-83.

precisely in the sense that, when the virtue of its original connotation seemed to have passed, it took on new meanings adapted to current needs.

The adaptation of the Address is apparent first of all in the selectiveness of focus. Relatively little attention, much less deference, has been given, for example, to Washington's warning against parties; his advice on foreign relations is presented as the substance of the Valedictory. But even Washington's criticism of special enmities and partialities in foreign relations was little quoted, relatively speaking, by a people for whom neutrality of thought was seldom more possible than it is today. The words which are quoted more often than any others of American literature are those elaborating " a conviction of long standing," [5] a principle of political reserve that would have continued even if the Farewell Address had never expressed it:

The great rule of conduct for us in regard to foreign nations is, in extending our commercial relations to have with them as little *political* connection as possible. So far as we have already formed engagements let them be fulfilled with perfect good faith. Here let us stop.

Europe has a set of primary interests which to us have none or a very remote relation. Hence she must be engaged in frequent controversies, the causes of which are essentially foreign to our concerns. Hence, therefore, it must be unwise in us to implicate ourselves by artificial ties in the ordinary vicissitudes of her politics or the ordinary combinations and collisions of her friendships or enmities.

Our detached and distant situation invites and enables us to pursue a different course. If we remain one people, under an efficient government, the period is not far off when we may defy material injury from external annoyance; when we may take such an attitude as will cause the neutrality we may at any time resolve upon to be scrupulously respected; when belligerent nations,

[5] J. Fred Rippy, *America and the Strife of Europe* (Chicago, 1938), p. 3.

under the impossibility of making acquisitions upon us, will not lightly hazard the giving us provocation; when we may choose peace or war, as our interest, guided by justice, shall counsel.

Why forego the advantages of so peculiar a situation? Why quit our own to stand upon foreign ground? Why, by interweaving our destiny with that of any part of Europe, entangle our peace and prosperity in the toils of European ambition, rivalship, interest, humor, or caprice?

It is our true policy to steer clear of permanent alliances with any portion of the foreign world, so far, I mean, as we are now at liberty to do it; for let me not be understood as capable of patronizing infidelity to existing engagements. I hold the maxim no less applicable to public than to private affairs that honesty is always the best policy. I repeat, therefore, let those engagements be observed in their genuine sense. But in my opinion it is unnecessary and would be unwise to extend them.

Taking care always to keep ourselves by suitable establishments on a respectable defensive posture, we may safely trust to temporary alliances for extraordinary emergencies.[6]

It has been suggested that the confusion over the meaning of these words arose from the fact that few who swear by their maxims " have ever carefully and critically read the words of their oracle." [7] But despite Washington's instruction to Hamilton to express his ideas in " plain " terms, it seems doubtful that the most careful and critical reading can fathom the precise meaning of certain of the propositions.[8] What, indeed, is the great rule itself? Is it to have as little political connection as possible in the sense of as little political relationship as possible? Or is the initial proposition to be understood in the light of the later thesis concerning our true policy, with the effect that it means merely to form no permanent alliances beyond

---

[6] James D. Richardson, ed., *Messages and Papers of the Presidents* (Washington, 1896), I, 222-23.

[7] Jones, in the *Forum*, XXVIII, 12.

[8] Washington to Hamilton, May 15, 1796, in W. C. Ford, ed., *The Writings of George Washington* (14 vols., New York, 1889-93), XIII, 191.

the existent French alliance? Even the apparently unde-
batable advice to steer clear of permanent alliances is in
certain respects so little definitive that throughout American history there were arguments over basic issues of its
meaning. This fact is not due necessarily to the careless-
ness of Washington and Hamilton in communication or
even to the fact that their divergences in interest called
for vagueness as a compromise. It may be due to the
inherent difficulty of making formulations in one temporal and logical context which will be clear in another,
or else to the hesitation of wise modesty to be too definitive. The fact remains, however, that the words are
at the same time inherently unclear, and yet, with certain
predispositions in the interpreter, sufficiently suggestive to
give the illusion of clarity to interpreters from the most
diverse schools of thought.

It is not even clear or a matter of consensus that the
warning against alliances was addressed to the nation
of the entire future rather than merely to Washington's
own generation. While Washington spoke of " the strong
and lasting impression " he could wish for his counsels,
he did not say that all of them were obligatory forever,
and he also expressed modest doubt that they would " control the usual current of the passions or prevent our nation
from running the course which has hitherto marked the
destiny of nations." [9] Scarcely had printer's ink dried
when William Duane, typical of many unfriendly readers
of the Valedictory, told the retiring President that " your
advice for the future is but a defence for the past." [10]
The past that seemed so indefensible comprised, on the
one hand, the negotiation of the Jay Treaty, which ap-

[9] Richardson, *Messages and Papers*, I, 223.

[10] William Duane, *A Letter to George Washington, President of the
United States: containing strictures on his address of the seventeenth of
September, 1796, notifying his relinquishment of the presidential office*
(Philadelphia, 1796), p. 42.

peared in effect an alliance with Great Britain, and, on the other, the Administration's unwillingness to strengthen or interpret to France's advantage the alliance of 1778. Even the great majority, by whom the counsel was " gratefully received," [11] seem to have thought of it primarily as " interesting to our Happiness " in a contemporary sense.[12]

It was chiefly upon evidence internal to the Address that not a few asserted in later times that the no-alliance rule, in contradistinction to Washington's maxims of virtue or stalwart nationalism, was meant to be valid only for the nation's period of immaturity. John Quincy Adams brought this view into general discussion when in his message urging attendance at the Panama Congress he maintained that Washington's advice was " founded upon the circumstances . . . at the time when it was given." [13]   While Adams was accused of denying the permanence of the no-alliance principle, he probably meant no more than that Washington, having called for a minimum of political connection with states entirely European, would not be opposed to mere consultation with the new American states. But in 1851 Senator Robert J. Walker, playing with the idea of an alliance with England to uphold the principle of non-intervention, maintained unequivocally that Washington never recommended that even his rule against permanent alliances should be observed permanently.[14] An official assertion that Washington's maxim was limited in time appears in a despatch of Seward in which, qualifying his rejection of

---

[11] John Jay to Judge Peters, March 29, 1811, in Henry P. Johnston, ed., *The Correspondence and Public Papers of John Jay* (4 vols., New York, 1890-93), IV, 352.

[12] Rufus King to John Quincy Adams, November 10, 1796, in Charles R. King, ed., *The Life and Correspondence of Rufus King* (6 vols., New York, 1894-1900), II, 104.

[13] Richardson, *Messages and Papers*, II, 337.

[14] *Cong. Globe*, Dec. 16, 1851, p. 105.

an alliance with American states, he observes concerning
the no-alliance principle:

It may well be said that Washington did not enjoin it upon us
as a perpetual policy. On the contrary, he inculcated it as the
policy to be pursued until the union of the States, which is only
another form of expressing the idea of the integrity of the nation,
should be established, its resources should be developed and its
strength, adequate to the chances of national life, should be
matured and perfected.[15]

Seward had in mind Washington's alternative to forming
alliances—that as "one people, under an efficient government" we await the period "not far off" when we
might "defy material injury from external annoyance." [16]
These words have been emphasized by interpreters disinclined to brook any permanent limitation of America's
capacity for international relationship. A distinct position
is that exemplified by Richard Olney who held without
concern for Washington's intent that, since the conditions
for which Washington made the rule no longer exist, the
rule itself should be considered as non-existent also.[17]
    The very fact that the great rule was canonized indi-
cates the preponderant assumption that Washington gave
it forth in "weighed and winged words directed to his
contemporaries and coming ages. . . ." [18] This assumption first became evident in the congressional debates on
the Panama mission, which also gave abundant evidence,
in encomiums and formal resolutions, that the process of
canonization had set in. One speaker declared that all his
constituents were familiar with the counsel of the Father
of his Country and regarded it as "oracular." [19]   Wash-

[15] John Bassett Moore, *A Digest of International Law* (8 vols., Washington, 1906), VI, 18.
    [16] Richardson, *Messages and Papers,* I, 222.
    [17] Olney, in the *Atlantic Monthly,* LXXXI, 581.
    [18] Charles A. Beard, *A Foreign Policy for America* (New York, 1940),
p. 15.
    [19] *Register of Debates,* April 22, 1826, p. 2512.

ington was like an oracle indeed in the equivocality of
his counsel. President Adams' policy towards the Latin-
American states seemed to many to tend towards an alliance, and his message urging attendance at Panama appeared to claim the blessing of the Farewell Address for
such an alliance. Among Adams' critics, Representative
Hamilton was typical in maintaining that Washington's
warnings " rest permanently on our immutable condition,
as a federative Republic." [20]   While recognizing Washington's argument that avoidance of alliances was particularly important during the nation's immaturity, Hamilton asserted that " he nowhere implies that when we do
become thus strong, we may go abroad and form foreign alliances." [21]   When the United States had reached
the strength of a world power, Woodrow Wilson in an
address of 1914 declared that " it was not merely because
of passing and transient circumstances that Washington
said that we must keep free from entangling alliances."
Washington said it also because " in our might and
majesty and in the confidence and definiteness of our
own purpose we need not and we should not form alliances with any nation in the world." [22]   Such arguments
seem more revealing of the mind of Washington's com-
mentators than of Washington. The words of the Farewell Address neither affirm nor deny that intention of
permanent warning which some interpreters wished to
believe in for good reasons of their own.

The words were ambiguous in respect not only to time
but also to space. As important as the temporal question was the problem whether the no-alliance maxim had
a universal validity or applied only to Europe, which in
Washington's day was the nation's entire political world.

[20] *Ibid.*, April 10, 1826, p. 2160.
[21] *Ibid.*, April 10, 1826, p. 2159.
[22] *Cong. Record*, May 26, 1914, p. 9243.

Adams' message on the Panama Congress appeared to limit the rule to Europe. Seeking to translate the Farewell Address into terms of the present, he inferred from it that America and not merely the United States should be declared to have a set of primary interests with no or only remote relation to Europe.[23]   What Adams merely intimated was stated explicitly by Secretary of State Clay in his instructions on the observance of the Washington policy.   While disclaiming any desire to form an alliance at Panama, he conceded that " long since the origin of the maxim, the new American powers have arisen, to which, if at all, it is less applicable."   Clay pointed out that in the adoption of the policy the attention of Americans was directed to Europe, which had a system of connections and of interests remote and different from theirs.[24]

But no doubt about the application of Washington's maxim to the American states was admitted by Adams' critics.   They pointed to the absence of any geographical qualification in Washington's words defining our true policy.   The fact that his supporting argument did refer to Europe seemed to Representative Rives irrelevant:

It is true that General Washington *illustrates* his advice by reference to European politics, but the advice itself is not confined to our relations with Europe. In its spirit and its principles, it is universal and immutable, acknowledging no distinction of time or place. In the comprehensive words used by him in a subsequent part of his address, " 'tis our true policy to steer clear of permanent alliances *with any portion of the foreign world."* [25]

As to the claim that our interests were not divergent from those of other American states, Martin Van Buren, later President, maintained that aside from their purely nomi-

[23] Moore, *Digest of International Law*, VI, 14.
[24] *International American Conference. Historical Appendix: The Congress of 1826 at Panama* (Washington, 1890), IV, 122.
[25] *Register of Debates*, April 6, 1826, p. 2082.

9

nal republicanism " the difference between us is infinitely greater, and the intercourse less and more difficult, than between us and several of the States of Europe." [26]   Van Buren's derivation from the Farewell Address of a meaning so unfavorable to Pan-Americanism was approved by his biographer, George Bancroft.[27]   And from 1826 to the present day it has seemed in general that a formal alliance, which the Monroe Doctrine is not, is as unallowable in the New World as in the Old.

The decision that the great rule was illimitable in space as well as in time did not, however, settle the issue that was most crucial for its development.   Whether it was to become a vitally significant and widely applicable principle of foreign policy depended upon judgment as to the scope of its content.   Was the rule directed solely against permanent alliances, which soon ceased to be an important issue, or did it go beyond and interdict more common forms of international relationship?   The former position was often taken, and from this point of view Olney deplored the attempt to give " an extension to the rule quite in excess of its terms as well as of its true spirit and meaning." [28]   But how great was the general extension of the rule, how far beyond the avoidance of permanent alliances, was indicated by the name by which Olney referred to the matured policy of reserve—isolation.   As two of its students have pointed out, " isolation is commonly represented as adherence to the principles laid down by Washington in his Neutrality Proclamation and his Farewell Address." [29]

Presidents and Secretaries of State, to be sure, have

[26] *Ibid.*, March, 1826, p. 262.

[27] George Bancroft, *Martin Van Buren to the End of His Public Career* (New York, 1889), pp. 137-38.

[28] Olney, in the *Atlantic Monthly*, LXXXI, 578.

[29] J. Fred Rippy and Angie Deboe, *The Historical Background of the American Policy of Isolation* (Smith College Studies in History, Northampton, 1924, IX), p. 71.

not used the term except to maintain that, in the words of Seward, the counsel of Washington could seem one of "isolation and indifference" only if "superficially viewed." [30] "Isolation" as a designation of American foreign policy was the coinage not of "isolationists" but of "anti-isolationists," who in the 1850's first used it as a means of discrediting opponents reluctant to undertake perilous adventures of international altruism. The fact remains, however, that "isolation" is only an exaggeration of a reserve that comprises avoidance of all commitments to force, non-intervention, non-participation in European politics, avoidance of joint action, abstention from "entangling" commitments, non-limitation of "essential" rights of sovereignty, and independence of any political super-authority. These seven policies are supplemented by still an eighth which prohibits any action or inaction that seems likely to lead to violation of any of them. An example of this preventive policy is Senator Gray's opposition to Philippine annexation on the ground that it "introduces us into European politics and the entangling alliances against which Washington and all American statesmen have protested." [31] So too, as Richard Olney pointed out, the Washington policy long served as an argument for protectionism in view of the difficulty of dissociating commercial ties from political relationships.[32] In more recent years this same difficulty has prompted the so-called neutrality legislation, which was "thought to be a means of escaping from the political entanglements against which George Washington warned." [33]

If one thinks of the Farewell Address only as a warning

[30] Moore, *Digest of International Law*, VI, 23.

[31] *Papers Relating to the Foreign Relations of the United States, . . . 1898* (Washington, 1901), p. 934.

[32] Olney, in the *Atlantic Monthly*, LXXXI, 583.

[33] Hanson W. Baldwin, "America Swings Back towards Isolation," *New York Times Magazine*, September 25, 1938, p. 14.

against permanent alliances, then it must seem that a veritable magic extracted so many shy rabbits from a hat that contained but one.   But at the very outset it really contained two.   With the no-alliance rule was associated a distinguishable principle which was amazingly prolific in implications.   The equivocality which permitted the conception of a broader principle of reserve appears in Washington's very statement of the great rule.   Political connection was a synonym in Washington's day for alliances, but at the same time it was understood in a much broader sense.   In the congressional debates of 1826 both Daniel Webster and Edward Everett maintained that the rule against political connection was more extensive than the injunction against permanent alliances.[34]   It is true that political connections were not regarded as including all international associations.   But they did comprise, to quote the paraphrase of the Senate Committee on Foreign Relations in 1826, " all entangling connections." [35]   If one investigates more closely this concept of the " entangling " one will come upon a version of the great rule that goes far beyond its literal content.

The word " entangling " harks back to the portion of the Address which sets forth the reasons why political connection is undesirable.   It is quoted in what seems to be the first congressional reference to Washington's advice on foreign affairs—that of Albert Gallatin in 1798.   Criticizing President John Adams' message proposing consultation with other neutrals, Gallatin spoke as follows: " The late President thinks it unwise, by interweaving our destiny with Europe, to entangle our peace—unwise to implicate ourselves by artificial ties—unwise and unnecessary to extend our engagements." [36]   The word " en-

---

[34] *Register of Debates*, April 14, 1826, p. 2275; April 20, 1826, p. 2429.

[35] *Ibid.*, Appendix, *Report . . . January 16, 1826*, p. 93.

[36] *Annals of Congress*, March 1, 1798, p. 1129.

tangle," of which "interweaving our destiny" is an equivalent, had been recurrent in the language of American reserve as far back as 1776, when John Adams warned against any treaty with France that would "entangle us in any future wars in Europe." [37] The phrase "entangling alliances," to be sure, was the coinage neither of Adams nor of Washington but of Jefferson in his inaugural address. Neverthless the phrase came to be ascribed to Washington—partly through ignorance and partly through the belief that, as Senator Vandenberg has written, "spiritually" at least it is present in the Farewell Address.[38]

The conception that the spirit of the great rule forbade entangling rather than merely permanent alliances permitted it to enter upon its career of expansion. For, while Jefferson as well as Washington apparently opposed only permanent alliances, which are preeminently entangling, the concept of entangling alliances may be so construed as to include other commitments to force as well. Thus in the congressional debates of 1826 one speaker declared that "every alliance is . . . entangling, which places our peace on the discretion or movements of any other Government." [39] In its resolution of that year against the formation of "any alliance," the House expressed its belief that Washington's maxim precluded any commitment, even if limited in duration, which would not leave the nation "free to act, in any crisis, in such a manner as their feelings of friendship towards these republics, and as their own honor and policy may, at the time, dictate." [40] More explicit still was the assertion of Senator Mason in

[37] C. E. Adams, *The Works of John Adams*, (10 vols., Boston, 1850-56), II, 505.
[38] Arthur H. Vandenberg, *The Trail of a Tradition* (New York, 1926), pp. 138-39.
[39] *Register of Debates*, April 17, 1826, p. 2323.
[40] *Ibid.*, April 4, 1826, p. 2029.

1852 that the first tenet of Washington's foreign policy
was " to preserve relations of peace and amity with all;
and that this is best subserved, by avoiding all alliances,
whether transient, or permanent." [41]   In the First World
War not even the existence of an extraordinary emergency
seemed to justify a temporary alliance, which was regarded as an entanglement with European aims despite
the fact that Washington had specifically sanctioned it.
In the making of peace, however, the President's project
seemed to Senator Lodge to mean that, " while passion
and emotion reign, the Washington policy is to be entirely
laid aside." [42]   Although in Washington's day a concert
of all nations to preserve world peace could scarcely have
been dreamed of, Senator Poindexter maintained that in
the light of Washington's counsel the League was " the
most entangling alliance that could be conceived, since it
binds us as one of the guardians and guarantors of every
right or interest of any of these nations which might be
involved in actual or threatened war." [43]

The concept of entangling alliances thus grew apace.
Still it does not account for the elephantiasis of a reserve
which extended far beyond the avoidance of commitments
to force.   The most far-reaching applications of the great
rule were based upon its identification with non-entanglement as a generic principle of which the no-alliance rule
is only one species.   Before long Americans came to
realize, with the multiplication of contacts and of forms
of international relationship, that entanglement was not
peculiar to alliances but inhered in other types of commitment and even in actions and relationships where an interweaving of destinies occurred through moral obligation
or the exigencies of events.   Then it became typical to say,

[41] *Cong. Globe*, Appendix, April 6, 1852, p. 407.
[42] Henry Cabot Lodge, *The Senate and the League of Nations* (New
York, 1925), p. 231.
[43] *Cong. Record*, Feb. 19, 1919, p. 3747.

as did the *Nation* in 1898, that " Washington . . . advised
us to avoid entanglements with foreign Powers." [44] The
ultimate extension of the concept beyond alliances is
evidenced clearly in the observation of Representative
Wood in 1917 that Washington warned this country to be
careful about our " foreign entanglements and alliances." [45] Most commonly the term is used to embrace
all the Washingtonian forms of reserve, and this use is
illustrated by Secretary Hull's reference to " our traditional policies of nonentanglement." [46]

If the meaning of entanglement was left vague by
Washington's merely metaphorical presentation, it received clarification in the commentary of the future.
Definitions vary in detail according to the historical context but in substance they are strikingly similar. In 1826,
applying Washington's principle to the issue of an American alliance, Representative Le Compte expressed his unwillingness that " the destiny of the People of the United
States should ever be connected with, or depend upon,
the will or destiny of any other nation or People whatever." [47] When the issue was one of dependence upon
European destiny the ideal of non-entanglement tended to
be presented as freedom from the influence of a sinister
history and political system. Thus in 1898 the historian
Von Holst, warning imperialists against viewing the Farewell Address as parochial, declared that if they hitched
their republic to the entangled politics of Europe they
would be fettering themselves voluntarily with the " un-
breakable chain " forged by the international history of
European nations in the by-gone centuries, " dragging
them, jointly and severally, all the while down and along

---

[44] " The Isolation of Our Country," *Nation* (Aug. 4, 1898), LXVII,
86-87.
[45] *Cong. Record,* April 5, 1917, p. 386.
[46] U. S. Dept. of State, *Press Releases,* August 20, 1938, p. 23.
[47] *Register of Debates,* April 22, 1826, p. 2512.

by its terrible weight." [48] Still later when the proposal was
that the United States join a world organization imagined
to be super-sovereign, the great rule was invoked as
a doctrine of unimpaired sovereignty resting upon what
a " passionate patriot " called " but one soul loyalty . . .
one flag." [49] Senator Arthur H. Vandenberg traced to the
Farewell Address the " trail of a tradition " which " demands the right of self-decision as to what America shall
do with her own national life in those concerns that are
the exclusive prerogative of a really free people." [50] When
the danger of membership in the League had been succeeded by that of participation in collective security in less
direct ways, Senator Borah, speaking in 1934, formulated
the policy of Washington in terms even broader than
those of the doctrine of sovereignty. This policy was said
to call for " freedom of action "—for avoidance in the
political sphere of " all commitments of any nature or
kind, which encroach in the slightest upon the free and
unembarrassed action of our people, or which circum-
scribe their discretion and judgment." [51] The common
denominator of all formulations of non-entanglement is
" the absence of voluntarily incurred relationships, formal
or informal, which remove the substantial control of the
nation's action, or even of its experience, from its own
choice by placing it in the will, influence, or career of
other nations." [52]

[48] Hermann Eduard Von Holst, *The Annexation of Hawaii.* An Address delivered before the Commercial Club of Chicago, January 29, 1898
(Chicago, 1898), p. 19.

[49] George Harvey, "Washington or Wilson?" An Address before
the Columbia Club of Indianapolis, March 17, 1919. Quoted in Willis
F. Fletcher Johnson, *George Harvey: 'A Passionate Patriot'* (Cambridge,
1929), p. 268.

[50] Vandenberg, *The Trail of a Tradition,* p. xix.

[51] William E. Borah, "American Foreign Policy in a Nationalistic
World." An Address before the Council on Foreign Relations, New York,
January 8, 1934. *Foreign Affairs* (Jan., 1934, special supplement), XII,
p. xi.

[52] Albert K. Weinberg, "The Historical Meaning of the American

This ideal is the major but not the only theme in the historical development of Washington's rule. Beside non-entanglement there was a minor theme which, surprisingly antithetic in character, sounded the note not of reserve but of international enterprise and cooperation. This is not merely to say that, as has been seen, there were a few who interpreted the great rule as forbidding only permanent alliances and thus as leaving a wide leeway for international relationship. There were scarcely any who did not see in the Farewell Address positive prescriptions of activity in foreign relations. Some of the interpretations were anathema to the adherents of reserve. But the method of loose construction which was sauce for the goose was also sauce for the gander.

A corollary which isolationist and anti-isolationist alike drew from the great rule is the Monroe Doctrine, which not only prohibits European interference in the Western Hemisphere but by implication threatens American intervention should this prohibition be disregarded. John Quincy Adams, who contributed so importantly to Monroe's doctrine, was the first officially to derive its principle from the Farewell Address. In his message justifying attendance at the Panama Congress, where a joint declaration against European interference was to be considered, Adams applied the counsel of Washington to the new situation presented by the growth of America's power and the independence of the Latin-American states:

> Reasoning upon this state of things from the sound and judicious principles of Washington, must we not say that the period which he predicted as then not far off has arrived; that *America* has a set of primary interests which have none or a remote relation to Europe; that the interference of Europe, therefore, in those concerns should be spontaneously withheld by her upon the same principles that we have never interfered with hers, and that

Doctrine of Isolation," *American Political Science Review* (June, 1940), XXXIV, 542.

if she should interfere, as she may, by measures which may have a
great and dangerous recoil upon ourselves, we might be called in
defense of our own altars and firesides to take an attitude which
would cause our neutrality to be respected, and choose peace or
war, as our interest, guided by justice, should counsel.[53]

The idea of Adams which attained the strongest hold in
later thought was that, to quote Olney, the Farewell
Address implied that " American nonintervention in European affairs necessarily implied and meant European non-
intervention in American affairs." [54]   This thesis was
reaffirmed by Senator Lodge in the League issue when
he declared that " if we put aside forever the Washington
policy in regard to our foreign relations, we must always
remember that it carries with it the corollary known as
the Monroe Doctrine." [55]

To Adams, however, the Farewell Address dictated not
only reserve towards Europe but also cooperation with the
states of the Western Hemisphere.   In reference to the
Panama Congress he maintained that " the acceptance of
this invitation . . . , far from conflicting with the counsel
or the policy of Washington, is directly deducible from
and conformable to it." [56]   For this counsel, as it seemed
to Adams, implied a separation of the two spheres which
could be maintained only through joint action of American
states.   While congressional critics of Adams held that
the rule regarding political connection forbade even consultation with one party to a war, the same rule was cited
by Adams' supporters.   Edward Everett argued that " because we ought to have as little political connexion as
possible with foreign States, from whom our distance
enables us to stand aloof, . . . therefore, it is not to be

[53] Richardson, *Messages and Papers*, II, 338.
[54] Moore, *Digest of International Law*, VI, 547.
[55] Lodge, *The Senate and the League of Nations*, p. 232.
[56] Richardson, *Messages and Papers*, II, 338.

assumed that we are to have no political relations whatever with any foreign State, however near our shores or
waters." [57] Daniel Webster felt that Washington's rule
had more than this permissive element. In words that
should be classic for anti-isolationist Washingtonians, he
maintained that " our neutral policy . . . not only justifies,
but requires our anxious attention to the political events
which take place in the world," as well as " firm and
timely assertion of what we hold to be our own rights and
our own interests." [58] Such ideas have tended from 1826
to the present day to make American policy toward nations of the Western Hemisphere less reserved, especially
in regard to joint action, than is our policy toward other
political areas.

Even in relation to Europe and Asia the words of Washington have not seemed a barrier without openings. One
of these is his sanctioning of temporary alliances in " extraordinary emergencies," which, to anti-isolationists, have
appeared to include more than times of actual or immi-
nent war. Thus Senator Walker held in 1851 that Washington " never condemned alliances temporary and for the
occasion," and proceeded to urge the propriety of forming
even in advance of war an alliance with England to give
pause to Continental interventionists.[59] In the same congressional discussion Seward, introducing a resolution
threatening American intervention to resist intervention,
questioned whether Washington enjoined his policy of
neutrality as one of absolute and perpetual obligation.
Seward cited Washington's statement that the motive of
this policy was to gain time to the nation to settle and
mature its institutions.[60]

While it has seemed generally that Washington was

[57] *Register of Debates*, April 20, 1826, p. 2429.
[58] *Ibid.*, April 14, 1826, p. 2266.
[59] *Cong. Globe*, Dec. 16, 1851, p. 105.
[60] *Ibid.*, March 9, 1852, p. 247.

opposed to interference designed merely to expand national interest, there has been no dissent from the view that Washington did not intend his counsel to preclude any justified defense of national interest.   Richard Olney was thus on scarcely challenged ground when in 1898 he observed that the Farewell Address did not interdict intervention to protect American citizens and commerce wherever such protection was needed.[61]   To be sure, Cleveland and other anti-imperialists regarded as contrary to " the tenets of a line of precedents from Washington's day " a program of meddlesome overseas or distant expansion.[62] Imperialists, however, reasoned that because the subject was not even mentioned the Address was " not a warning against extra-continental expansion." [63]   Indeed Robert Ellis Jones put forth the brilliant argument that, since annexation of the Philippines would give pause to European nations which coveted South America, " there can be little doubt that Washington's Farewell Address indirectly favors our retention of the Philippines." [64]

Humanitarian and peaceful collaboration with Europe occasioned less exegetical controversy even if the demonstration that Washington's blessing was upon it had to be no less indirect.   In declining the invitation of England and France to exert diplomatic influence in behalf of oppressed Poland, Seward qualified his refusal by an observation which was to be much quoted:

It is true that Washington thought a time might come when, our institutions being firmly established and working with complete success, we might safely and perhaps beneficially take part in the consultations held by foreign states for the common advantage of the nations.[65]

[61] Olney, in the *Atlantic Monthly*, LXXXI, 579.
[62] Moore, *Digest of International Law*, III, 198.
[63] Jones, in the *Forum*, XXVIII, 20.
[64] *Ibid.*, p. 28.
[65] Moore, *Digest of International Law*, VI, 23.

These words became the subject of debate in the Senate in 1935 when Senator Borah attacked as a " forgery " the careless ascription of these words to the author of the Farewell Address by a Washington newspaper as well as an American historian.[66]   But Seward was not the only authority for such an interpretation of the Valedictory. In 1900 Woodrow Wilson, contemplating the beneficent rôle in world politics for which America seemed destined, declared the Address to mean: " Wait . . . until you need not be afraid of foreign influence, and then you shall be ready to take your part in the field of the world." [67]   Commerce was a less lofty call to this field than humanity and yet participation in European deliberations concerning commercial matters seemed clearly justified by Washington's advice to extend our commercial connections.   To be sure, such deliberation as that at Algeçiras in 1905 seemed to some, as to Senator Bacon, to have political ramifications which ran afoul of the Washingtonian doctrine of non-entanglement.[68]   But Senator Spooner held with the majority that to send representatives to foreign congresses of this kind was " not to entangle us, not to violate in any manner the doctrine of Washington," but to conserve American interests by sharing only in that part of the deliberations which concerned us.[69]

Even in respect to political questions the concept of entanglement was by no means always antagonistic to international relationships.   One mode of reconciliation was indicated by an anti-isolationist who, in view of the pejorative connotation of entanglement in the Farewell Address, maintained that " helpful relationships are not

[66] *Cong. Record*, Feb. 22, 1935, pp. 2447-48.
[67] Ray Stannard Baker and William E. Dodd, eds., *The Public Papers of Woodrow Wilson: College and State* (2 vols., New York, 1925), I, 367.
[68] *Cong. Record*, Jan. 15, 1906, p. 1074.
[69] *Ibid.*, Jan. 23, 1906, p. 1427.

entanglements: entanglements are injurious relationships from which it is difficult to withdraw." [70]   Even more suggestive was the fact that in its original context entanglement referred to special and partial relationships or, as it was once expressed, " entanglement with one nation." [71]   Thus when the World War prompted certain philanthropic Americans to promote a league of nations to insure a better international society, even Henry Cabot Lodge did not—at first—see any danger of entanglement. On the contrary, he declared that he could " not believe that when Washington warned us against permanent alliances he meant for one moment that we should not join with the other civilized nations of the world if a method could be found to diminish war and encourage peace." [72] Entrance into the World War to end war was proclaimed in Congress to be no violation of Washington's rule against foreign entanglements. Washington himself, as was observed by James M. Beck, one-time Solicitor General, envisaged extraordinary European vicissitudes which would involve the United States because they involved civilization itself.[73]   This trend of thought reached its climax in Wilson's ingenious dialectics justifying membership in the League of Nations. Wilson consistently presented the League as the perfect consummation of the spirit of traditional policy:

> I shall never myself consent to an entangling alliance, but I

[70] Jones, in the *Forum*, XXVIII, 19.

[71] " That great man perfectly understood the dangerous tendency of forming political connexions and alliances with foreign nations, and how easy it was, by an entanglement with one nation, to excite the hostility and jealousy of others." *Register of Debates*, April 18, 1826, p. 2356.

[72] Lodge, *The Senate and the League of Nations*, p. 132.

[73] " If Washington had been living in 1914, he would not have questioned the propriety of this country intervening in this war and sending its soldiers to Europe to defend the basic principles of civilization." James M. Beck, " The League of Nations." Address before the Union League of Philadelphia, May 8, 1919. Reprinted in *Cong. Record*, July 21, 1919, p. 2918.

would gladly assent to a disentangling alliance—an alliance which would disentangle the peoples of the world from those combinations in which they seek their own separate and private interests and unite the people of the world to preserve the peace of the world upon a basis of common right and justice.[74]

Though Wilson's pretension to traditionalism was rejected, his critics by no means permitted him the entire field in the discovery of humanitarian implications in the Washington policy. They differed with Wilson only as to the means consistent with Washington's counsel. James M. Beck resented the imputation that adherents of Washington's reserve believed in a selfish isolation:

When one speaks of the traditional isolation of this country as Washington's policy, the Farewell Address is misinterpreted. Its doctrine is that of independence, not isolation. Isolation is such complete detachment from the world as would make us a hermit nation, but independence is freedom from entanglement by " artificial ties " which impair our freedom of action.[75]

The view that Washington's doctrine was independence and not isolation has seemed to receive confirmation from the recent studies of academic historians, many of whom have been anti-isolationist. Especially noteworthy is the conclusion of Professor Bemis that " the immediate purpose of the Address was to strike a powerful blow against French intermeddling in American affairs," and that " in Washington's time avoidance of foreign alliances and of foreign entanglement was a question of independence and national sovereignty." [76] Calling attention similarly to Washington's concern with dangers peculiar to his coun-

[74] Ray Stannard Baker and William E. Dodd, eds., *The Public Papers of Woodrow Wilson: The New Democracy* (2 vols., New York, 1926), II, 195.

[75] Beck, in the *Cong. Record*, July 21, 1919, p. 2918.

[76] Samuel Flagg Bemis, " Washington's Farewell Address: A Foreign Policy of Independence," *American Historical Review* (Jan., 1934), XXXIX, 263, 268.

try's immaturity, other historians have proceeded to the conclusion that he could scarcely have intended his rule to fetter the powerful America of the future to her own and the common hurt. " It is hard to believe," Professor Garner writes, " that he meant to condemn American co-operation with other states for the promotion of common policies for the betterment of mankind." [77] Elbert D. Thomas, scholar as well as Senator, has collected evidence indicating that Washington subscribed to ideals of inter-nationalism characteristic of the eighteenth-century theory of progress. He not only cites Washington's letter to Lafayette of August 15, 1786, recording belief that en-lightenment and commerce would some day unite all man-kind in " fraternal ties." He finds also that the idea of growth is dominant in the Farewell Address itself with its words " the period is not far off." So interpreting the Valedictory to the Senate on February 22, 1937, Senator Thomas pointed to America's cooperation with individual nations and with the League as the fulfilment of Wash-ington's " dream of the nations working together." [78]

On the other hand, it has also been held that the ideas of the Farewell Address are rendered anachronistic by the alteration in American national interest concomitant with modern forces making for the greater political as well as economic interdependence of the peoples. Tech-nology is said to belie in particular the present validity of Washington's thesis of a divergence of America's primary interests from those of the European world. The editor of a popular magazine has argued, to be sure, that the Farewell Address should not be considered outdated

---

[77] James W. Garner, *American Foreign Policies* (New York, 1928), p. 50. See also John H. Latané, *From Isolation to Leadership* (New York, 1922), p. 11; George H. Blakeslee, *The Recent Foreign Policy of the United States* (New York, 1925), pp. 19-20; Louis M. Sears, *George Washington* (New York, 1932), p. 474.

[78] *Cong. Record*, Feb. 22, 1937, pp. 1459-60.

merely because the time of crossing the Atlantic has greatly decreased. Standing on a continent mainly ruled by Europe, George Washington " was not farther from Europe than we are. He was closer to it." Independently of geography he advised us to " mind our own business." [79]   But the scope of our own business seems to most to have increased proportionately to the undeniable lessening of America's geographical isolation—a diminution which has profound consequences for national security. By implication President Franklin D. Roosevelt apparently repudiated one element of Washington's doctrine of two spheres of interest when he characterized as a false teaching of geography " the thought that a distance of several thousand miles from a war-torn Europe gave to us some form of mystic immunity which could never be violated." [80]

But the central element in Washington's teaching has not been repudiated. It could be accepted independently of any antiquated assumption as to the geographical immunity of America's interests and still serve as the foundation of all the Washington policies. It is the doctrine of freedom of action—the teaching that the nation should avoid voluntary entanglement of its peace and prosperity with those of other nations to an extent which places their control utterly beyond America's reach. President Roosevelt subscribed to this doctrine when in 1935 he expressed as the unanimous sentiment of the American people the determination that " despite what happens in continents overseas, the United States of America shall and must remain—as long ago the Father of our Country prayed that it might remain—unentangled and free." [81]

The combination of the traditional ideal of freedom of

[79] " Washington Was Closer to Europe than We Are," *Saturday Evening Post*, August 26, 1939, p. 212.
[80] *New York Times*, May 11, 1940.
[81] *New York Times*, October 3, 1935.

10

action with the modern doctrine of the interdependence
of nations has given its distinctive character to the most
recent phase in the evolution of the great rule. This
character may be formulated in terms of the doctrine of
some philosophers of history that ideas evolve through a
conflict of thesis and antithesis which issues into synthesis.
The conflict between the isolationist and the anti-isolationist interpretations of the great rule has appeared to
be yielding to a synthesis embracing elements of both.
This tendency towards harmonization appeared clearly
as early as the cooperative policies of the Hoover Administration, which in 1932 evoked from Ambassador
Walter E. Edge the explanation that " the United States,
while adhering to its historic Washington policy of dis-
association and detachment, has very clearly manifested
its willingness to cooperate where cooperation may be
productive of constructive results." [82] Even more clearly
is this ambivalent ideology revealed in the pronounce-
ments of Secretary Hull, who has declared that we must
" become . . . increasingly effective in our efforts to con-
tribute along with other peoples—always within the range
of our traditional policies of nonentanglement." [83] In
justifying such contributions to world peace and order,
Mr. Hull has consciously or unconsciously, paraphrased
words of the Farewell Address. Attempts at national
isolation, he asserted, would lead to a world so threatened
by international anarchy as to " impair our ability to control our own affairs." [84]

The outbreak of the world war which Hull strove to
prevent has, indeed, weakened for the time being the
factors making for balance in American foreign policy. It

[82] Department of State, *Press Releases*, February 27, 1932, p. 210.
[83] *Ibid.*, August 20, 1938, p. 123.
[84] Cordell Hull, " The Spirit of International Law." Address before
the Bar Association of Tennessee, Nashville, June 3, 1938. Dept. of State,
Publication 1190, p. 14.

has suggested to large sections of national opinion that the United States must choose a single course and follow it rigidly and wholeheartedly.   Our situation is in some respects similar to, in others different from, that in which the great rule was given forth.   In a striking letter, written in the year following the Valedictory, Washington declared: " With respect to the nations of Europe, their situation appears so awful, that nothing short of Omnipotence can predict the issue; although every human mind must feel for the miseries it endures.   Our course is plain; they who run may read it." [85]   Today as in Washington's time Europe flames in war, but no longer does our course seem plain except to extremists and dogmatists of two opposing schools.   Not even Washington's message seems to speak plainly as we listen confusedly to conflicting interpretations.   To Senator Borah, to adhere closely to the advice of Washington meant the determination to send neither men, munitions, or money to the irrelevant holocaust abroad.[86]   To Rupert Hughes, on the other hand, the essential implication of that advice is that Washington was " committed to no policy of unalterable neutrality." [87]

If the complexity of the present situation gives rise to confusion, it may well be that the outcome of the war will cause the great rule once more to seem plain.   But we cannot foresee that future clarification since nothing short of Omnipotence can predict the denouement which will determine its form.   Shall we find ourselves isolated in a world of enemies with the result that a minimum of political connection will, even more than in the beginning, seem not merely wisdom but necessity?   Or will there

[85] George Washington to Oliver Wolcott, May 29, 1797; Ford ed., *Writings of George Washington,* XIII, 394.

[86] *New York Times,* March 26, 1939.

[87] Rupert Hughes, "Washington — and Entangling Alliances," *New York Times Magazine,* February 18, 1940, p. 7.

be a victory of our friends, with promise so great for beneficent international cooperation that the rule will shrink to its smallest range of restriction? The few years still to intervene before the Valedictory reaches its sesquicentennial will probably be the most decisive of all our national history for its further evolution.

We may be certain only that this continuing evolution need never be obstructive of America's needs. While in form the rule is a restriction, the extent ascribed to its restrictiveness varies in accordance with the circumstances and at times appears negligibly slight. In spirit, moreover, and for this reason it is great, the rule is the expression of an emancipative ideal. This ideal determines the precise degree of restriction that will minister to an ulterior purpose of liberation. Like a compass the prohibition of political connection has ever pointed toward the nation's "command of its own fortunes." A rule informed by this ideal will endure and evolve as long as will the caution of Americans for their nationality.

HILDRETH, DRAPER, AND "SCIENTIFIC HISTORY"

BY

DONALD E. EMERSON

". . . The object at which I aim is neither more nor less than a total revolution in the whole system of philosophy relative to man considered as an intellectual and active being. My principle is, to apply to the philosophy of man's nature the same inductive method which has proved so successful in advancing what is called natural philosophy. Man is a part of nature: the philosophy of man is a part of natural philosophy, and it ought to be investigated by the same methods."

Richard Hildreth [1]

". . . I have therefore endeavored to treat of man according to the methods accepted in Physical Science. . . ."

John William Draper [2]

By the middle of the nineteenth century the Muse of History "began to fall under the potent spell of natural science" and even "began to talk of raising her chaotic mass of information to the rank of a science."[3] To make of history a science was the noble task of the day, and

[1] Richard Hildreth to Caroline Weston, Jan. 8, 1841, MS, Anti-Slavery Weston Papers, Boston Public Library.

[2] *Human Physiology, Statical and Dynamical* (New York, 1856, citations to 7th ed., 1865), p. viii.

[3] James Harvey Robinson, *The New History, Essays Illustrating the Modern Historical Outlook* (New York, 1913), pp. 43-44, 47, 75; W. Stull Holt, "The Idea of Scientific History in America," *Journal of the History of Ideas* (1940), I, 354-355; Harold Temperly, ed., *Selected Essays of J. B. Bury* (Cambridge, 1930), pp. 5, 9-10, 23-31; Ernst Troeltsch, *Der Historismus und seine Probleme* (*Gesammelte Schriften*, III, Tübingen, 1922), p. 371.

139

many turned their minds to it.[4] So active was the pursuit by the sixties that Charles Kingsley felt impelled to point with alarm to *The Limits of Exact Science as Applied to History*.[5] But to be " scientific" remained the great desideratum.

The prestige of science furnished an irresistible temptation. The glories of seventeenth century studies of God's handiwork, particularly the treatment of mechanical displacement, established the hegemony of science in modern thought. In succeeding years the methods of the scientist became an object of devoted imitation and uncomprehending devotion. To make of a subject a *science* was to raise it to the pinnacle—and to obtain for it a plenary indulgence. As moral philosophy sought to follow natural philosophy up to the heights of science, historians strove to give the same elevation to their work.[6]

What those historians meant by " scientific history" is far from clear. They seem to have been interested not so much in exploring the relations of science to history as in sharing the prestige of science. The cold hard light of logical thinking might have dispersed the fog in which they moved. But " from the vague allusions, the oblique comments, and the occasional clear statements" of American historians of the last quarter of the nineteenth century, Professor Holt has identified " two distinct and contradictory conceptions of scientific history." At one extreme was " the belief that scientific history consisted of a search for facts alone, with no laws or generaliza-

---

[4] Among the first to use the phrase " science of history" were P. J. B. Buchez, *Introduction à la science de l'histoire* (Paris, 1833), and the anonymous author (William B. Greene) of *Remarks on the Science of History* (Boston, 1849).

[5] London, 1860.

[6] Troeltsch, pp. 371-72; Edward Fueter, *Geschichte der Neueren Historiographie* (Munich and Berlin, 1911), pp. 334, 344, 575-80, 583-85; Henry Thomas Buckle, *History of Civilization in England* (2 vols., New York, 1876), I, 25-26, 636.

tions and with a renunciation of all philosophy "; at the other, " the belief that there were historical laws or generalizations which could be formulated." [7]

Not everybody talking about history as a science was writing it. But in the middle of the nineteenth century in the United States Richard Hildreth and John William Draper were writing history, and both were pursuing the ideal of science. As the quotations at the head of this essay declare, these two men were intent on treating the affairs of man according to the methods accepted in the realm of mechanical matter. In a day of advance in geology and biology, the model science of both men was physics, though Draper was close to the new currents of evolution. In the middle of the nineteenth century in America Hildreth furnished an example of the first type of " scientific history," Draper of the second.

In Hildreth's own day his *History of the United States of America* found little favor.[8] In the next generation it was widely popular, and the standard historical bibliography of the last quarter of the nineteenth century declared:

These volumes, completed as early as 1850, still probably form the most valuable single work on American history.[9]

Indeed, even as late as 1911 a professor of history decided:

If I had to dispense with all the older books of American history that could be got on without, I could let most of them go, with only moderate tears and grief, save three: [in the first

[7] Holt in the *Journal of the History of Ideas,* I, 356-57.
[8] 6 vols., New York, 1849-1852. Successive editions 1856, 1863, 1880. Cited hereafter as *History,* in 1856 edition.
[9] Charles Kendall Adams, *A Manual of Historical Literature* (New York, 1889), p. 569. *Guide to Historical Literature* (New York, 1931) omits Hildreth.

place] Richard Hildreth, for the as yet unrivalled comprehensiveness and accuracy of his information.[10]

For historians of the last quarter of the nineteenth century, the man, Richard Hildreth, was merely a name on six substantial volumes of history.[11] He had written many other things, but the Schoulers and the Channings had not read them. If they had, they would have discovered that his history was a curious contrast, a contrast presenting a problem. Edward Everett Hale happened to have read Hildreth's *Archy Moore, or the White Slave*,[12] the first of the anti-slavery novels, and the difference in style of the history and novel was so striking that he recalled, a bit solicitously:

When the novelist Smollett was set to the job of writing the history of England, he made one of the stupidest books which it has been the duty of people afterward to read. Walter Scott did not fare much better when he wrote the " Life of Napoleon." Mr. Hildreth's book is much more readable than either of these, but . . . .[13]

Present-day scholars looking at Hildreth for special purposes have struck the same problem from a different side. Examining Hildreth as a historian, Professor Alfred H.

[10] William MacDonald, " Some Bibliographical Desiderata in American History," *Proceedings of the American Antiquarian Society* (New Series, 1911), XXI, 267.

[11] Born at Deerfield, Massachusetts, June 28, 1807, the son of the Congregational clergyman and academy preceptor there, and educated at Phillips Exeter and Harvard, Hildreth earned his living as a journalist of parts, helping to found the *Boston Daily Atlas* and serving as " principal editor " for Horace Greeley's *Tribune* in the fifties.

The most complete biographical account is by William S. Thayer, " Richard Hildreth," in Evart A. and George L. Duyckinck, eds., *Cyclopaedia of American Literature* (2 vols., New York, 1866), II, 459-62.

[12] *Archy Moore, The White Slave or Memoirs of a Fugitive* (New York and Auburn, 1855), pp. viii-xxii.

[13] Edward Everett Hale, *Memories of a Hundred Years* (2 vols., New York, 1902), II, 67.

Kelly noticed the contrast between the apparent Federalism of parts of the history and the concealed tendency to socialism of another writing. He could explain this opposition only by the fact that Hildreth's " mind was conveniently departmentalized." [14] Professor Michael Kraus noted, in addition, that the treatment of Jefferson in the history seemed markedly different from that in still another writing.[15] Recently, Mr. Arthur M. Schlesinger, Jr. pointing directly to the striking difference between Hildreth's history and his other works has furnished the key for understanding the contradictions, though he has not used it for all the doors which it fits.[16]

Hildreth's history was " a plain, unvarnished narrative of facts as they were understood by its author, devoid of all attempts at rhetorical finish or philosophical digression." [17]

Rhetorical grace and effect [as another critic put it], picturesqueness and the impress of individual opinion, are traits which the author either rejects or keeps in abeyance. His narrative is plain and straightforward, confined to facts which he seems to have gleaned with great care and conscientiousness. The special merit of his work consists in the absence of whatever can possibly be deemed either irrelevant or ostentatious.[18]

A critic of the first series wrote:

The three volumes before the public everywhere display the

[14] Alfred H. Kelly, " Richard Hildreth," in William T. Hutchinson, ed., *The Marcus W. Jernegan Essays in American Historiography* (Chicago, 1937), pp. 25-42, 39-40.

[15] Michael Kraus, *A History of American History* (New York, 1937), pp. 247-50, 252-53.

[16] Arthur M. Schlesinger, Jr., " The Problem of Richard Hildreth," *New England Quarterly* (1940), XIII, 223-45, especially pp. 226, 229, 232, 233, 237-38.

[17] James Baldwin, *An Introduction to the Study of English Literature and Literary Criticism* (2 vols., Philadelphia, 1883), II, 83.

[18] Henry T. Tuckerman, " A Sketch of American Literature," in Thomas B. Shaw, *Outlines of English Literature* (Philadelphia, 1852), p. 450.

marks of profound original research, a critical comparison of authorities, a strenuous devotion to the subject of inquiry, a calm and temperate judgment in the balancing of evidence, and a sturdy adherence to the common-sense view of the facts and events that pass under the notice of the writer, with a rigid abstinence from all excursions of the fancy, or indulgence in theory and conjecture.[19]

In contrast with the Olympian coolness and crispness of the history, Hildreth had in other works

exhibited a glow and depth of feeling, a facility of vivid picturesque description, and a power of poetic eloquence, that give him an eminent rank in the department of graphic and pathetic composition.[20]

His anti-slavery novel left upon William Dean Howells " an indellible impression of his imaginative verity." Forty years after reading it Howells felt " no misgiving in speaking of it as a powerful piece of realism . . . which treated passionately, intensely, though with a superficial coldness, of wrongs. . . ." [21] The icy reserve of the history appeared almost never in Hildreth's other writings. It was said of his journalism:

His articles were remarkable for the vehemence of their tone, the closeness of their reasoning, their elaborate historical illustrations, and the point and vigor of their diction. If strongly partisan in their spirit, it was impossible, with his earnest nature, to have been otherwise. His perceptions were clear, his convictions of an iron strength, and he hated compromise. His love of controversy was also innate and genuine; it had the force of a passion.[22]

[19] *Littell's Living Age* (1849), XXIII, 365 (reprinted from the New York *Tribune*).

[20] *Ibid.*, p. 366.

[21] William Dean Howells, *Literary Friends and Acquaintances* (New York, 1900), p. 97.

[22] *The American Annual Cyclopaedia and Register of Important Events of the Year 1865* (New York, 1869), p. 427.

This was no less true of Hildreth's pamphlets and some of his longer writings.[23] If in the history Hildreth abstained from philosophical generalization, he had sufficiently demonstrated in his *Rudiments of the Inductive Science of Man* that he was not incapable of a high order of theoretic consideration.[24]

Some characteristics, to be sure, run throughout all Hildreth's writings—the same hatred of slavery, though in the history the denunciation is suppressed; the same contempt of mystical ideas, of theocracy, though in the history, again, vituperation is omitted.[25] In the other writings is the view " that our respected ancestors were not altogether that pure, honest, and simple-minded people we are taught to believe them," and it appears hard-headedly throughout the history.[26] In the other writings is the same economic realism, in one place carried even to a sweeping view of an economic interpretation in modern history.[27] Despite these common traits the history is evidently in striking contrast with the other writings,

[23] *A Joint Letter to Orestes Brownson and the Editor of the North American Review* (Boston, 1844); *Letter to Andrews Norton on Miracles* (Boston, 1840); *Despotism in America* (Boston, 1840, 1854).

[24] Planned on occasion in 6-10 volumes, " Notebook and Literary Memoranda," MS, Hildreth Papers. Only *Theory of Morals* (New York, 1844) and *Theory of Politics* (New York, 1853) were published; manuscripts survive of parts of " Theory of Wealth " and " Theory of Taste." I am indebted to the generous courtesy of Mrs. Louisa M. Hildreth for these and other materials used in the preparation of this essay.

[25] *Despotism in America* and *History, passim*; Kelly in the *Jernegan Essays*, pp. 33, 35; John Spencer Bassett, *The Middle Group of American Historians* (New York, 1917), p. 46. *Theory of Politics, Theory of Morals, Letter to Andrews Norton, Despotism in America, History* (especially first three volumes); *North American Review*, LXXIII (1851), 414 ff.

[26] *Banks, Banking, and Paper Currency* (Boston, 1840), p. 54; *Despotism in America*.

[27] *Banks, Banking, and Paper Currency*, p. 64; *Despotism in America*, pp. 64, 97; *Theory of Politics*, pp. 158-226. This section is probably part of a projected work on " Universal History," " Notebook and Literary Memoranda," MS, Hildreth Papers.

in its plain, unimpassioned style, its rejection of imaginative description and picturesque detail, its abjuration of philosophical generalization, in short, with its predominant matter-of-factness.

These peculiar characteristics of Hildreth's history become all the more clearly a problem if his volumes are compared with the works of his contemporaries. Writing in the days of Bancroft and Prescott, of the early Motley and Parkman, Hildreth constructed windows of flint glass, reinforced with steel ribs, through which to view the past; his fellows lovingly set up stained glass casements with leaded panes. Their volumes were works of art, and so they were meant to be. Writing in elegantly flowing style, which could, on occasion, become florid, the authors made the most of drama, rousing narration, and description with picturesque detail. Often they enjoyed the grand sweep, the breadth of " philosophical generalization," which in the case of Bancroft led one critic to remark that his *History of the United States* " should be entitled, ' The Psychological Autobiography of George Bancroft, as Illustrated by Incidents and Characters in the Annals of the United States.' " [28] The finger of God could be seen in the accounts they narrated, and Platonic ideas rolling to realization down the halls of time. Their contemporaries read their works and liked them; liked, too, the colors of the panes in their windows upon the past, fired from popular pigments—" manifest destiny," glowing meliorism and optimism, and liberalism not often libertarian. These were the Romantic Historians, dominating the Middle Group of American Historians.[29]

Hildreth was with them, but not of them. Only in the search for facts were their chief characteristics also his.

[28] Edwin Percy Whipple, *American Literature and Other Papers* (Boston, 1887), p. 92.

[29] Bassett, *passim*; Kraus, pp. 221-39.

In this, indeed, he must yield to some of them, at least
for breadth of research and attention to manuscript
sources, if not for criticism and comparison of authorities.
In everything else he varied from the Middle Group. He
" belongs by spirit to a later generation," declares G. P.
Gooch, surveying *History and Historians in the Nineteenth Century.*[30]

The characteristics of Hildreth's history were a matter
of principle with him, the consequence of a deliberate
aim, as some of his more acute critics saw.

> Mr. Hildreth undertook to present a rigid narrative of events
> from the earliest development of American history, until a period
> not far remote from our own times. Abstaining from philosophi-
> cal analysis and generalization and from the embellishments of
> rhetoric and poetry, he has aimed to give a coherent and accurate
> representation of facts.[31]

Another reviewer continued:

> The frigid tone of the composition, we are confident, proceeds
> from principle, and not from inability. It was essential to the
> realization of Mr. Hildreth's conception of a genuine historical
> work.

> .   .   .   .

> It is a rare thing for an author to be so consistent with himself,
> throughout the construction of a laborious work, as Mr. Hildreth
> has been in the composition of this history. He is never seduced
> for a moment from the plan which he has adopted. He accom-
> plishes whatever he undertakes. He pursues the idea which he has
> chosen for his guide with an austere tenacity of purpose, which,
> applied to the moral relations of life, would make one a very
> anchorite of virtue.[32]

Hildreth himself had aimed as his critics perceived. In
the advertisement to his second series he states,

[30] London, 1913, p. 407. See also Kraus, p. 251.
[31] *Littell's Living Age* (1852), XXXV, 28.
[32] *Ibid.*, pp. 366, 315.

It has been my earnest endeavor, now, as formerly, guarding, so far as might be, against these current illusions, to present, through a pure medium of impartial truth and justice, the events and characters of the times of which I write, undistorted by prejudice, uncolored by sentiment, neither tricked out in the gaudy tinsel of a meretricious rhetoric, nor stretched nor shortened to suit the purpose of any partial political theory.

.   .   .   .

It is due to our fathers and ourselves [he stated in another place], it is due to truth and philosophy to present for once, on the historic stage, the founders of our American nation unbedaubed with patriotic rouge, wrapped up in no fine-spun cloaks of excuses and apologies, without stilts, buskins, tinsel, or bedizenment, in their own proper persons, often rude, hard, narrow, superstitious, and mistaken, but always earnest, downright, manly, and sincere; their best apology is to tell their story exactly as it was.[33]

It was not simply that Hildreth was penning history in answer to Bancroft—" the Federalist facing the Democrat, fact against rhapsody, the dull, precise prose against the turbulent, windy rhetoric." [34] The conscious anti-Romanticist in a day of Romanticism, Hildreth was opposed to the whole way of thinking and writing which Bancroft and his fellows represented.[35] He found his central aim and

[33] *History,* IV, vii. The whole advertisement is of interest. *History,* I, vii. The inclusion of "truth and philosophy" seems significant in an author who used his words sparingly. Note the addition to the advertisement in 1853, I, x-xi.

[34] Schlesinger in the *New England Quarterly,* XIII, 226. See also pp. 226-29. Mr. Schlesinger's ascription to Richard Hildreth of *An Abridged History of the United States of America* (Boston, 1831) is quite right, as witnessed by "Manuscripts of Publications of the Class of 1826, Deposited by W. H. Tillinghast, '77," MS, Harvard Archives, and "Notebook and Literary Memoranda," MS, Hildreth Papers.

[35] Hildreth, "National Literature," *American Monthly Magazine* (1829), I, 379 ff., the authorship of which is witnessed by "Notebook and Literary Memoranda." The "Theory of Taste" is also distinctively anti-Romantic, but there some peculiarly "Romantic" characteristics such as the admiration of the Laocoon creep in.

principle in the depths of his convictions; his was a different philosophy.

Of George Grote, the historian of Greece and a leading Utilitarian, Professor Bain once declared, " His earnest devotion to mental science . . . had no small share in the characteristic excellencies of his historical compositions." [36] So, too, with Hildreth, the philosophy which he developed in other writings helps to explain the characteristics of his history. He turned to writing history from his " scientific work," the treatises on the *Rudiments of the Inductive Science of Man,* which, for a time, he thought his great task and life achievement.[37] In these works, his goal was high.

> The peculiarity of these treatises will consist in an attempt to apply vigorously and systematically to their several subjects the Inductive Method of Investigation,—a method which in Physical science has proved successful beyond expectation; but which, hitherto, . . . has been very partially employed . . . upon the yet nobler and more important science of Man. The daily increasing interest with which that science is regarded, and the great social problems which depend upon it for solution, seem to demand for its several branches a more patient, thorough, comprehensive, experimental investigation than they have yet rereived. Such will be the aim of these treatises.[38]

When these treatises are examined the chief characteristic that appears is their systematization; the manuscript of the " Theory of Taste," indeed, is notable as probably the only attempt by an American of the period to deal systematically with the problems of criticism. Primarily, the *Inductive Science of Man* was an attempt to systema-

---

[36] Alexander Bain, ed., *The Minor Works of George Grote* (London, 1873), p. 67.

[37] " Recent American Historians," *Christian Review* (1850), XV, 194; Hildreth to Caroline Weston, Jan. 8, Nov. 26, 1841, MS, Anti-Slavery Weston Papers.

[38] *Theory of Morals,* Advertisement.

tize human actions under the dogmas of the Utilitarian school. The analysis it contained was based upon the principle of utility, not on any thorough-going induction. An unsparing and generally acute critic, well versed in the schools of philosophy, Orestes Brownson, placed the endeavor immediately. " Mr. Hildreth," he shrilled,

is, substantially, a Benthamite,—for his slight modification of Benthamism amounts, practically, to nothing at all. . . . He has studied Bentham till his head is more confused, if possible, than was ever Bentham's own head, and till even his heart appears to have lost all of its native appreciation of right and wrong.[39]

" So acurately did Hildreth reproduce the subtleties and nuances of Bentham's thought," Mr. Schlesinger says of another book, " so completely did he enter into the spirit of Benthams' argument, that, as C. K. Ogden, editor of the most recent edition of the Theory of Legislation, writes: ' The present translation . . . has so long been a classic that it has become an almost integral part of the Bethamite canon. . . . By Hildreth's work alone is Bentham known to the majority of lawyers and to the wider public.' " [40]

Writers as different as Stephen, Troeltsch, and Scott have pointed to the influence of Utilitarianism upon historical writing, without making clear the nature of that influence.[41] Langlois and Seignobos declare that George Grote wrote " the first model of a ' history ' thus defined," meaning that by renouncing literary ornaments and state-

[39] *Brownson's Quarterly Review* (1844), I, 333, 329-30.

[40] Schlesinger in the *New England Quarterly,* XIII, 237-38; Hildreth translated from the French of Dumont, Bentham's *Theory of Legislation.* See Hildreth, " Etienne Dumont," in George Ripley and Charles A. Dana, eds., *New American Encyclopaedia* (16 vols., New York, 1858-1863); " Jeremy Bentham," *ibid.,* III, 136-42, especially p. 142.

[41] Leslie Stephen, *The English Utilitarians* (3 vols., London, 1900), III, 317-75; Troeltsch, *Der Historismus und seine Probleme,* pp. 392, 415; Ernest Scott, *History and Historical Problems* (Oxford, 1925), p. 32.

ments without proof Grote had introduced "scientific methods of exposition." [42] "If Grote wrote a model history," Stephen suggests, "it was because he thoroughly embodied the Utilitarian spirit." [43]

The effect upon style seems most evident and indisputable.[44] It was the very first principle of the Utilitarians, according to Stephen, "to rely upon fact pure and simple, and to make it precede speculation and to minimize 'sentiment,' 'vague generalities,' and *a priori* theories." [45] "Grote war kein Stilkünstler wie Macaulay," says Fueter, and continues: "An den rigorosen Stilprinzipien der Benthamisten hielt er unentwegt fest." [46] With the empiricist's aim of presenting the facts the Utilitarian writing history would be expected to be interested not in the artistic organization of the facts so much as in direct presentation. "The artistic aim is incompatible with scientific history," Stephen continues, "so far as it interferes with the primary aim of giving the unadulterated facts." [47] The Utilitarian would be disinclined to lose himself in exciting narration or vivid description with picturesque detail.

Furthermore, in the world-view of Benthamite thought there was no systematic formulation of historical development. The references to history *per se* in Bentham's writings are almost negligible.[48] Benthamism was in an important sense a-historical, if not actually anti-historical.[49] Consequently there was no broad and conspicuous

[42] Charles V. Langlois and Charles Seignobos, *Introduction to the Study of History* (New York, 1907), p. 310.
[43] Stephen, III, 338.
[44] *The Minor Works of George Grote*, p. 101.
[45] Stephen, III, 338.   [46] Fueter, p. 518.   [47] Stephen, III, 339.
[48] John Bowring, ed., *The Works of Jeremy Bentham* (11 vols., Edinburgh, 1843), VIII, 7; XI, cliii.
[49] Elie Halévy, *Growth of Philosophical Radicalism* (New York, 1928), p. 273; Stephen, I, 296-99, 304, III, 374-75; Ernest Albee, *A History of English Utilitarianism* (London, 1902), pp. 212-14.

framework into which the story of the past must be fitted. The Utilitarian aim of presenting the facts could realize itself, limited only by the ability and prejudices of the writer of history. There would be little tendency to interlard the account of the past with extended disquisitions inspired by any systematically formulated theory of historical development. No Utilitarian could have written rhapsodies like George Bancroft's delineation of the hand of God pushing forward Americans in their progress. Historical development in Hildreth's history is rigidly naturalistic.

To argue in this vein about Benthamism is not to maintain that the system of ideas would fail to suggest certain points of emphasis in relating the story of the past. Quite the contrary. The self-interest motivational scheme of pleasures and pains might well appear in the account of past actions, as might the stress on the conditions under which human action occurred. This emphasis on the conditions of action could operate as a stimulus to an economic interpretation of history, especially in the simple "economic motives" form.[50] From Utilitarianism might come other emphases. A democratic political philosophy is one of the characteristics most frequently associated with the Benthamite system of thought, and a Utilitarian might well give most favorable treatment to the elements of democracy in history, as George Grote had done, even indulging in near disquisitions.[51] But such a characteristic would depend upon the particular writer. Though democratic philosophy was most closely associated with Utilitarianism by the time Grote was a foremost representative of it, it was not an unavoidable principle of the system.

[50] Stephen, III, 342.
[51] Fueter, pp. 516-18. A good instance is George Grote on the Kleisthenes constitution and Athenian democracy, *History of Greece* (12 vols., London, 1869-1870), IV, 169-244.

One could be a Benthamite without being a democrat, as
Bentham himself was before 1808.[52] The system of ideas
would still tend to exclude dominant artistic purposes from
historical writing, to eliminate grandiose formulations
of historical development, and to put no others in their
place, allowing and stimulating a presentation of the facts
in a generally " factual " tone.

To be sure, no system of ideas works in a vacuum, and
Hildreth, sometime editor of the leading New England
Whig sheet of the thirties, could have found in the
Federalist-Whig tradition an inclination to some of the
characteristics which he displayed. An economic interpretation of politics, for instance, was a part of the Federalist tradition. To the extent that Hildreth was preju-
diced in favor of Federalist policies that tradition certainly did play a part in his history; but it does not offer a
satisfactory explanation of the striking difference between
Hildreth's history and his other writings.[53] Utilitarian
philosophy in its application does offer an explanation
why Hildreth wrote the sort of history he did. From that
dogma, striving toward the method of post-Newtonian
physics, Hildreth drew the aim which he pursued in his
" scientific work," seeking to create an " Inductive Science of Man." His history stands as an early attempt at
the first type of " scientific history."

If Hildreth foreshadowed the first type, John William
Draper owes his position in American historiography to
his exemplification of the second. An exception in the
group of American historical writers, he has been called
the " Buckle of America "—sufficient praise or damnation
according to one's view of the English historian. But
Draper was not imitating Buckle; rather he was accom-

[52] *Halévy,* pp. 249 ff.
[53] See Schlesinger in the *New England Quarterly,* XIII, 233-45, which
faces well and directly the emphasis many have put upon Hildreth's
Federalism.

panying him upon the same path.[54] The remarkable fact is that figures so different—professional scientist and *Privatgelehrter*—produced histories with so much in common.[55]

When Draper could remark that " it was discovered by the author of this book that the spectrum of an ignited solid is continuous," he gave his volumes a kind of prestige which no other writers of " scientific history " could equal.[56] Best known in the world of science for his researches on radiant energy, his activities included pioneer work on spectrum analysis and studies on the chemical action of light, with particular attention to the growth of plants.[57] His researches also had most immediate practical consequences. He was, for instance, the first to take a portrait by the use of light, using for that purpose the silver bromide plate by which he improved the newly announced daguerreotype.[58] By his experiments upon the resistance of wires to electrical currents he aided in the practical development of the telegraph.[59] His researches upon the

[54] John W. Draper, *Human Physiology, Statical and Dynamical*, pp. v, viii, and *History of the Intellectual Development of Europe* (2 vols., New York, 1863), I, iv. This work, in 1876 ed., cited hereafter as *HIDE*.

[55] See " Buckle, Draper and the Law of Human Development," *Continental Monthly* (1863), IV, 529-45; " Buckle, Draper, and a Science of History," *ibid.*, IV, 610-24 (1864), V, 161-80; J. M. Robertson, *Buckle and His Critics* (London, 1895).

[56] *HIDE*, II, 283.

[57] George F. Barker, *Memoir of John William Draper, 1811-1882*. Read before the National Academy, April 21, 1886; Ellwood Hendrick, " John William Draper," *Dictionary of American Biography*, V, 438-41. W. Jerome Harrison, " John William Draper," *Dictionary of National Biography*, XVI, 3-4.

In the preparation of this essay I have been aided by an unpublished paper on Draper, written by Mr. Jerome Blum, a graduate student in the Johns Hopkins Department of History, which called my attention to materials I might otherwise have missed.

[58] John W. Draper, *Scientific Memoirs* (New York, 1878), p. x.

[59] *Silliman's American Journal of Science and Arts*, December, 1843; E. L. Morse, *S. F. B. Morse, his Letters and Journals* (Boston, 1914), I, 45-46; Barker, pp. 377-78.

production of light by heat were the basis from which Thomas A. Edison developed the incandescent electric light bulb.[60] If no greater honor could be paid to the pursuit of history as science than to have the scientist him-self participate, few more distinguished scientists could be found in nineteenth-century America than John William Draper.

The History of the Intellectual Development of Europe, which first won Draper fame as a historian, sprang from the attempt to demonstrate, or as he sometimes said, to teach

that the civilization of Europe has not taken place fortuitously, but in a definite manner, and under the control of natural law; that the procession of nations does not move forward like a dream, without reason or order, but that there is a predestined, a solemn march, in which all must join, ever moving, ever restlessly advancing, encountering and enduring an inevitable succession of events; that individual life and its advancement through successive stages is the model of social life and its secular variations.[61]

He aimed to construct a science of history, armed, like all science, with prevision, and he was confident that

Historical foresight is not denied to man. As the Astronomer from recorded facts, deduces the laws under which the celestial bodies move, and then applies them with unerring certainty to the prophesying of future events, so may the Historian, who relies on the immutability of Nature, predict the inevitable course through which a nation must pass.[62]

Like many of his fellows in the nineteenth century

[60] In 1875 he was awarded the Rumford medal for these investigations, and the following year he was chosen first president of the American Chemical Society.

[61] *HIDE,* II, 175, 186, 395. See also *ibid.,* pp. 392-93.

[62] *Thoughts on the Future Civil Policy of America* (2d ed., New York, 1866), p. iv (Cited hereafter as *TFCPA*); *History of the American Civil War* (3 vols., New York, 1867-1870), I, 37. Cited as *HACW*.

Draper had a profound conviction that there was a pattern in the affairs of men.

Our actions are not the pure and unmingled results of our desires; they are the offspring of many various and mixed conditions. . . . From this more accurate point of view we should therefore consider the course of these events, recognizing the principle that the affairs of men pass forward in a determinate way, expanding and unfolding themselves.[63]

De Tocqueville, too, believed that there was a plan in the affairs of men, leading, as he saw it, to the realization of equality.[64] Karl Marx, also, saw a design in history.[65] But the ends which different observers thought were being realized were diverse. Such a belief in patterns of history was fundamental for any conviction of " scientific history " in terms of laws or generalizations; but it was a faith which the theological historians also shared. The question was how the simple scheme of nature was to be discovered. Like his fellow Positivists, following their precursors of the Enlightenment, Draper discovered it by reasoning on the analogy of natural science.

Such historical views were a consequence of profound faith and an assumption. Draper was convinced that everything developed subject to law, and he assumed that the operation was the same in society as in individual men.[66] He believed in the immutability of nature: that

[63] *HIDE*, I, 388, 389; see also p. 390.

[64] John Stuart Mill, *Dissertations and Discussions* (5 vols., New York, 1874-1882), II, 82-90.

[65] Karl Marx and Friedrich Engels, *The German Ideology* (Parts I and II, New York, 1939), pp. 4-69. See also Marx's preface to the *Critique of Political Economy* (New York, 1904).

[66] *HIDE*, I, iii, 1-22, II, 358-59 and *passim; Report of the Thirtieth Meeting of the British Association for the Advancement of Science* (London, 1861), pp. 115-16 (cited hereafter as *BAAS*). Draper was invited to deliver this sketch of his physiological theory of history in the meeting of 1860 which exploded into the battle between T. H. Huxley and the Bishop of Oxford over the Darwinian hypothesis—obscuring the

there were invariants in the unceasing flux; and he believed in the scrutability of nature: that man could read the book of the Lord, and had by 1860 perused a good many pages.[67] Aware of the " temporalizing of the great chain of being " with which the nineteenth-century scientists were busying themselves, he was greatly impressed with development according to law. He saw " not only the evidences, but also the proofs of the dominion of law over the world of life "

first, in the successive stages of development of every individual from the earliest rudiment to maturity; second, in the numberless organic forms now living contemporaneously with us, and constituting the animal series; third, in the orderly appearance of that grand succession, which in the slow lapse of geological time has emerged, constituting the life of the earth. . . .[68]

Evidently all mundane events were the results of the operation of law.[69] And

Man, thus, is the last term of an innumerable series or organisms, which, under the dominion of law, has, in the lapse of time, been evolving.[70]

In this evolution, this progress, as he frequently viewed it,

the general principle is to differentiate instinct from automatism, and then to differentiate intelligence from instinct. In man himself three distinct instrumental nervous mechanisms exist, and three distinct modes of life are perceptible, the automatic, the instinctive, the intelligent. They occur in an epochal order, from infancy through childhood to the more perfect state.[71]

---

paper. *HIDE*, I, iii and L. Huxley, *Life and Letters of Thomas Henry Huxley* (2 vols., New York, 1901), II, 196, 202.

[67] *HIDE*, I, 18; *TFCPA*, pp. 16, 238; *Scientific Memoirs*, pp. xii-xiii. See also Draper's early lecture at Hampden-Sydney on the History of Science, *Southern Literary Messenger* (1837), III, 693-98.

[68] *HIDE*, II, 358; *TFCPA*, pp. 241-42; *BAAS*, p. 115.

[69] *HIDE*, I, 5.

[70] *Ibid.*, II, 359.

[71] *Ibid.*, pp. 394-95; *BAAS*, p. 115.

" Man," Draper then went on to assume, " is the archetype of society." [72] Since it was physiologically impossible
to separate the individual from the race, " what holds
good for the one must also hold good for the other too.
Hence man is truly the archetype of society. His development is the model of social progress." [73]   And " social
advancement is as completely under the control of natural
law as is bodily growth." [74]

   This assimilation of history to physiology Draper had
presaged in the companion volume which preceded his
historical work, *Human Physiology—Statical and Dynamical.* " The practice of Medicine," he there declared,
" must rest on an exact Anatomy and a sound Physiology,"
and his text aimed

to treat Physiology as a branch of Physical Science; to exclude
from it all purely speculative doctrines and ideas, . . . from which
the more advanced subjects of human knowledge, such as Astro-
nomy and Chemistry, have long ago made themselves free. . . .

.   .   .   .

Physiology, however, in its most general acceptation, has another
department connected with problems of the highest interest. Man
must be studied not merely in the individual, but also in the race.
There is an analogy between his advance from infancy through
childhood, youth, manhood, to old age, and his progress through
the stages of civilization. In the whole range of human study
there are no topics of greater importance, or more profound, than
those dealt with in this second department or division. It is also
capable of being treated in the same spirit and upon the same
principles as the first. I have nearly completed a volume, which
will serve as a companion to this, in which in that manner the
subject is discussed, and the laws which preside over the career
of nations established. . . .[75]

In the last chapter, " Social Mechanics," Draper sketched

[72] *Ibid.;* HIDE, I, 2.   [74] *HIDE,* I, iii.
[73] *TFCPA,* p. 248.   [75] *Human Physiology,* I, v, viii.

the argument which needed only to be clothed with facts to become his account of the intellectual development of Europe in the companion volume.[76]

From this assimilation of history to physiology Draper drew a cyclical interpretation of history, based on " organic patterns."

The intellectual progress of Europe . . . being like that of an individual, we may conveniently separate it into arbitrary periods, sufficiently distinct from one another, though imperceptibly merging into each other. To these successive periods I shall give the titles of—1, the Age of Credulity; 2, the Age of Inquiry; 3, the Age of Faith; 4, the Age of Reason; 5, the Age of Decrepitude.[77]

Upon this scheme he sketched the political events in each period and examined at some length the ideas of the particular individuals who seemed representative according to his construction. Draper ignored art and literature.[78] His concern was with speculative thought, religious, philosophic, or scientific, and his favor lay obviously with the last.

But Draper never faced the problems to which his cyclical theory gave rise; the historian was satisfied with the physiologist's analogy. The physiologist's assumption that the nation, or what he sometimes called the race, lived and died like a man, obscured for the historian the difference between man and social groups.[79] The number

[76] *Ibid.*, pp. 602-37. The argument was repeated in substantially the same words in the paper before the *British Association*, the last section of the *Intellectual Development*, and the *Thoughts on Civil Policy*.

[77] *HIDE*, I, 19.

[78] To the especial annoyance of at least one critic. See Johannes Scherr, *A History of English Literature* (London, 1882), pp. 311-12.

[79] For his units Draper took groups of people which he called sometimes races, sometimes nations. *TFCPA*, p. 47. Though he viewed their common characteristics as the outcome of similar adjustment to environment (*HIDE*, I, 11-12), he tended to reify the characteristics and make them a separate factor, *race*. His assumption would imply a uniformity of characteristics of a people in the same environment, but he recognized

of cycles observed in the development of Europe could be one or many, according to the unit taken, and the period from neolithic man to Napoleon III might easily have been viewed as a single cycle. Draper envisaged two cycles clearly and suggested others. He presented the life and death of Greece and brought Europe to maturity, and he implied that the Mohammedans, the Ancient East, China, and India had all had cycles of their own. But his attention wandered little from European civilization. Outside of Europe he devoted extended consideration only to the Mohammedans, presenting on the subject of Arabian science some of the freshest parts of his book.[80] He offered no justification of the units he had chosen, and the distinction between the ages of Europe and the successive Hellenic, Hellenistic, and Hellenistic-Roman civilizations in the eastern Mediterranean throws little light upon the progress of races or nations. It is seldom clear whether he is considering the intellectual development of western civilization or the progress of nations, to which intellectual development is the chief clue.

Besides the ambiguity of what exactly is going in cycles, there is the question of fact whether anything really so proceeds, and Draper too evidently forms, rather than finds, the variations he discusses. The analogies furnished by any pattern of cycles may be immensely stimulating, but an organic cyclical theory of history is a confession of mystification about historical development, rather than an explanation. Like other holders of a cyclical interpretation, Draper did not reveal why development should follow such ups and downs, unless, indeed, such is the nature of the unfolding of the universal spirit. But the " outgoing of the will of the immutable Creator " has

also the existence of classes, without facing the problem they represented for him. *HACW*, I, 21, 36, 92, 110, 111; *HIDE*, I, 13, II, 99.

    [80] These sections were translated into Arabic. *Popular Science Monthly* (1874), IV, 36.

never furnished notably useful explanations. What satisfied the historian would have startled the chemist.[81]

Although this " physiological interpretation of history " with its cyclical theory was the dominant aspect of Draper's historical speculation, another current ran with it, also proceeding on a " physiological base." [82] There was in the *Intellectual Development* occasional mention that the conditions under which men acted limited, and, indeed, determined their development. Thus the explanation of the success of Mohammedan imperialism was " to be found in the social conditions of the conquered countries." [83] In the Renaissance " the ensuing development of Europe was really based upon the commerce of upper Italy, and not upon the Church." [84] And there were other such instances.[85] The primary condition influencing development was geography. " The permanence of organic forms is altogether dependent on the invariability of the material conditions under which they live." [86] ". . . the mode of life of man is chiefly determined by geographical conditions, his instinctive disposition to activity increasing with the latitude in which he lives.[87] " With differences of climate there must be differences of manners and customs, that is differences in the modes of civilization." [88] " All over the world physical circumstances control the human race." [89] Thus Draper indicated the basis for explaining

[81] For a criticism of cyclical theories see Frederick J. Teggart, *Journal of the History of Ideas* (1940), I, 494-503; Vilfredo Pareto, *Traité de sociologie générale* (2 vols., Paris, 1917-1919), II, parts 2330-2331 (cited by Teggart), and *passim*.

[82] The clearest recognition of the fact that Draper had not one but two formulations of historical development seems to be in Charles Dudley Warner, ed., *Library of the World's Best Literature* (31 vols., New York, [c. 1913]), pp. 4865-66.

[83] *HIDE*, I, 332.

[84] *Ibid.*, II, 110.

[85] *Ibid.*, I, 84-86.

[86] *Ibid.*, p. 8.

[87] *Ibid.*, pp. 11, 237.

[88] *Ibid.*, p. 11.

[89] *Ibid.*, p. 26; *HACW*, I, 30.

historical development in terms of climate, by which he meant the aggregate of all circumstances, natural and artificial, in which man lives.[90]

This climatic theory, only indicated in his first historical writing, Draper applied in his *History of the American Civil War*. When he was surveying the development of Europe his

attention was often drawn to facts illustrating how much the national life of the American people had been influenced by uncontrollable causes, and how strikingly it exemplified the great truth that societies advanced in a preordained and inevitable course.

Encouraged by the favorable reception of his survey of European intellectual development, he declared, his intention to treat American history became a resolve during the Civil War. By revealing

how much the actions of men are controlled by the deeds of their predecessors, and are determined by climate and other natural circumstances,

he hoped that animosities would lose much of their asperity and the return of kind feelings would be hastened.[91] He devoted the first of his three volumes to demonstrating how the opposition of North and South arose from the wide disparity in their climates, which necessarily occasioned " race-diversity " and consequent political oppositions.[92] Using as his especial instrument of

[90] *HACW*, I, 80. For a discussion of Draper's climatic theory see Franklin Thomas, *The Environmental Basis of Society* (New York, 1925), pp. 95-97.

[91] *HACW*, I, iii.

[92] The other two volumes contained fairly straight military history not always displaying the author's realization that he would " have to describe military operations eclipsing in magnitude and splendor those of the French empire; a revolution in the art of war through the introduction of the steam engine, the locomotive, the electric telegraph, rifled ordnance, iron-clad ships, and other inventions of this scientific age, sustained by

analysis isothermals—lines of common mean temperature at a given time—he demonstrated the sharply varying climatic conditions of the United States, and his historical account attempted to relate political variations to these divergent conditions—without notable success.[93]

Draper seems never to have realized that this climatic theory of history in his later writings could conflict fundamentally with the " organic " cyclical theory of his earlier work. He was not, to be sure, a notably rigorous thinker. In the field of natural science he is now given credit for his experiments, not for his theories.[94] The opposition of his two historical interpretations, both founded in his physiological groundwork, was a basic contradiction. If climate determines actions, if the permanence of organic forms is, indeed, dependent on the invariability of the material conditions under which they live, it is certainly not immediately evident that the development of individuals or of groups will follow the presupposed " organic " patterns with their five stages. Environmental conditions may prevent some of the supposed " ages " from ever appearing.[95] If climatic conditions should not

the development and use of financial resources on a scale that has no parallel in the history of the world." (HACW, I, 17.)

Special historiographical survey of Draper, which he deserves, might well consider his History of the American Civil War his chief work. It is the only one written actually from the documents, and the admission which he had to sources suggests the volume is of considerable interest simply for that reason, if he used much of what he had available.

[93] Isothermals had been mentioned only once in HIDE, I, 35.

[94] H. Kayser, Handbuch der Spectroscopie (6 vols., Leipzig, 1900-1912), I, 34, 35. " Wenn so die Arbeiten Drapers eine ganze Reihe wichtiger Fortschritte bringen, so sind doch die Anschauungen, welche er entwickelt, fast durchweg recht verkehrte " (I, 39). " Wir kommen nun zu Untersuchungen von J. W. Draper, die im Gegensatz zu dessen sonst meist so tüchtigen Arbeiten ganz verfehlt sind. . . . So falsch all diese Ideen von Draper sind, so interessant ist es anderseits, dem Gedankengang des Autors nachzugehen . . . (I, 57, 58). See also Nation (1865), I, 407-409 reviewing TFCPA.

[95] Thus some species of tadpoles spend their whole existence in that

vary so as to produce development after the pattern of the
" organic cycles," either the climatic interpretation must
be dropped, or vice versa. Thus is implicit, on the one
hand, a determinism of a radically materialist character and on the other a developmental dynamic that
approaches an essentially emanationist idealism.[96]

This basic contradiction is characteristic of Positivism,
and Draper was caught in Positivistic currents of
thought.[97] Orestes Brownson placed Draper as sharply
as he had Hildreth.[98] Other critics, too, lined him up with
the Positivists.[99]

What exactly were Draper's debts to other Positivists
it is impossible to state with any conclusiveness. His
papers were destroyed at his own request.[100] Like Comte
he believed that the science of history consisted in the
discovery of laws on the model of physical science, and
he believed that such a science formed part of the science
of man. If his " organic pattern " be substituted for
Comte's mechanical one, his physiological theory of development followed substantially the same lines as Comte's
developmental scheme.[101] The only difference between the
three stages of theology, metaphysics, and science, and the

form without ever becoming frogs, unless placed in a special environment.
There are other instances of the same sort of interaction of organism and
environment—as in one type of salamander.

[96] *TFCPA,* pp. 60, 157, 159, 178-79.

[97] Troeltsch, pp. 371 ff.

[98] " Professor Draper's Books," *The Catholic World* (1868), VII, 155-
74, especially p. 158; Henry F. Brownson, ed., *The Works of Orestes
A. Brownson* (20 vols., Detroit, 1882-1907), IX, 547-66 (reviewing
Draper's last book, *Conflict of Science and Religion*).

[99] " Buckle, Draper, and the Law of Human Development," *Continental
Monthly* (1863), IV, 529-45; " Buckle, Draper, and a Science of History," *ibid.,* pp. 610-24; (1864), V, 161-80, especially IV, 529; *Manual
of Historical Literature,* pp. 44, 575.

[100] Mrs. Dorothy Draper Nye to the writer, Sept. 20, 1940.

[101] Robert Flint, *History of the Philosophy of History* (New York,
1894), pp. 579-615.

four ages of credulity, inquiry, faith, and reason was that
Draper realized that after maturity came death. To be
sure, Draper's was a cyclical theory and Comte's, at least
by implication, was one of unilateral progress. But Draper did not stress the decrepitude of Europe, as have those
holders of cyclical theories such as Spengler, who gloried
in death. Instead his concern was the intellectual maturity of Europe, its tremendous age of reason, which should
reach its fullest development in the new empire arising
in the United States out of the Civil War.[102]

Draper's science of man drew more from physiology
than Comte's. His views strikingly approximate those of
the master to whom Comte owed so much of his system,
Saint-Simon. In Saint-Simon's *Mémoire sur la science de
l'homme*, he sketched a physiological interpretation of
history.[103] The science of man had two parts, the first
treating the individual physiologically and psychologi-
cally; the second, the science of history, dealing with the
human race. The whole science of man was a part of the
comprehensive science of physiology, and physiology in
this comprehensive sense was the last in a series of sciences
which had gradually achieved a "positive and properly
scientific state"—on the model of physics.[104] This was
exactly Draper's view.

There are, to be sure, sources other than Positivistic
thought for Draper's historical views, but the combination
he made was in easy accord with that system. Thus the
assumption that "man is the archetype of society" goes
back at least to Plato's *Republic*. But for Draper this
assumption seemed the natural consequence of the estab-

[102] *TFCPA*, pp. 239-40, 248, 251; *HACW*, III, 675.
[103] Flint, pp. 397-400; *Oeuvres choisies de C. H. de Saint-Simon* (3
vols., Brussels, 1859), II, 5-166.
[104] Flint, pp. 397-98; for comparison with Comte, *ibid.*, pp. 579-601.
John Stuart Mill, *The Positive Philosophy of Auguste Comte* (New York,
1875), pp. 32-41.

lishment of scientific history upon a physiological basis.[105] From the point of view of physiology " society is only an aggregate of individuals; whatever affects, whatever regulates each of them, must regulate and affect it also. Its actions are the sum of their actions." [106] But such an identification of physiology and a science of society is a characteristically Positivistic assumption, the consequence of which is to reduce society to the sum of the conditions under which it exists.[107] In the same way, geographic determinism, as Draper well knew, could be found in Bodin and Montesquieu, to mention only two, but in Draper it was an aspect of the reduction of society to its conditions, carried, indeed, to the logical extreme.[108]

Like Comte's follower, Buckle, Draper was writing Positivistic history. Although the classical political economy did not appear in Draper's scheme, and the climatic interpretation took a different tack, both Draper and Buckle were showing forth the laws of history in a strikingly similar fashion.[109] For both the path from history to science led through the bounds of Positivistic philosophy, a system which, in contrast with Utilitarianism, had a formulation of historical development.

Like other Positivists Draper viewed the past from the vantage point of his own time, which it had been the particular achievement of history to evolve.[110] He valued in the past that which approximated most closely the chief achievement of his own day, natural science. Consequently the high points of history were the Hellenistic

[105] See his treatment of Plato (*HIDE,* I, 159, 162-63), and of society as organism, *TFCPA,* pp. 254, 260, 261, 263.
[106] *TFCPA,* p. 258.
[107] Talcott Parsons, *Structure of Social Action* (New York, 1937), pp. 60-69, 115-21.
[108] *HIDE,* I, 6, 245; *HACW,* I, 93.
[109] See footnote 55.
[110] *HIDE,* I, 341; *TFCPA,* p. 248.

period of scientific discoveries after Aristotle and the period of Mohammedan interest in science; those were ages of reason in which the " races " reached their maturity. He scorned Platonic philosophy and concern with ethical problems almost as much as he did Europe under the Roman Church. He could find some favor for the pre-Socratics since they had been occupied in physical speculations. With the rise of experimental science Europe reached her day of glory. If Draper's cyclical theory was more sophisticated than his fellow Positivists' view of unilateral progress, he was no less convinced that the aim of Nature's simple plan was to evolve a Europe in an age of experimental science—a conviction which, as an experimental scientist, he might hold more deeply than those who simply reflected other men's glories. Intellectual advancement was the law of development, the inevitable tendency of nature.[111] Thus he could conclude his survey of the intellectual development of Europe with a plea for nations to realize this tendency and to further it by the organization of intellect.[112] The logical conclusion from his cyclical theory, that an age of decrepitude was inevitable, did not appear.

The generalizations which Draper achieved in his historical writing remained excrescences. So far as his theories were not simply paragraphs inserted in pauses of the running account, they represented not so much a searching of hypotheses to fit the facts as a search for facts to fit hypotheses arising from his formulas of historical development. In part, at least, the virtual disappearance of Draper's theories of climatic determinism in the two volumes of his civil war history dealing with detailed events is no doubt a tribute to the intractability of historical facts to the simple purposes of the investi-

[111] *TFCPA*, p. 297.
[112] *HIDE*, II, 395; *TFCPA*, p. 304; *HACW*, III, 671-72.

12

gator. When the scientist came to make a science of history he deserted scientific method.

Draper's critics did not fail to notice the fatal deficiency of his high aim of " scientific history." A reviewer of the first volume of his civil war history declared:

> Dr. Draper has furnished, during the last few years, more striking examples of sweeping and fallacious generalization than any modern author of equal pretensions; and some of his fallacies have been of a kind which one would not have expected a gentleman to fall who was as familiar as he with physical science, even if he had not prepared himself for the work of moral and political speculation into which he has so largely entered, by a study of formal logic.[113]

Critics of Draper's volumes laid bare many weaknesses, and the historians of the last quarter of the nineteenth century put him in his place with fitting disdain.[114] But he continued to be read, in part, no doubt, because of the sheer lack of any works even beginning to treat of intellectual history, possibly also because of his prestige as a scientist.[115] And his *Intellectual Development* was stirring stuff, with its ringing appeals to the greatness of free thinking in history, and its accompanying scorn for the restrictive tyranny either of governments or religions.[116]

For such effective passages alone, Draper could find

[113] " Draper's Civil War in America (I)," *Nation* (1867), V, 207.

[114] *Nation* (1865), I, 407-09, reviewing *TFCPA; ibid.* (1867), V, 207-08; (1869) VIII, 234-35; (1870) XI, 94-95, reviewing *HACW*. *Atlantic Monthly* (1864), XIII, 642-47; *Scribner's Monthly* (1875), IX, 635-37. *New Englander* (1866), XXV, 26 ff. on *TFCPA*. *North American Review* (1865), CI, 587-97 on *TFCPA* (1867), CV, 664-70, on *HACW*, I; John Fiske, " The Laws of History," *ibid* (1870), CIX, 197-230; *Manual of Historical Literature,* p. 575. *HIDE* was translated into French, German, Italian, Russian, Polish, and several other languages, *Eclectic Magazine* (New Series, 1875), XXII, 759-60.

[115] Robinson, *The New History,* pp. 103-06.

[116] Max Lerner, *Ideas Are Weapons* (New York, 1940), p. 260, remarking Mr. Justice Black's interest in Draper.

readers, regardless of the weaknesses of his science of history. In his own field of science he was continually concerned with the methods of establishing relations; when he came to write history he was satisfied to reason upon analogy, making no investigation of the nature of historical relations, but assuming them of the same order as in natural science. It was his achievement, however, to have attempted to make a science of history, and his failure was at least witness to the fact that history could not become scientific without careful consideration of the nature of its realm.

While American historians of the last quarter of the nineteenth century so largely scorned Draper, Hildreth found high favor with them. Whether they liked him because of his approximation to their idea of scientific history or because of the Federalism they had little difficulty seeing in him if they wished, it is impossible to say. At any rate, if one recalls the characteristics of his history it is not surprising that it should be popular with the generation which joined to a greater or less degree with Henry Adams in his effort to " satisfy himself whether, by the severest process of stating, with the least possible comment, such facts as seemed sure, in such order as seemed rigorously consequent, he could fix for a familiar moment a necessary sequence of human movement." [117] But that generation did not heed the lesson which Hildreth could have taught them. For his belief that scientific history was a search for facts alone, with no laws or generalizations, did not arise from the belief that he had no philosophy. It issued from a very definite philosophy. And the weaknesses of that philosophy had been pointed out in one of the first reviews of his volumes. The philosopher and sometimes historian, Francis Bowen, hurled against Hildreth the two challenges to be reiterated

---

[117] *The Education of Henry Adams* (New York, 1918), p. 382.

against the historians of the last quarter of the nineteenth century, an issue of fact and an argument.

A naked record of facts must also be untrustworthy; it will be not merely incomplete, but deceptive. It will give rise to undue impressions, and create false judgments.

. . . .

. . . it is impossible to write history without seeking, either avowedly or stealthily, or unawares, to verify some hypothesis, or establish some theory, which furnishes a reason and a guide for the selection and arrangement of materials. It is not necessary to draw the inference, or set forth the doctrine, which the course of the narrative is calculated to illustrate or defend. What is skillfully left to implication generally strikes the reader's mind with more force than that which is boldly and earnestly inculcated. The facts have no connection with each other, and the story has no unity, unless some doctrine lies at the bottom to which they are all, more or less related. Without giving one false assertion or positive misstatement, a writer may give any tone to a narrative that he pleases, simply by an artful choice of events to which predominance is given, and a studied collocation of the circumstances. And he may do this unconsciously, or while sincerely striving to elucidate the truth.[118]

Bowen went on to argue that real history required " a large view of the facts, including their connection with each other, and with the causes in which they had their origin and the consequences to which they lead." [119] Thus the middle nineteenth-century representative of the first type of " scientific history " called forth the basic objections to that conception.

[118] *North American Review* (1851), LXXIII, 412-13.
[119] *Ibid.*, p. 411.

SCHOOL HISTORIES OF THE MIDDLE PERIOD

BY

ALFRED GOLDBERG

History textbooks have not always been written by professional historians. In the forty years before the Civil War, when this type of writing first flourished, preeminence belonged to a publisher, a clergyman, a politician, and four people interested primarily in general education. The publisher was Samuel G. Goodrich, who printed on his own presses some of the famous " Peter Parley " series.[1] The clergyman was Peter Parley's brother, Charles A. Goodrich. Having abandoned the ministry soon after entering it, this Goodrich wrote what was probably the most popular of all history texts of this period.[2] Salma Hale held public office in New Hampshire. For his text he received a prize from—of all institutions!— the American Academy of Languages and Belles Lettres.[3] Emma Willard, though well-known for her school history, is far more famous as a promoter of secondary education for girls.[4] John Frost, Jesse Olney and Marcius Willson were school teachers who found textbook writing a profitable enterprise. Frost made so much at it, that he was able to give up his position as Professor of Belles Lettres at the Philadelphia Central High School and devote all of his time to turning out history manuals.[5] Like

[1] *Dictionary of American Biography,* VII, 402-03. See also Goodrich, *Recollections of a Lifetime* (2 vols., New York, 1856).

[2] *Dictionary of American Biography,* VII, 397.

[3] *New England Historical and Genealogical Register* (1867), XXI, 292.

[4] Alma Lutz, *Emma Willard, Daughter of Democracy* (Boston, 1929), *passim.*

[5] S. A. Allibone, *A Critical Dictionary . . .* (Philadelphia, 1871), I, 639-40.

Frost, Jesse Olney earned enough from his histories and geographies to retire from teaching at a comparatively early age. Olney then went into politics and helped lead the fight for a public school system in Connecticut.[6] Marcius Willson, besides his history, published textbooks in four other school subjects.[7]

The textbooks of these writers were an answer to one of the demands of American public education in its first great phase of growth. The expanding school curriculum created a market for history textbooks, particularly manuals of American history, and these began to flow from the presses in quantity during the 1820's. Between 1821 and 1861 at least sixty-one texts in the history of the United States were published—twenty-two in the last decade of the period.[8] The works of the seven people mentioned led all this group in importance because of their widespread sale and use.[9]

[6] *Dictionary of American Biography*, XIV, 31-32.

[7] Allibone, *Critical Dictionary*, III, 2762-63. Also *National Cyclopaedia of American Biography* (New York, 1909), X, 39.

[8] C. A. Jacquith, *The Development of History Teaching in the United States up to the Civil War* (Chicago, 1911), p. 31. Between 1821 and 1861, 220 history textbooks were published. Jacquith found that 61 of these were United States histories. In the decade 1821-1831, 46 textbooks were published, of which 11 were histories of the United States. In the decade 1851-1861, 75 textbooks were published, of which 22 were histories of the United States. For the latest and most complete bibliography of history textbooks published in this country prior to 1861, see Agnew O. Roorbach, *The Development of the Social Studies in American Secondary Education Before 1861* (Philadelphia, 1937), pp. 246-60. A criticism of Roorbach's bibliography may be found in Alice W. Spieseke, *The First Textbooks in American History* (New York, 1938), pp. iv-v.

[9] Rolla M. Tryon, *The Social Sciences as School Subjects* (New York, 1935), pp. 120-23. Tryon finds that the works of Hale, C. A. Goodrich, Olney, Mrs. Willard, and Willson were among the most popular and widely used textbooks of the period. Clifton A. Johnson, *Old Schools and Schoolbooks* (New York, 1904), p. 372, singles out Charles A. Goodrich's *History* as the most popular for a long time. He also found that the books of Hale, Olney, and S. G. Goodrich were widely circulated.

What kind of histories did this popular group of writers offer the public? In the main, they were straightforward narratives, relating in some detail what the authors regarded as the " essentials " in American history appropriate to the instruction of youth. Political and military personalities and events occupy from seventy-five to ninety-five percent of the contents.[10] The American Revolution, described almost exclusively in terms of military campaigns, was usually given about one-fourth of the total space.[11] The War of 1812, almost solely in its military aspects, occupies as much as ten or twelve percent of some of these books.[12] Social and economic history assumes important proportions only in the *History* of Charles A. Goodrich, who devoted twenty-five percent of his work to it.[13] As might be expected, all of the histories

Charles A. Goodrich, *History of the United States* (Boston, 1834), said in the Preface that in the little more than ten years since its publication, the book had passed through " forty-four editions comprising more than one hundred and fifty thousand copies." See also Tyler Kepner, " The Influence of Textbooks Upon Method," *5th Yearbook of the National Council for the Social Studies* (Philadelphia, 1935), pp. 159-63. Kepner says 500,000 copies of C. A. Goodrich's *History* were reported sold before 1870. He also found that Frost's *History* was still being published in 1890. As measured in editions, the works chosen for the present study were the most popular of the period. See Roorbach, *Development of the Social Studies*, pp. 246-60.

[10] *22nd Yearbook of the National Society for the Study of Education* (1920), p. 320. Table XII was prepared by Dr. Earl U. Rugg. It shows the proportion of political, military, and social history in eight leading textbooks of the pre-Civil War era. The two Goodriches, Olney, Mrs. Willard and Willson are among the eight. An analysis by the present writer confirms Dr. Rugg's figures and finds them to be true in the cases of Frost and Hale also.

[11] An examination revealed the following percentages: Mrs. Willard (1831)—30%; Frost (1837)—30%; C. A. Goodrich (1834)—23%; Willson (1846)—23%; Olney (1836)—23%; S. G. Goodrich (1859)—23%; Hale (1827)—24%.

[12] For example, Olney (1836) devotes 12% to the War of 1812; Frost (1837)—13%; S. G. Goodrich (1859)—12%; Mrs. Willard (1831)—19%.

[13] Earl Rugg, *22nd Yearbook,* p. 320. A check by the present writer confirms the accuracy of Dr. Rugg's figure.

in this group give at least sixty per cent of their space
to the Colonial and Revolutionary periods.[14] The treatment of Massachusetts is invariably extended; all of the
writers in this group were New Englanders.[15]

Similarities in the texts are not surprising, for the
authors borrowed readily from one another. Marcius
Willson, when accused of plagiarism by Emma Willard,
showed that both of them had used common sources—
among them the textbooks writers Frost, Hale, Charles
A. Goodrich, and William Grimshaw.[16] Charles A. Goodrich and John Frost also borrowed from other textbook
historians.[17] A rôle more important for our present interest was played by Bancroft's *History of the United
States.* This early period of history textbooks was also
an era of more critical historical scholarship in the United
States, when the plagiarized histories of Ramsay, Gordon
and Marshall gave way to the original histories of Bancroft, Sparks and Hildreth.[18] The value of Bancroft's

[14] The percentages arrived at by the present writer are as follows:
Olney (1836)—63%; C. A. Goodrich (1834)—64%; Frost (1837)—
77%; S. G. Goodrich (1859)—63%; Mrs. Willard (1831)—69%;
Hale (1827)—72%; Willson (1846)—85%.

[15] For example, S. G. Goodrich (1859) devotes 55% of the Colonial
Period to Massachusetts; Frost (1837)—34%; C. A. Goodrich (1834)—
55%.

[16] Marcius Willson, *A Reply to Mrs. Willard's Appeal* (New York,
1847), pp. 18-21.

[17] Compare Emma Willard, *History of the United States* (1831), p.
315 with C. A. Goodrich, *History of the United States* (1834), pp. 274-
75. John Frost, *History of the United States* (Philadelphia, 1837). See
the bibliography. Another textbook writer of the period, Noah Webster,
complained that his competitors were lifting passages from his historical
publications. See Harry R. Warfel, *Noah Webster Schoolmaster to
America* (New York, 1936), p. 398.

[18] Orin Grant Libby, "Ramsay As a Plagiarist," *American Historical
Review* (1902), VII, 692-703. Also Libby, "A Critical Evaluation of
William Gordon's History of the American Revolution," *Annual Report
of the American Historical Association for 1899,* pp. 367 ff. On Marshall,
see William A. Foran, "John Marshall as a Historian," *American Historical Review* (1937), XLIII, 51-64.

History as a source for the textbook writers lay in its uniqueness; it was incomparably the best of the few general American histories available. In its synthesis of colonial history it represented the accumulated knowledge of hundreds of works. The books of its chief rivals, Abiel Holmes,[19] George Chalmers,[20] and James Grahame,[21] offered none of its advantages. Holmes' and Chalmers' *Annals*, chiefly collections of facts, could not rival Bancroft's integrated narrative. Grahame's *History*, written by an Englishman and never popular in the United States, lacked the glow of Bancroft's romantic nationalism. Bancroft's first three volumes appeared from 1834 to 1840, and by the late 1840's Bancroft had come to be followed by the textbook historians as *the* authority in American history.

Some of the textbook writers paid explicit tribute to Bancroft as their guiding star. Marcius Willson wrote of the *History*, " We regard it as the best for its purposes that has yet been written." [22] Emma Willard acknowledged that she revised her *History* in 1840 largely according to Bancroft's. " The earlier part [of the history] was reexamined by several new lights which had appeared, chiefly Mr. Bancroft's extended history of colonial America, and much of this portion was rewritten." [23] " In the present work," explained Samuel G. Goodrich in the 1859 edition of his manual, " the author has adopted

[19] *The Annals of America* (2 vols., Cambridge, 1829). The original edition appeared in 1805 under a slightly different title.

[20] *Political Annals of the Present United Colonies from Their Settlement to the Peace of 1763* (London, 1780).

[21] *The History of the United States of North America from the Plantation of the British Colonies till their Revolt and Declaration of Independence* (4 vols., London, 1836). The first two volumes were originally published in 1827.

[22] Marcius Willson, *Report on American Histories* (New York, 1847), p. 2.

[23] Emma Willard, *Answer to Marcius Willson's Reply* (New York, 1847), pp. 3-4.

the plan [of organization] followed by Bancroft and other leading writers upon our national history." [24]   These writers had the grace to acknowledge their debt to Bancroft either in their histories or elsewhere. Others, not out of keeping with the habit of the time, did not trouble themselves with this detail.

Whether the writers hailed Bancroft or not, they industriously worked his volumes. Mrs. Willard's *History*, in the editions after 1840, probably owed more to Bancroft than to any other historian. She revised her textbook with the aid of many unquoted phrases and sentences from Bancroft; numerous other passages were paraphrased. Pages 41-46 in Mrs. Willard's *History* (1844) are almost an abridgement of pages 130-146 in Bancroft's Volume I (1843).[25]   One of the few authorities C. A. Goodrich referred to in his footnotes was Bancroft.[26] Hale inserted new materials from Bancroft into his narrative, including a detailed account of the settlement of Delaware by the Swedes, an account of Bacon's rebellion, and a description of the condition of Virginia in the last quarter of the seventeenth century.[27]

Of the writers who published after 1834, John Frost, Samuel G. Goodrich, and Marcius Willson, made extensive use of information from Bancroft. Frost virtually abridged Bancroft's first volume into sixty-eight pages, though he mentioned his source only three times in connection with quotations.[28]   Samuel G. Goodrich likewise

[24] *Pictorial History of the United States*, p. iv.

[25] For specific examples compare Willard (1844), p. 37 with Bancroft (1843), I, 130; Willard, p. 42 with Bancroft, I, 136.

[26] *History of the United States* (1859), pp. 47, 81.

[27] Salma Hale, *History of the United States* (Aberdeen, Scotland, 1848). Compare this with the 1827 edition published in New York. For borrowing from Bancroft, compare Hale (1848), p. 37 with Bancroft (1843), II, 211-13; Hale, pp. 88-89 with Bancroft, II, 288-93; Hale, pp. 30-31 with Bancroft, II, 217-33.

[28] John Frost, *History of the United States* (Philadelphia, 1837).

drew heavily on this new mine of information for his narrative of seventeenth-century colonial America. Most of his account of King Philip's War, and of the landing of the Pilgrims, for instance, is taken from Bancroft, long passages often being quoted.[29] These quoted passages are usually attributed to Bancroft or to " the historian," always Bancroft.[30] The text of Marcius Willson reflected to a marked degree the influence which Bancroft's *History* exercised upon the textbook writers.[31]

These writers not only went to Bancroft for information. Mrs. Willard, Samuel G. Goodrich, and John Frost owed something to him for the organization of their books. Mrs. Willard and Goodrich acknowledged this debt either in their books or elsewhere.[32] Frost, though he did not admit his indebtedness, adopted *in toto* the scheme of Bancroft's first volume. Even some of the chapter headings in Frost are slight modifications of Bancroft's.[33] The single exception in this group of writers was Jesse Olney. An examination of his *History* reveals no dependence on Bancroft for organization or facts.

In 1847, Marcius Willson published his *Report on American Histories,* a critical survey of textbooks in

Frost's first twelve chapters, through p. 68, follow Bancroft's organization in Vol. I. The materials within the chapters are a condensation of Bancroft's chapters.

[29] Compare S. G. Goodrich (1859), pp. 85-88 with Bancroft (1843), II, 102-09; Goodrich, pp. 48-49 with Bancroft, I, 312.

[30] See for instance pp. 47, 81, 85, 105.

[31] Marcius Willson, *History of the United States* (New York, 1846). Willson, for instance, takes his accounts of the settling of Delaware, of the Dutch-Indian War of 1637, and of the Pequod War of 1637, from Bancroft. Compare Willson, p. 121 with Bancroft (1837), II, 284-86; Willson, pp. 122-23 with Bancroft, II, 288-93; Willson, p. 106 with Bancroft (1834), I, 432--33.

[32] Emma Willard, *Answer to Marcius Willson's Reply,* pp. 3-4. S. G. Goodrich, *Pictorial History,* p. iv.

[33] Compare the titles of Frost's first twelve chapters with those in Bancroft's first volume.

American history.[34]   In his criticisms and corrections of
these histories, Willson appealed constantly to Bancroft's
authority.   Willson published a long list of errors he had
found in such textbooks as those of the Goodriches, Salma
Hale, Emma Willard, Jesse Olney, and John Frost.   Of
the thirty-five corrections for which Willson gives authority, Bancroft appeared in seventeen—far oftener than
any other historian.   Abiel Holmes, Bancroft's only real
rival, was cited but eight times.[35]   This gives a kind of
statistical measure of Willson's evaluation of Bancroft in
comparison with other authorities in American colonial
history.   It is likely, furthermore, that Bancroft was the
chief source for many of the corrections Charles A Goodrich and Emma Willard made in their later editions as a
result of Willson's criticisms.[36]   To the extent that textbooks made intelligent use of scholarly history, especially
that of Bancroft, they brought closer to the American
people the best critical history of the period.

But it was not only facts and organizational suggestions
that the textbook writers took from Bancroft.   Some were
sufficiently alert and respectful of his scholarship to adopt
his view of events in American history.   A striking example of this is the treatment of Bacon's Rebellion.   Prior
to Bancroft, American historiography had rendered an
unfavorable verdict on the movement.   Abiel Holmes,
George Chalmers, and James Grahame considered Bacon
a rebel against legally constituted authority, and therefore
a seditious and evil influence.[37]   The earlier textbook

[34] Part of this Report was first published in the *Biblical Repository,*
July, 1845, under the title, "A Critical Review of American Common
School Histories."
    [35] *Report,* pp. 24-32.
    [36] C. A. Goodrich and Mrs. Willard corrected some of the errors
pointed out by Willson, for which Bancroft was given as authority.
    [37] Holmes, *Annals of America,* I, 385-86.   Chalmers, *Political Annals,*
pp. 332-36.   Grahame, *History of the United States* (1836), I, 118-26.
The terms used by the textbook writers in describing Bacon and his
movement may be found in these books.

writers, Charles A. Goodrich, Emma Willard, and Salma Hale described Bacon's movement in the same terms.[38] " It pleased the Supreme Ruler," Goodrich wrote typically, " to withdraw Bacon by a natural death. The malcontents, thus left to recover their reason, now began to disperse." [39] Bancroft's second volume, published in 1837, contained a new and favorable interpretation of Bacon's Rebellion.[40] To this Romantic nationalist, Bacon was a pioneer of freedom and liberty against tyranny and, as such, his revolt foreshadowed the approved events of a century later.

Charles A. Goodrich, while cognizant of Bancroft's new approach to Bacon, refused to change his verdict on the rebellion, maintaining that Bacon was a " rebel," and hence, by inference, an evil influence in society.[41] Samuel G. Goodrich, like his brother, did not change his original unfavorable view of Bacon.[42] But Bancroft's interpretation was accepted by others of the textbook group, Salma Hale and Emma Willard revising their accounts to accord with it.[43] Among those who began publishing after Bancroft, Marcius Willson, adopted Bancroft's view of the rebellion *in toto*, even using Bancroft's words.[44]

The object of writing these history manuals was " to cultivate the memory, the intellect, and the taste," according to Mrs. Willard:

[38] C. A. Goodrich (1834), pp. 71-72; Emma Willard (1831), pp. 71-72; Salma Hale (1827), pp. 28-30, and (1843), pp. 24-25.

[39] C. A. Goodrich (1834), p. 72.

[40] Bancroft (1843), II, 217-34.

[41] C. A. Goodrich (1859), p. 34.

[42] S. G. Goodrich (1859), pp. 88-89. Goodrich's acquaintance with Bancroft must have included knowledge of Bancroft's new interpretation of Bacon's rebellion. It could not have been ignorance of Bancroft's work which caused Goodrich to retain his unfavorable view of Bacon.

[43] Hale (1848), pp. 30-31; Willard (1844), pp. 90-91.

[44] Willson (1846), pp. 64-66. Jesse Olney was also unfavorable to Bacon. See his *History* (1836), pp. 33-34.

But much more anxious have we been to sow the seeds of virtue, by showing the good in such amiable lights, that the youthful heart shall kindle into desires of imitation. And we have been careful to give clear conceptions of those deeds, which are proper to imitate; while, with regard to bad actions, we have, as far as possible, given the result, rather than the detail.[45]

In choosing between "deeds, which are proper to imitate" and "bad actions," the textbook writers showed no wide departure from the dominant ideas of their fellow New Englanders of the Middle Period.

This becomes clear in their conception of change, an idea fundamental in the construction of any history. Where these textbook writers expressed opinions or where their attitudes can be discerned, they are agreed upon the revolutions of 1688 and 1776 as good revolutions.

The British nation [wrote Emma Willard] putting aside the fiction of the divine right of legitimate sovereigns, asserted that of human nature, by declaring that an oppressed people may change their rulers. They forced the king to abdicate and completed what is called the English "Revolution," by placing William and Mary on the throne.[46]

Marcius Willson believed that "the revolution in England restored the liberties of the people."[47]   John Frost wrote, "The political freedom, which the revolution confirmed and established in England, extended many of its blessings to Virginia. . . . "[48]   The echo of these opinions by the other textbook writers leaves no doubt of their enthusiasm for the "Glorious Revolution."[49]   Of course,

[45] Willard (1844), pp. v-vi.
[46] Willard (1860), p. 111.
[47] Willson (1846), p. 110.
[48] Frost (1847), p. 44. "The Revolution of the British government which took place in 1688, was highly beneficial to Virginia, in common with the other American colonies."
[49] See Olney (1836), p. 44; C. A. Goodrich (1859), pp. 79, 90; S. G. Goodrich (1859), p. 97.

The American Revolution was ecstatically praised. It " is doubtless the most interesting event in the pages of modern history," Charles A. Goodrich typically wrote. " Our independence was *won by the people* who fought for the natural rights of man." [50]

But other revolts in American history received different treatment. Participants in Shays' Rebellion in 1786 were described variously as " insurgents," " rebels," " malcontents," and " rioters." [51] " In some parts of the State, the people, convened in tumultous assemblies, obstructed the sitting of courts, and, finally, took Arms in opposition to the laws of the state. . . ." [52] The " insurgents " performed " outrages " which made it necessary to call out troops to " suppress the insurrection." [53] Finally, the rebels, after " abandoning their seditious purposes, accepted the proferred indemnity of the government." [54] The story of the Whiskey Rebellion was told in similar terms. Not only were the Pennsylvania farmers " rebels," " insurgents," and " malcontents." [55] Charles A. Goodrich was certain that they were " chiefly foreigners, and consequently less disposed to submit to the taxation necessary to the support of government." [56] The " open defiance of the laws " [57] was overcome by the militia [who] instituted salutary terror." [58] " The government acquired the respect of the people by this exer-

---

[50] C. A. Goodrich (1834), pp. 226-27. See also Olney (1836), p. 123; Hale (1827), p. 265; Willard (1831), pp. 141-42; Willson (1846), pp. 194 ff.; Frost (1837), pp. 127 ff.; S. G. Goodrich (1859), pp. 132 ff.

[51] See Frost (1837), p. 233; Willard (1860), pp. 251-52; Hale (1843), p. 219; C. A. Goodrich (1834), p. 230.

[52] C. A. Goodrich (1859), p. 230.

[53] *Ibid.*

[54] Hale (1843), p. 219.

[55] Olney (1836), pp. 189-90; Hale (1843), pp. 230-31.

[56] C. A. Goodrich (1859), p. 256.

[57] Willson (1846), p. 290.

[58] Willard (1860), p. 264.

tion of its force, and their affection, by . . . display of its lenity." [59]

Professor Merle Curti has pointed out that conservative thought in the Middle Period disliked changes that contained threats to the economic status quo, whether they were in the past or the present.[60]   1688 and 1776 were such movements in fact but not in tradition.   1688 had become the " Glorious Revolution " of purely political significance and 1776, looked at exclusively as the founding of the American nation, could hardly be disapproved by its patriotic heirs. Shays' Rebellion and the Whiskey Rebellion, in the text books as in the general conservative thought of the day, enjoyed no such immunity from social implications, and Bacon was glorified only after Bancroft had started the tradition of making the Virginian the " Torchbearer of the American Revolution."

Slavery, too, was an issue fraught with peril for people who disliked violent shifts in property. Four of the seven textbook writers under discussion—Emma Willard, John Frost, Jesse Olney, and Marcius Willson—expressed no positive attitude toward slavery. Indeed, they mentioned slavery only three or four times. Typical of their neutrality is Marcius Willson's statement that " In the month of August, 1620, a Dutch man-of-war entered the James river, and landed twenty negroes for sale. This was the commencement of negro slavery in the English colonies." [61]   John Frost recognized that negro slavery had been one of " those prolific sources of disquiet in all periods of our history," [62] but beyond that expressed no

[59] Hale (1843), p. 231.
[60] Curti, " The Great Mr. Locke: America's Philosopher, 1783-1861," *Huntington Library Bulletin* (No. 11, 1937), pp. 143-46.   Professor Curti refers specifically to the American Revolution, Shays' Rebellion, and the Whiskey Rebellion.
[61] Willson (1846), p. 57.
[62] Frost (1837), pp. 100-01.

opinion on the subject. Only in the 1860 edition of Mrs. Willard's history did she take cognizance of the crucial nature of the slavery question; then she begged for moderation in the interest of preserving the union.[63] Frost, Olney and Willson, not carrying their histories as far in time as did Mrs. Willard, escaped the necessity of treating the slavery question at length.

The other three writers under examination were forthright in their opposition to slavery. In Hale's book it was denounced as "abhorrent to humanity, disgraceful to civilization, and . . . the foulest stain upon the character of the age and the people." [64] Samuel G. Goodrich regarded the introduction of slavery into America a " serious mistake," and lauded the abolition of slavery in Pennsylvania during the Revolution as another victory for liberty.[65]

> Since the beginning of the present [nineteenth] century [wrote Goodrich], attempts have been made, both by legislation and benevolent effort, to open a door to the general manumission of slaves in the United States, by establishing colonies in distant parts, especially on the western shore of Africa. Others, however, have opposed such efforts and labored with much zeal in behalf of immediate and universal emancipation.[66]

Of the seven textbooks, then, four stood for the great compromise on slavery which was broken only by the election of 1860. Three violated it, with a denunciation of slavery. None of the three lent any countenance to the abolitionist point of view, to violent social change.

To these textbook writers the most desirable form of change was material progress. For Olney, " science and the mechanic arts " symbolized a more perfect future for America:

[63] Willard (1860), p. 456.   [65] S. G. Goodrich (1859), p. 220.
[64] Hale (1827), p. 24.   [66] *Ibid.*, p. 221.

13

Our manufactures already rival those of Europe in variety and importance; and have even, in some cases, superseded those of the Mother country in her own home markets. Our commerce, speeded by the magic power of steam, furrows every sea and port with its restless keels. Magnificent palaces glide over our great rivers and lakes. Our fiery coursers unite the wildest valleys of the interior with the rich and busy ports that line our coasts. Broad and deep chasms are spanned by bridges of fairy lightness, but wonderful strength. Impatient thought, already dissatisfied with the swiftness of steam . . . sends messages over *electric* highways with a speed rivaled only by light.[67]

The Goodrich brothers and Marcius Willson also revelled in the material progress of the United States.

We have seen [marvelled Samuel G. Goodrich] our country advancing with unparalled rapidity in the march of civilization. We have seen the arts spring up. . . . We have seen innumerable inventions, ingenious and useful, brought to light. We have seen manufactures of vast extent and wonderful ingenuity, spread over our land.[68]

Charles A. Goodrich was certain that no country

ever possessed, in a higher degree, the means of national prosperity. . . . Thus circumstanced, what should prevent our country from advancing to that eminence of national happiness beyond which national happiness cannot extend—" Manufactures may here rise—busy commerce, inland and foreign, distribute our surplus produce, augment our capital, give energy to industry, improvements to roads, patronage to arts and sciences, vigor to schools, and universality to the institution of religion; reconciling civil liberty with efficient government; extended population with concentrated action; and unparalleled wealth with sobriety and morality." [69]

[67] Olney (1836), p. vii.
[68] S. G. Goodrich (1859), p. 240.
[69] C. A. Goodrich (1834), pp. 351-52. See also Willson (1846), " Concluding Remarks."

This was progress, this was change which the textbook writers considered desirable.

" Unparalleled wealth "—but it was not only America's wealth which made her seem uniquely good to these writers.

The citizens of this republic [admonished Salma Hale] should never forget the awful responsibilities resting upon them. They constitute the oldest nation on this western hemisphere, the first on the list of existing republics. They stand forward the object of hatred to some, of admiration to many, of wonder to all; and an impressive example to the people of every country.[70]

Marcius Willson was equally certain that

For all these blessings we are bound to acknowledge and adore the invisible hand of Almighty power that has directed and sustained us; for every step in our progress has been distinguished by manifest tokens of providential agency.

Let our prayer then be that the same God who brought our fathers out of bondage, into a strange land to found an empire in the wilderness may continue his protection to their children.[71]

Important crises in American history were decided by Divine Providence, so that the failure of the people to fall into anarchy during the period 1783-89 may be ascribed to that deity who continued to watch over them.[72]

A God-inspired, ingenious, and energetic people was, of course, superior to other nations. John Frost was of the opinion that " As a nation we hold the highest rank in the world, so far as intelligence, energy, and civil freedom are concerned. It should, therefore, be the earnest endeavor of every citizen to maintain a position so exalted." [73] Jesse Olney made it clear that " The people at large are proud of the government, because it is a

---

[70] Hale (1827), pp. 466-67.
[71] Willson (1846), " Concluding Remarks."
[72] C. A. Goodrich (1834), pp. 87, 239. S. G. Goodrich (1859), p. 340.
[73] Frost (1859), p. 358.

monument of their superiority to other nations." [74]   But
more than this, America gave to its people a greater share
of material benefits than did any other nation.   " The
population of no country in the world ever enjoyed the
necessaries and comforts of life in such abundance as that
of the United States." [75]   " The people of no country on
the globe," boasted Charles A. Goodrich, " are better, or
so well fed as the Americans.   It is emphatically a land
of plenty. . . .   In general, the people of the United
States are better clothed than the people of any other
country." [76]

The logical extension of the feeling of uniqueness and
superiority was the doctrine of the mission of America.
Salma Hale felt that to the citizens of the United States
was " committed an experiment, successful hitherto, the
final result of which must have a powerful influence upon
the destiny of mankind; if favourable and happy, the
whole civilized world will be free; if adverse, despotism
and darkness will again overshadow it." [77]   Jesse Olney
stated the doctrine of mission in its most positive terms.

Here, for the first time in human history, man will be *truly*
man, protected and honored as man, developed in all his powers,
and enabled to realize the prophetic dreams of his infancy, and the
growing hopes of his youth.   Here shall be realized the long-
prophesied, long-expected *Golden Age,* which shall perfectly
reconcile Order with Liberty, Individual Interests with the
General Good, and make Justice and Fraternity the supreme
principles in the intercourse, as well of nations, as of men.   From
this Free and Happy Land shall go forth the power to perfect the
Civilization of the World. . . .   The inferior races shall be
educated by this friendly intercourse, and made fellow-laborers
in the great work of human progress.   To the portal of this

[74] Olney (1836), p. 256.
[75] *Ibid.* p. 257.
[76] C. A. Goodrich (1859), pp. 320, 322.
[77] Hale (1827), pp. 466-67.

Golden Future, the consummation of man's earthly destiny, America holds the key. *She* only can accomplish the work to which she is pledged, and thus make the sublimest prophecies and aspirations of the Past the brightest *realities* of the Present, and the foundation for a yet nobler Future.[78]

The textbook writers recognized that certain forces in American life could be utilized in accelerating and safeguarding the march of progress. In particular, they recognized that universal public education would help to ensure steady and peaceful progress. In the words of Marcius Willson, " The education of youth, upon which the well-being of society and the perpetuity of our republican institutions so greatly depend, is receiving that share of attention which its importance demands." [79] The need of universal free education for this purpose was clear to Jesse Olney, writing in 1836.

Another great advantage [of public schools] is, that the schools are supported by a tax upon property, which is the case in all those states which have not a permanent school-fund. The arrangement is eminently beneficial to the poorer classes of the community. In most towns, one-fifth of the inhabitants pay at least one-half of the tax, while they do not send one-sixth of the scholars. Of course, the school tax is substantially a tax on the rich to educate the children of the poor, and it is thus equally beneficial in its operation, to both parties. The poor have the promise of the law and the constitution that their children shall be educated, and thus preserved from the greatest temptation to crime,—the rich are assured that they shall live in a community,

---

[78] Olney (1851), p. vii. For a discussion of the idea of the mission of America, see Ralph H. Gabriel, *The Course of American Democratic Thought* (New York, 1940), pp. 22-25. Professor Gabriel couches his discussion almost exclusively in terms of the moral and political aspects of the idea, neglecting the important economic facet. Frederick J. Turner, *The United States 1830-1850* (New York, 1935), pp. 334-35, discusses a modification of the idea of the mission of America in the West during the Middle Period.

[79] Willson (1846), " Concluding Remarks."

where universal education shall keep the foundation of society safe, and afford them a greater personal security than the law can afford.

In this way the system of free schools, as practically carried into operation in some parts of this country, is to be regarded as a great moral police, to preserve a decent, orderly, and respectable population; to teach men from their earliest childhood, their duties and their rights; and, by giving the whole mass of the community a sense of character and a general intelligence, make them understand the value of justice, order, and moral worth, and more anxious to maintain them, than the law itself can be.[80]

The other textbook writers, whether or not because of their personal interest in a universal school system, concurred in the Willson and Olney statements.[81]

Many advocates of the universal public school movement pointed out that such a system would bulwark the premises upon which American society was founded. They believed that the framework of American society was entirely satisfactory—it was only necessary to make the great masses of the people aware of the fact in order to obtain a powerful insurance of the perpetuation of that society. The extension of public education they believed necessary in order to prevent violent change in the structure of society.[82] With this school of thought the articulate textbook writers found themselves in agreement. The principles which they hoped the free schools would instill in society, they themselves offered in their textbooks—" justice, order, and moral worth."

[80] Olney (1836), p. 259.
[81] See for instance S. G. Goodrich (1859), p. 340; C. A. Goodrich (1834), p. 122.
[82] Merle Curti, *Social Ideas of American Educators* (New York, 1935), pp. 55-61.

EDWARD EGGLESTON: PIONEER IN
SOCIAL HISTORY

BY

CHARLES HIRSCHFELD

Toward the end of 1879, Edward Eggleston closed another chapter of his varied career. He resigned from the pastorate of the Church of Christian Endeavor in Brooklyn. For nearly five years he had led the members of what was once the Lee Street Presbyterian Church in the uncharted paths of a Christianity which he was trying to fit to the social problems of his day. But the steady progression of Eggleston's own unbelief balked at the very wisp of the supernatural, and the pulpit of even this undenominational church was bounded by heaven and hell. No longer, even by taking thought, could he preach an acceptable minimum Christianity. So in deference to his conscience, he bade farewell to his parishioners.[1]

The old impulsions were gone. " I find myself in middle life with my ambition in a state of relaxation," he wrote to his daughter. " I've rather lost interest in this thing we call life." [2] His health had broken down once more. The

---

[1] For the facts of Eggleston's life, the reader is referred to George Cary Eggleston, *The First of the Hoosiers: Reminiscences of Edward Eggleston* (Philadelphia, 1903); the article on Eggleston by Prof. Ralph L. Rusk in the *Dictionary of American Biography*; Washington Gladden, " Edward Eggleston," *Scribner's Monthly* (1873), VI, 561-64; Meredith Nicholson, " Edward Eggleston," *Atlantic Monthly* (1902), XC, 804-09; Edward Eggleston, " Books That Have Helped Me," *Forum* (1887), III, 578-86; Edward Eggleston, " Formative Influences," *Forum* (1890), X, 279-90. A scholarly, full-length biography is in preparation by Mr. William Peirce Randel of the University of Minnesota.

[2] Eggleston to his daughter, Mrs. Elizabeth Eggleston Seelye, July 5,

old ailment, consumption, that in youth had sent him to Minnesota, had festered again under the strain of his characteristic methods of work. He needed a rest, a change, if only to preserve the physique that was the delight of his friends and admirers, that supported his large expenditures of nervous energy.

He decided to take a trip to Europe. Shortly before he sailed, Roswell Smith, publisher of *Scribner's,* offered him an unlimited subsidy to continue his literary work. Eggleston pleaded that he did not wish to go on writing novels. Smith then suggested that he " connect [his] name with a great historical work." The suggestion made no great impression on Eggleston at the time.[3]

In Europe, Eggleston was concerned chiefly with recovering his health. In the calm of French village life, in restful sojourn on a history-cushioned continent, he found again both health and peace. But health and peace were not all he found. From abroad, at the beginning of 1880, he revealed to his brother his decision to write a " History of Life in the United States." He added solemnly that it " will require a great deal of research, but I stand ready to give ten years of my life to the task, if necessary." [4]

To his daughter, not long after, he wrote in a similar vein, " My project of a ' History of Life in the United States ' interests me much and amuses me. . . . But it is a life work almost. . . . I am ripe for it. Everything in my life seems to have prepared me for it." [5] Smith's sugges-

1880, Eggleston MS. The author wishes to thank Mr. E. E. Seelye for permission to use the Edward Eggleston manuscript collection at the old Eggleston family home at Joshua's Rock, Lake George, N. Y. He also gratefully acknowledges the coöperation of Mr. William Peirce Randel, of the University of Minnesota, who graciously permitted the use of his notes as a guide to the voluminous Eggleston correspondence. All letters cited hereafter are from the collection at Lake George.

[3] " Edward Eggleston: An Interview," *Outlook* (1897), LV, 433.

[4] George C. Eggleston, *The First of the Hoosiers,* p. 363.

[5] Eggleston to Mrs. Seelye, June 14, 1880.

tion, it seems, had germinated and flowered into a grand conception, to the realization of which Eggleston devoted the remaining years of his life. His health restored, his vision cleared, he found once more a directive.

The task to which Eggleston dedicated himself was not to be an easy one. For years he assiduously collected his materials in the British Museum, in the Public Record Office, the Bibliothèque Nationale, the public libraries of New York and Boston, and the historical societies of Massachusetts, New York, Pennsylvania, Maryland, and Virginia.[6] He soon discovered that " New England history and all colonial history is a horrible labyrinth," and wryly contemplated reaching " the settlement of Boston in the course of ten or fifteen years of work." [7] Through sixteen years, he persevered in the face of discouragement and delay. There were financial demands that sent him barnstorming around the country in fatiguing but remunerative lectures, that sidetracked him into writing serial novels for the *Century Magazine* and improvising textbooks and revised editions of textbooks. There were sieges of ill-health, with nervous attacks and sleepless nights which made sustained scholarly efforts a torture. There were domestic afflictions, the death of his wife, and the jealousies attendant on his second marriage. Above all, there was advancing age with its encroaching pall of disillusion.[8]

But Eggleston was kept to his task by a hard bright flame of ambition. Through all distractions he continued to work on his history, which was to contain the best that was in him. In 1894, sighing " Poor history! no one man's life is long enough for it, certainly not the life of a sick-

[6] Edward Eggleston, *The Beginners of a Nation* (New York, 1896), pp. ix-x.

[7] Eggleston to Mrs. Seelye, February 3, 1881.

[8] The details of Eggleston's life in this period can only be found in his manuscript correspondence.

ish man like myself with a dozen other irons and no wealth to come and go on," [9] he set to work on the final stages of his book. Two years later, the first volume of *A History of Life in the United States* appeared, *The Beginners of a Nation: A History of the Source and Rise of the Earliest English Settlements in America with Special Reference to the Life and Character of the People.*

The volume, long-awaited, was well received. Its publication was celebrated by a reception at the Authors Club of New York at which John Bach McMaster and Henry Van Dyke spoke. Eggleston's friends, Moses Coit Tyler and Justin Winsor, sent messages of congratulation. The history department of the Johns Hopkins University, the Bethlehem of "scientific history" in the United States, sent word to the effect that it had recommended the work for adoption in its courses.[10] Herbert L. Osgood, while denying that the work contained many new facts or positive additions to historical knowledge or even a new point of view, characterized it as "an able discussion in outline of the political and social history of the earliest Anglo-American achievements in colonization . . . presented to the reader in a style of such beauty and force as to make [it] at once a history and a contribution to literature." [11] The more popular reviews were highly favorable.[12] The sales were not mean, totaling close to 10,000 between 1898 and 1902.[13] The capstone of recognition was Eggles-

[9] Eggleston to Mrs. Seelye, March 20, 1894.

[10] *The Critic* (1896), XXVI, 389.

[11] *The American Historical Review* (1897), II, 528-30.

[12] W. P. Trent, "Dr. Eggleston on American Origins," *Forum* (1897), XXII, 590-99; *Independent* (1897), XLIX, 89; *Outlook* (1897), LV, 462-63; *Chicago Tribune,* December 26, 1897; *Rochester Post Express,* January 2, 1897; *Boston Herald,* February 27, 1897; *Baltimore News,* January 30, 1897; *Brooklyn Eagle,* January 10, 1897. The newspaper reviews are selected from hundreds which were originally collected by a clipping bureau and are to be found among the Eggleston papers.

[13] These figures are taken from the royalty accounts with D. Appleton and Co. found in the Eggleston correspondence.

ton's election in 1898 to a vice-presidency of the American Historical Association and his automatic promotion to the presidency two years later.

Eggleston would not, however, rest on his honors. Moved by the fear that " the darkness of age and death " would cover his work and himself, he painfully continued his labors, hastily preparing for publication the material he had amassed. The result was presented to the public in 1901 as the second volume of the *History of American Life, The Transit of Civilization from England to America in the Seventeenth Century.* The author himself is reported to have been gravely dissatisfied with his last effort.[14] To a scholar like Charles M. Andrews, the essays that made up the work exhibited a lack of organization, an unscientific approach, and a lamentably outdated scholarship.[15] The work, in fine, despite its appeal to non-scholarly reviewers impressed by the author's fame and lively style, was far below the level of *The Beginners of a Nation.*[16]

These two volumes represent the sum of Eggleston's scholarly labors, which, though still cited by scholars, are a legacy too meagre to give him the reputation of a great historian.[17] It is rather as a pioneer in American historiography that Eggleston must be considered, a specimen whose dissection is uncommonly revealing of the genesis and structure of an important development in the history of American history.

[14] G. C. Eggleston, pp. 368-69.

[15] *Political Science Quarterly* (1902), XVII, 162-66; see also the review by F. H. Hodder in *Dial* (1901), XXXI, 51-52.

[16] *Nation* (1901), LXXII, 221; *Independent* (1900), LII, 3108-09 are examples of popular reviews.

[17] Eggleston's two books are still cited as reference works in Curtis Nettels, *The Roots of American Civilization* (New York, 1938), pp. 161, 191; Carl Becker, *The Beginnings of the American People* (Boston, 1915), p. 124; and Thomas Wertenbaker, *The First Americans* (New York, 1929), p. 331.

The ideal that gave Eggleston strength and direction through the long, distracted years was not simply that of writing history. He wished to write a certain kind of history. " Not a history of the United States, bear in mind," he emphasized to his brother, " but a history of life there, the life of the people, the sources of their ideas and habits, the course of their development from beginnings." [18]

> What chapters, [he exulted as he surveyed the vista opening up before him], what chapters I can write on " Religious Life in New England," " The Great Kentucky Revival," " Flight of Emigrants Across the Mountains," " Indian Wars and Cabin Life in the Interior," " Early Fur Traders," " The Old Gentry in the South," " Social Changes of the Revolution. . . . . " [19]

The subjects that flitted through Eggleston's mind were strikingly and essentially of the stuff known as social history, history overflowing the bounds of politics and diplomacy, the affairs of the state, and merging with the broad stream of the social and economic life of the people. " The domestic and social life of the people, their dress, their food, their modes of thought and feeling, and their ways of making a livelihood " were at the core of his interest. " Of primary importance " to him " in any history written in the modern spirit " was " the story of the progress of civilization, as marked by the introduction of new inventions and by changes in modes of living." [20] By thus bringing " into relief the social, political, intellectual, and religious forces . . .," he also wished to make his histories reflect the character of the age.[21] Whether in the series of twelve popular historical articles entitled

---

[18] G. C. Eggleston, p. 363.

[19] Eggleston to Mrs. Seelye, June 14, 1880.

[20] Edward Eggleston, *A History of the United States and Its People for the Use of Schools* (New York, 1888), p. iv.

[21] Edward Eggleston, *The Beginners of a Nation,* p. vii.

" A History of Life in the Colonies," [22] or in the eight lectures on the " Culture-History of the American People " delivered at Columbia College in 1893,[23] or in his two published historical works, Eggleston's conception of history was broader than that of any American historian of his time except McMaster.

What were the springs of Eggleston's conception of history? What events and ideas of Eggleston's life dissolved with what conditions and impulsions of the America of his day to precipitate social history? The answer is doubly important, for it must throw light not only on the particular phenomenon of Eggleston's enthusiasm, but also on the writing of social history in America. It may suggest some of the factors in the milieu which were conducive to similar work by other American historians.

Eggleston himself believed, at the time he first conceived the idea, that everything in his life had prepared him for the writing of social history.[24] More specifically, in later life, he linked his historical works with his novels, among the earlier realistic fictional studies of the American scene. In 1890, discussing the formative influences of his career, he concluded,

I find this bond between them [my historical studies] and my novels—that in history, as in fiction, I am mainly interested in the evolution of society; that in either sort of writing this interest in the history of life, this tendency to what the Germans call "culture-history," is the one distinguishing trait of almost all that I have attempted.[25]

[22] These articles appeared in *Century Magazine,* XXV, XXVI, XXVII, XXVIII, XXIX, XXX, XXXIII, and XXXVI (1882-1888). Some of the titles are: " Indian War in the Colonies," " Husbandry in Colony Times," " Commerce in the Colonies," " Social Conditions in the Colonies," " Church and Meeting House Before the Revolution."

[23] Columbia College, *Fourth Annual Report of President Low to the Trustees, October 2, 1893* (New York, 1893), p. 42.

[24] Eggleston to Mrs. Seelye, June 14, 1880.

[25] E. Eggleston, " Formative Influences," *Forum* (1890), X, 287.

He was convinced, moreover, that whatever aesthetic value might be ascribed to his novels, they "would always have a certain value as materials to the student of social history." [26] Some seven years later, after the publication of *The Beginners of A Nation,* he told an interviewer that, judged objectively, "what distinguished them [the novels] specially was that these characters were all treated in their relation to social conditions—something of which I was quite unconscious at the time; they were forerunners of my historic studies. . . ." [27]

Eggleston was not altogether unconscious of the sociological settings of his novels at the time he wrote them nor was the link between his histories and his novels imposed by the logic of hindsight. In the preface to his *Mystery of Metropolisville,* published in 1873, he contended that

> A novel should be the truest of books. It partakes in a certain sense of the nature of both history and art. . . . It needs to be true to human nature in its permanent and essential qualities, and it should truthfully represent some specific and temporary manifestation of human nature; that is, some form of society. . . . I have wished to make my stories of value as a contribution to the history of civilization in America.[28]

This passage clearly postulates the close relation between modern literary realism and social history, as well as Eggleston's recognition of that relation. The realist, in attempting to portray his characters truthfully, to make them correspond to reality as he sees it, must of necessity include the social background in which they exist. That background, documented and transposed to the foreground, becomes social history. And such was, roughly, the course followed by Eggleston.

[26] *Ibid.,* p. 286.
[27] "Edward Eggleston: An Interview," p. 433.
[28] E. Eggleston, *The Mystery of Metropolisville* (New York, 1905), Preface. This was first published in 1873.

That the course was neither unique nor fortuitous is suggested by an episode in the history of French literature. The same course was followed by the Goncourt brothers, the first conscious realists in French literature, who came to their first realistic novel, *Germinie Lacerteux* (1865), through history. They had previously written historical monographs on the social life of eighteenth-century France. The transition from social history to literary realism was for them a natural one, feeling as they did that "L'histoire est un roman qui a été; le roman est de l'histoire qui aurait pu être. . . ." [29]

To relate literary realism and social history does not solve the problem of the genesis of the latter. It merely transposes the question to a more basic level. What were the impulses that led Eggleston to both realism in literature and an expanded view of history?

In the external circumstances of Eggleston's life are to be found some of the elements that formed the matrix of his conception of history.[30] "In my early life," he wrote in 1897, " I rapidly changed from one environment to another. . . . That preparation, quite as much as any natural bent, gave me the tendency to write a history of life." [31] His early youth was spent in a flourishing Ohio River town and in the backwoods of Indiana. A visit to his uncle's plantation in Virginia in the '50's brought him first-hand knowledge of slave economy. Years on the frontier, as a circuit rider in Indiana and as farm-hand, chain-carrier on a surveying gang, and Methodist minister in Minnesota, must have formed a sharp contrast to his life in New York City, as editor and littérateur, in the

---

[29] P. Martino, *Le naturalisme français* (*1870-1895*) (Paris, 1923), p. 18.

[30] Eggleston himself said, "This marked bent [for social history] was no doubt given to my mind by the circumstances of my youth and early manhood. "Formative Influences," p. 287.

[31] "Edward Eggleston: An Interview," p. 433.

last twenty years of the century. And all these environments must have seemed raw when brought up against the ripe civilization of Europe. Passing thus from one society to another, Eggleston saw no dynast carving up history to suit his fancy, but change, broad and immanent, transforming the lives of whole communities. "You are the only man that can write a history of life in the United States," Parkman once told Eggleston, "you are the only man who has seen so many forms of our life." [32]

From the well of his youth and early manhood Eggleston drew also a democratic impulse which moved him to write history in terms of the life of the people. It was this democratic sensibility that made him an abolitionist when he first saw slavery, even in its benevolent form, on his uncle's plantation in Virginia, that sent him from Minnesota to help free Bloody Kansas. It was the middle-western egalitarian that resigned from the editorship of *The Independent* when his opposition to Grant's imperialist designs in San Domingo clashed with the policy of the publishers. [33] It was the agrarian democrat that spoke out determinedly for the popular election of senators in the hope of displacing the "lumber barons" and the "silver kings," [34] who expressed his satisfaction at the Populist victories in 1890. [35]

To the fund of personal experience that led Eggleston to social history were added congeries of ideas which he absorbed from the intellectual atmosphere. Eggleston responded eagerly to the claims of the biological and geological sciences and to the parallel secularization of

[32] *Ibid.,* p. 432.

[33] "Edward Eggleston," *Independent* (1902), LIV, 2206.

[34] E. Eggleston, "A Full Length Portrait of the United States," *Century Magazine* (1889), XXXVII, 791, a review of Bryce's *American Commonwealth*; see also *Critic* (1897), XXVII, 87.

[35] Eggleston to Mrs. Seelye, November 6, 1890.

thought and life. Far back in his youth, coming to the close of his teens, Eggleston and his younger brother, George Cary, would go on little geological expeditions along the rivers near their home in Indiana. They chipped the rocks and studied the formations, comparing what they saw with what they had read in books like *The Testimony of the Rocks* and Chambers' *Vestiges of Creation*.[36] Eggleston's strait and scrupulous fundamentalist Methodism was puzzled and then perturbed at the conclusions that were suggested.[37] When he later remarked to the Presiding Elder that Bishop Ussher's chronology was not perhaps inspired, the old man could only propose " earnest prayer for the salvation of a young soul. . . ."[38] " The long and painful struggle for emancipation from theological dogma," as Eggleston himself later characterized it, started while he was still a minister. He read the works of Dr. Thomas Chalmers and of the broad churchmen and gravitated to an undogmatic interpretation of Christianity.[39] His views almost brought a heresy prosecution on his head while he was preaching in Minnesota.[40] In 1879, his Christianity, compounded of the Sermon on the Mount and boys' club and settlement work, was too thin even for the heterodox Church of Christian Endeavor. By 1880 he had confessedly lost all religion.[41] And his histories subsequently gave voice to his soft disdain for the puerilities of hidebound dogmatism and his admiration for the toler-

---

[36] Professor A. O. Lovejoy considers *The Vestiges of Creation* the most cogent and advanced argument, consonant with the religious thought of the day, for the theory of organic evolution before the publication of *The Origin of Species*. " The Argument for Organic Evolution before *The Origin of Species*," *Popular Science Monthly* (1909), LXXV, 499-514, 537-49.

[37] G. C. Eggleston, p. 232.

[38] *Ibid.*, p. 237.

[39] E. Eggleston, " Books That Have Helped Me," *Forum* (1887), III, 584, 585.

[40] G. C. Eggleston, p. 338.

[41] Eggleston to Mrs. Seelye, July 5, 1880.

ance and Christ-like piety of men like John Robinson and
Roger Williams.[42]

When Eggleston lost religion, he found science. And
science meant Charles Darwin. In 1887 he declared publicly that he no longer found solace and inspiration in
Thomas à Kempis, as was his wont when astride a horse
on the Indiana circuit, but would "rather walk in wide
fields with Charles Darwin."[43] He came to regard Darwin
as "the intellect that has dominated our age, modified
our modes of thinking, and become the main source of
all our metaphysical discomforts."[44] Thus, willingly if
somewhat painfully, Eggleston had accepted the whole
Darwinian theory and its implications.

Inspired by the work of Darwin and under the influence of the ideals of Science, Eggleston was eager to
bring human history within the ordered confines of the
new faith. When he read, in preparation for his history,
John Stuart Mill's dictum that the highest stage of historiography was "not simply to compose histories, but to
construct a science of history," he agreed entirely.[45] He,
too, would make history "a reasonable science."[46] He
was not interested in "a recital of occurrences that [were]
presented like beads unstrung." His *History of Life in
the United States* would "answer the questions 'How?'
and 'Whence?' and 'Why?'"[47] He would, in short,

[42] E. Eggleston, *The Beginners of a Nation,* pp. 108, 156, 245, 277-
78, and Book III, chapter 2; *The Transit of Civilization,* Preface and
p. 164.
[43] E. Eggleston, "Books That Have Helped Me," *Forum* (1887), III,
586.
[44] E. Eggleston, *The Faith Doctor* (London, 1891), p. 16.
[45] "Edward Eggleston: An Interview," p. 434. The essay Eggleston
refers to in this interview is Mill's review of "Michelet's History of
France," in *Dissertations and Discussions; Political, Philosophical, and
Historical* (2 vols., London, 1867), II, 120-80. It first appeared in
The Edinburgh Review, Jan., 1844.
[46] E. Eggleston, *A History of the United States and Its People,* p. iv.
[47] G. C. Eggleston, p. 363.

put human history on the same basis as natural history by giving it form, direction, and perhaps purpose.

The way to make history a science, Mill again suggested, was to conceive it as "a progressive chain of causes and effects." [48] Eggleston, too, declared that only by understanding "the action of cause and effect and the continuity of institutions and usages" could one penetrate "the history that underlies history." [49] And so, in his histories, he strove "to make the causes and effects of public events clear and to trace with simplicity our present institutions from their springs downward." He paid special attention to "those events, great or small, which have exerted an influence on the general current of our history or modified our institutions . . . in order to keep in mind that chain of causes and effects which makes history reasonable and intelligible." [50] Eggleston made the great nineteenth-century assumption that all life could be explained in naturalistic terms as a continuum of observable cause and effect. And he wished to do for American institutions what Darwin had done for biological species, to trace their development from their original simplicity to their present complexity by means of continuous adaptations to successive stimuli.

Thus he declared at the 1890 meeting of the American Historical Association that "American institutions were all historical developments from colonial germs," a revolutionary step in turning American historiography away from Teutonic towards native origins, the direction in which Turner was to point a few years later.[51] His *Beginners of a Nation* did not "pretend to be the usual account of all the events attending early colonization; it

[48] J. S. Mill, *Dissertations and Discussions*, II, 129.

[49] E. Eggleston, "A Full Length Portrait of the United States," *Century Magazine* (1889), XXXVII, 791.

[50] E. Eggleston, *The Household History of the United States*, p. iv.

[51] *Annual Report of the American Historical Association for 1890*, p. 7.

[was] rather a history in which the succession of cause
and effect [was] the main topic—a history of the dynamics
of colony-planting. . . ."[52] "The procession of motives"
of colonization was viewed with a wide-ranging eye: the
commercial, imperial, religious, and visionary aspects were
all noted.[53] Puritanism and dissent, as ideas, were tracked
to their ideological sources in the theological controversies
of central Europe and followed through their development in the shifting kaleidoscope of English political and
social history of the sixteenth and seventeenth centuries.[54]
What Eggleston considered the unlovely asperities of the
New England theocracy he attributed to the opportunities
and exigencies of an unsettled land.[55] Virginian liberty
was traced to the liberalism of Sir Edwin Sandys and the
sufferings at Jamestown.[56]

It is clear that the conception of history as a "continuous, genetic, causal process," based on the theory of
Darwin and the assumptions of biological science, greatly
enlarged the scope of written history. In the first place,
that theory was concerned with the "origin of species"
and not individual creatures; it traced "the descent of
man," not men. Eggleston, too, conceived history in
terms of the evolution of society and the origin of institutions, social groups, customs, and ideas and not in terms
of outstanding individuals. The latter were important
for him only in so far as they modified the general course
of social patterns. In the second place, social structures,
like species, evolved only by responding to stimuli in their
total environment, whether political, social, or economic.
History was thus broadened to include all of man's observable life. The state was removed from the center of

[52] E. Eggleston, *The Beginners of A Nation*, p. vii.
[53] *Ibid.*, Book I, chapter 3.
[54] *Ibid.*, Book II, chapter 1.
[55] *Ibid.*, pp. 178, 212-15, 275-78.
[56] *Ibid.*, Book I, chapter 2.

the historical stage and became but one of the institutions that made up society; politics were but one of the many human activities that affected these institutions. History as science, as biological science, one might say, became a study of the origin and development of human institutions and ideas in the play and interplay of natural, social, and intellectual events.

Eggleston was not content to trace the development of institutions merely in time and space. Like other American social scientists, like Lester Ward and Simon N. Patten, for example, he turned to psychology for the key to the history of society.[57] In his study of colonization, what vitally interested him were the "propulsions" that sent the colonists to the wilderness, the "visions that beckoned them," "the story of their hopes, their experiments and their disappointments."[58] He wished to explain "the complex states of knowing and thinking, of feeling and passion," to understand "the little world as seen by the man of the seventeenth century."[59] Medieval credulity, Puritan intolerance, general religious scrupulosity, the romantic Elizabethan spirit of adventure, are what Eggleston emphasized repeatedly.[60] He used such phrases as "the character of the age," "the time-spirit," in dealing with such characteristics. They explained many matters for him, without, however, assuming the immanent and decisive attributes of Lamprecht's collective *Massengeist*. As one reviewer stated, Eggleston attempted "to put behind the phenomena of early colonial life on this continent, the impulses, convictions, forces, traditions,

[57] H. E. Barnes, *The New History and the Social Studies* (New York, 1905), p. 79; see also E. W. Dow, "Features of the New History: Apropos of Lamprecht's *Deutsche Geschichte*," *American Historical Review* (1898), III, 447. Dow remarks that "it seems pretty well agreed that psychology must be taken as the basis of historical science."

[58] E. Eggleston, *The Beginners of A Nation*, p. vii.

[59] E. Eggleston, *The Transit of Civilization*, p. vii.

[60] E. Eggleston, *The Beginners of A Nation*, pp. 1, 2, 20, 98-103, 298, 342.

and social impulses which gave those phenomena form, order, and significance.[61]   In the vast complex of causes and effects that formed the living stream of history, the emotions of men, their ideas, their patterns of behavior, stood foremost.   They were the essential features in a recreation of the past, the essence of verisimilitude, without which history remained a dry husk.

The resurrection of the psyche of the past, Eggleston believed, was possible only by the exercise of the vision of the poet and the imagination of the man of letters. For him, the construction of the historical narrative was " based on a new perception of the relation and significance of facts."   " It is one thing," he contended, " to unearth new facts . . . it is another to see what the facts collectively amount to, and to mass them so as to carry that impression in its wholeness into the mind of the reader.   This is the function of the man of letters in the domain of history." [62]   As a man of letters, interested in bringing history " into oneness," in writing of the mind and temper of the people " with the vividness of personal experience," he felt it was necessary to saturate himself in the documents and then "transform fact by imagination." [63]   Only by seeing the facts " through the medium of his own thought, experience, and temperament," could the historian achieve an individual, incisive picture of the character of the age.[64]   And that picture could, in turn, be conveyed to the reader only by " ingenious eavesdropping and peeps through keyholes," by the judicious selection of pertinent, varied details from the life of the people.[65]

Eggleston differed sharply from the growing body of academic historians, not only with regard to the content of

---

[61] *The Outlook* (1897), LV, 462.

[62] Eggleston to his wife and daughter, February 14, 1883.

[63] " Edward Eggleston: An Interview," pp. 434, 436.

[64] *Ibid.*, p. 432.

[65] E. Eggleston, *The Beginners of a Nation,* pp. viii-ix.

history, but also in his conception of the methods of writing history. American historians were then under the sway of Ranke and *Geschichtswissenschaft*. Eggleston rejected the example of Ranke and the "scientific" historians. He accepted of course, the "scientific" method of establishing the facts. Beyond that, he agreed rather with Augustin Thierry that

> La recherche et la discussion des faits, sans autre dessein que l'exactitude, n'est qu'une des faces de tout problème historique; ce travail accompli, il s'agit d'interpréter et de peindre, de trouver la loi de succession qui enchaine les faits l'un à l'autre, de donner aux événements leur signification, leur caractère, la vie enfin. . . .[66]

He shared, too, Thierry's acceptance of the claims of art in writing history.[67] He never fully approved "the new school of historians, men of large and accurate scholarship, who are destitute of skill in literary structure, . . . who hold style in contempt . . . [and] dump the crude ore of history into their ponderous sentences." In Thierry's *Le tiers état* and *Récits des temps mérovingiens*, two of the outstanding works of the French romantic, narrative, historical school, he found many suggestions amplifying and bolstering his own ideas of the kind of history he wished to write.[68] In general, Eggleston's interest in the people, his preoccupation with the innermost character of the age, the organismic theory of society implicit in his conception of history as science, and his concern for the literary effects of his historical work, class him as a

[66] Augustin Thierry, *Récits des temps mérovingiens précédés de considérations sur l'histoire de France* (Paris, 1868), p. 132. Eggleston read this work and was greatly impressed by the lengthy introduction from which the passage was quoted. "Edward Eggleston: An Interview," p. 434.

[67] E. Eggleston, *The Beginners of A Nation*, p. ix; E. Eggleston, "Note on the Completion of Mr. Parkman's Work," *Century Magazine* (1892), XLV, 46.

[68] "Edward Eggleston: An Interview," p. 434.

disciple of Thierry and the French romantic narrative historians, Michelet and Barante.[69]

It is not strange that Francis Parkman should have had the enthusiastic approval of Eggleston. Parkman's own distrust of what might be called factual atomism, his concern for the total impression conveyed by a series of individual facts, his insistence on the necessity for the historian of personal identification with the characters and events he was describing, are evidence of his intellectual kinship with Eggleston.[70] The two were, in fact, acquainted with each other and exchanged letters. When Parkman completed his monumental series, Eggleston wrote a short appreciation praising the several works highly.[71] Moreover, Parkman's preference, expressed through his fictional *alter ego*, Vassall Morton, for Thierry's *History of the Norman Conquest*, suggests a common intellectual influence.[72] It suggests, too, that French history and historians, as against German history and historians, have played a more significant rôle in American historiography than they have hitherto been assigned.[73]

As Eggleston approached the end of his life, the weights of the various elements that formed his conception of history shifted. The resultant could still be characterized as social history, but was in inspiration and in

[69] Louis Halphen, *L'histoire en France depuis cent ans* (Paris, 1914), pp. 17, 39, 41, 50, 54, 55, 83; G. Monod, *Les maîtres de l'histoire, Renan, Taine, Michelet* (Paris, 1903), p. ix.

[70] Francis Parkman, *The Pioneers of France in the New World* (Boston, 1871), p. xii.

[71] E. Eggleston, "Note on the Completion of Mr. Parkman's Work," *Century Magazine* (1892), XLV, 46.

[72] Joseph Schafer, "Francis Parkman, 1823-1923," *Mississippi Valley Historical Review* (1924), X, 355.

[73] Doubts on the uniqueness of the influence of German historians on American historiography have been expressed by W. Stull Holt, ed., *Historical Scholarship in the United States, 1876-1901: As Revealed in the Correspondence of Herbert B. Adams* (Baltimore, 1938), p. 11.

essence something quite different from what Eggleston had originally conceived.

In his address as president of the American Historical Association in 1900, Eggleston once more proclaimed his faith in " The New History." [74]   He declared that the time had come to brush aside " the domination of the classic tradition of history," to dispense with the details of political and military campaigns, with " history hung in the air . . . written in the manner of the early eighteenth century."   He looked forward to the day when there would be " gifted writers of the history of the people " and " we shall have the history of culture, the real history of men and women."   The words were the same words, but the meanings were different.   His original fervent ideal had turned into a penchant for " felicitous detail " and " delightful particularity."   Macaulay was now accounted the greatest historian of the nineteenth century " for the brilliant putting in of particulars."   His famous third chapter was " worth the whole history beside . . . [because] it [was] so particular, so minute, so extraordinary."   He admired Scott, Michelet, and Thierry, historians of the people, because when they wrote, " men read with delight."   Another historian was praised for " his touches of folk history."   The whole conception of social history seemed to have been watered down to the search for quaint, folksy, literary effects.   The evolution of society and the science of history were nowhere mentioned.

A year before his death Eggleston brought out his second and last volume.   It consisted of essays on the mental outfit of the colonists, their quaint notions of behavior and education, their amazing medical beliefs and practices, their antiquated legal structure.   One often

[74] Edward Eggleston, " The New History," *Annual Report of the American Historical Association for 1900,* I, 37-47.

has the feeling of reading illustrations of nothing in particular.[75]

It was, in truth, a tired, sick old man who descanted somewhat incoherently on the "New History," a man who was too ill to appear in person to deliver his presidential address. And *The Transit of Civilization* was almost a death-bed effort to preserve in print the results of scholarly labors which a dying author could not bear to see moulder in the oblivion of manuscript literary remains.

Much of the transformation, however, was inherent in the life and ideas of the earlier Eggleston. He was, after all, for many years a novelist and littérateur and, indeed, published two novels after he had begun his historical work. Eggleston's principle of historical reconstruction offered, moreover, a constant temptation to depart from the sober effort at objectivity which he professed to regard as fundamental. To limn the character of the age was a noble experiment. To refract the past through one's own imagination was, in truth, only submission to the inevitable. But to combine that end with this method and hope to produce more than a commentary on one's own time and a reflection of one's own personality required a genius and a scholarship that was not Eggleston's. When he characterized the religious ardor of the seventeenth century as intolerance and petty scrupulosity, he was not pinning down the elusive *Zeitgeist*, but telling us that he, Eggleston, child of Darwin, had only contempt for that ardor. When he canonized Roger Williams, he invited approval perhaps of his own sense of right and justice, but hardly conveyed the spirit of the time. The combination of a literary orientation and the subjective approach to an iridescent time-spirit produced a result that seemed almost

[75] Compare Charles M. Andrews' review in the *Political Science Quarterly* (1902), XVII, 162-63.

inevitable: history became a collection of colorful details interlarded with the value-judgments of a tolerant, kindly personality.

The democratic sentiment that underlay his original conception of social history was also weakening. Something had happened to the frontier democrat. The one-time abolitionist had come to sneer at reformers, who, as he in effect put it, having abolished slavery or noisily approved its abolition by others now wished to abolish capital punishment and the marriage relation.[76] He praised Cleveland for calling out the Federal troops in the Pullman strike. The quondam agrarian democrat had nothing but violent condemnation for the Populist upsurge of 1896 and for Bryan, the leader of the embattled farmers joined in the rear by labor. Eggleston the democrat was, in short, for the people, but for him the people meant essentially the pioneer settlers who had braved the wilderness, the aroused colonists who had thrown off the British yoke, the self-reliant citizen-farmers who had broken the tough prairie soil and struggled to preserve their gains from the grasp of slaveowners and monopolistic railroads and banks. His democracy was sympathy for that struggle. It did not extend to the urban proletariat, the scum of the cities, the sweating aliens. These were not the American people. To Eggleston they seemed a bastard product of civilization gone awry. His democracy, his values, his ethics, were repelled and confused by this new smoke-stained America and those who seemed to represent it.

Out of his confusion grew pessimism. The channels of democracy seemed choked. The American dream seemed to have dissolved in the acid of greed and unlovely struggle. He turned in angry disgust from the present

---

[76] E. Eggleston, *The Graysons* (New York, 1905), p. 136. This novel was first published in 1888.

and despaired of the future of his country.   A devoted
friend testified in stilted verse that

> The rage for gold, the strife for power, the greed
> Of luxury—three vultures cursed of old—
> He saw them ere he died, with pinions bold
> Trail ominous shadows o'er his native mead.[77]

"The Lord Almighty help us, what are we coming to?"
was his pained comment on the state of the country on the
occasion of the Washington inaugural centenary celebra-
tion.[78]   The coming of the Spanish War moved him to
bitter outburst.

> Living right at the door of Congress in this tiresome time, I
> don't seem to care much for American citizenship; it is a brand
> that covers a discouraging lot of clap-trap; . . . . You will not
> take this too seriously—it only means that I am constitutionally
> not interested in politics.[79]

The country seemed in an ugly impasse.   And as disease
and weary age came upon him, Eggleston left democracy
and history to shift for themselves.

[77] O. C. Auringer, *Friendship's Crown of Verse, Being Memorials of
Edward Eggleston* (Clinton, N. Y., 1907), p. 16.

[78] Eggleston to Mrs. Seelye, April 30, 1889.

[79] Eggleston to Herbert B. Adams, April 14, 1898, printed in W. Stull
Holt, ed., *Historical Scholarship in the United States: As Revealed in the
Correspondence of Herbert B. Adams* (Baltimore, 1938), p. 253.

MIDDLE STATES REGIONALISM AND AMERICAN HISTORIOGRAPHY: A SUGGESTION

BY

ERIC F. GOLDMAN

Thousands of words have been written about the influence of regionalism on American historiography, but few of these words concern the Middle Atlantic states. This is hardly surprising. Long before the Civil War, New England, the South, and the West each contained a dominant pattern of thought which is generally referred to a dominant pattern of living. In the Middle States there was no equally dominant way of making a living and of living on what you made. Scholars inquiring into "The Mind of the Middle East" find themselves stopped, as Parrington was, by the realization that

Irving and Paulding and Cooper and Melville and Whitman reveal none of that strong community of taste and purpose that marks the Concord group, or the Boston-Cambridge group, or even the Charleston group. They expressed no common culture, they had been disciplined in no common faith, and they were held together by no common economic or political or intellectual interests. . . . [1]

Certainly the history written in the Middle States before the Civil War showed few marks of a positive regionalism. Typical in this respect was Edmund B. O'Callaghan, the man who put New York local history on its feet. In his *History of New Netherland*, O'Callaghan attacked the

[1] Vernon L. Parrington, *Main Currents in American Thought* (3 vols., New York, 1927-30), II, 183.

211

contention of George Bancroft that the colony owed its
municipal liberties to migrants from Connecticut, but the
New Yorker did not combat New England regionalism
with a Middle States regionalism. Instead O'Callaghan,
in a minimum of un-emotional words, traced the liberties
to the Dutch feudal code.[2] Even this negative approach
to regionalism was more likely the result of an Irish Catholic's dislike for English Puritans than any Middle States
feeling.[3] Boston's *North American Review* promptly
showed how different positive regionalism was by its comment on the *History of New Netherland.* The reviewer,
self-described as on " the New England side of this question," devoted most of his seventeen pages to fervent
support of the Bancroft contention and concluded with a
lyric of cultural imperialism.[4]

Perhaps the Middle States deserve attention in the history of regional influences just because they were not a
region in the sense that other sections of the country were.
By the time American historiography entered its enor-
mously productive period in the late nineteenth century,
the men of the Middle States had only this in common:
theirs was the tradition of being inbetween. Struck by
the middleness of the Middle States before the Civil War,
Frederick Jackson Turner wrote,

> The Middle region, entered by New York harbor, was an open
> door to all Europe. The tide-water part of the South represented
> typical Englishmen, modified by a warm climate and servile labor,
> and living in baronial fashion on great plantations; New England
> stood for a special English movement—Puritanism. The Middle

[2] Edmund B. O'Callaghan, *History of New Netherland* (2 vols., 2d
ed., 1855), I, 393.
[3] For O'Callaghan's strong Irish and Catholic attitude, see Francis S.
Guy, *Edmund Bailey O'Callaghan, A Study in American Historiography*
(The Catholic University of America Studies in American Church History,
XVIII, Washington, 1934), *passim.*
[4] *North American Review* (1846), LXII, 456, 464.

region was less English than the other sections. It had a wide mixture of nationalities, a varied society, the mixed town and county system of local government, a varied economic life, many religious sects. In short, it was a region mediating between New England and the South, and the East and the West. It represented that composite nationality which the contemporary United States exhibits, that juxtaposition of non-English groups, occupying a valley or a little settlement, and presenting reflections of the map of Europe in their variety. It was democratic and nonsectional, if not national; " easy, tolerant, and contented "; rooted strongly in material prosperity. It was typical of the modern United States. It was least sectional, not only because it lay between North and South but also because with no barriers to shut out its frontiers from its settled region, and with a system of connecting waterways, the Middle region mediated between East and West as well as between North and South. Thus it became the typically American region. Even the New Englander, who was shut out from the frontier by the Middle region, tarrying in New York or Pennsylvania on his westward march, lost the acuteness of his sectionalism on the way.[5]

Of course, this paragraph in Turner's famous essay is an explanation of the sentences, " The economic and social characteristics of the frontier worked against sectionalism. The men of the frontier had closer resemblances to the Middle region than to either of the other sections." [6] One need not wholly accept Turner's interpretation of the Middle States to suggest that the Inbetweeners were left by their tradition comparatively free to go along with, and often to lead the nationalization of American history after the Civil War.

Strikingly national in his interests was Herbert Baxter Adams, the founder of the colonial empire of history over which he presided at Johns Hopkins. By genealogy and

[5] " The Significance of the Frontier in American History," in *Annual Report of the American Historical Association for 1893* (Washington, 1894), p. 220.
[6] *Ibid.*, p. 219.

early education Adams was tied close to Plymouth Rock, but he completed his education in Europe and spent the mature years of his life in Baltimore. The violent Teutophilism Adams contracted in Europe was not a sectional disease but it could have been, and often was confined within sectional limits. Had Adams established his school of history at his alma mater, Amherst, he might well have concerned himself chiefly with the Anglo-Saxon origins of New England institutions. Working in the Middle States, Adams sent his students to ferret out Teutonic origins in Georgia and Wisconsin as well as in Massachusetts. Indeed, of the studies published under his direction, less than one-fourth treated New England subjects.[7] One of Adams' eulogists was doing more than eulogizing when he attributed to this adopted Inbetweener a large share of the credit for the revival of interest in Southern local history.[8] All sectional lines were cut across in other studies edited by Adams—for example, the work of young Nicholas Murray Butler. Already interesting himself in the promotion of unity within institutions, Dr. Butler produced a monograph entitled, *The Effect of the War of 1812 Upon the Consolidation of the Union*.[9] Not only as a teacher but also as an historical organizer, Adams' interests proved to be as broad as at least the eastern half of the continent. It was appropriate that he should be the moving spirit in organizing the American Historical Association which, as its friends exulted, was to " be neither local nor sectional, but truly national." [10]

[7] During Adams' editorship (1882-1901), the *Johns Hopkins Studies in Historical and Political Science* showed the following division of monographs on the basis of regional subject: Middle States—15; New England—15; the West—17; the South—32.

[8] B. J. Ramage, "Professor Herbert Baxter Adams," in *Herbert B. Adams, Tributes of Friends* (Baltimore, 1902), p. 63.

[9] Johns Hopkins University Studies in Historical and Political Science, Fifth Series, VII, Baltimore, 1887.

[10] The quotation is from an editorial in the *Nation,* reprinted in

Equally national in scope was the work of John Bach McMaster. Born in Brooklyn, educated at The College of the City of New York, for over thirty years a professor at the University of Pennsylvania, McMaster was nothing if not Middle Atlantic, and his *History of the People* gave space to sections which had been slighted. Though violently anti-slavery, McMaster was the first major historian born outside the South who gave as much space to that region as to New England.[11] Of life on the frontier he wrote so much and so sympathetically that he has been called a precursor of Turner.[12] This Inbetweener even remembered what both Northern and Southern history had usually forgotten—that something lay between the North and the South.

> [McMaster] brought to notice . . . [tart William Dunning, of New Jersey and New York, put it], the neglected fact that on rare occasions a gleam of intelligence had been discernible in other parts of the country than Massachusetts and South Carolina. Even New York and Philadelphia were assigned by him to a humble place in the broad picture of the national development.[13]

The wide focus of the *History of the People* appeared also in McMaster's influential school texts. The pub-

---

Papers of the American Historical Association (New York, 1886), I, i. For Adams' role in founding the Association, see W. Stull Holt, ed., *Historical Scholarship in the United States: As Revealed in the Correspondence of Herbert B. Adams* (Baltimore, 1938), p. 12.

[11] William T. Hutchinson, " John Bach McMaster," in William T. Hutchinson, ed., *The Marcus W. Jernegan Essays in American Historiography* (Chicago, 1937), p. 139.

[12] Michael Kraus, *A History of American History* (New York, 1937), p. 394.

[13] Dunning's letter in *Testimonial Dinner to John Bach McMaster . . . Letters Received* (Philadelphia, 1913), a pamphlet among the McMaster Papers. I have been permitted to use these papers through the generous courtesy of the historian's son, Dr. Philip D. McMaster, of the Rockefeller Institute for Medical Research, New York City.

15

lishers, appropriately enough, had gone to him for a book "in which the middle colonies and the country to the westward should receive more adequate treatment than they do in most of the current textbooks prepared from the ultra New England standpoint." [14] McMaster did not disappoint his publishers.

This Inbetweener contributed to the nationalization not only of the scope of American history but also of its interpretation. The large-scale as well as the textbook story of America's past had been written largely by New Englanders and they had made it read, as one Middle States historian phrased it, like the "Expansion of New England." [15] The conception that brought fame to Mc-Master was emphatically national—a story of the people of all the classes of all the sections. Quite obviously this historian preferred Northerners to Southerners, and William McKinley to William Jennings Bryan, but no one who took the *History of the People* seriously—as thousands did—could believe that America's past was essentially either the expansion of New England or the restriction of the South. [16]

With less research but far more literary skill, Woodrow Wilson added to the de-regionalizing influence of Middle States historiography. Perhaps the young historian was led in this direction by a Southern boyhood, but equal emphasis may be placed on his training under Adams and his manhood in Maryland, Pennsylvania, and New Jersey. If America was really the expansion of New England, Wilson told the New England Society of New

[14] Russell Hinman, of the American Book Co., to McMaster, Nov. 3, 1894, MS, McMaster Papers.

[15] Woodrow Wilson, "The Proper Perspective of American History," *Forum* (1895), XIX, 544.

[16] For a discussion of McMaster's prepossessions, see the author's Master's thesis, "John Bach McMaster, The Emergence of Non-Political American History," MS, Johns Hopkins Library, pp. 111-33.

York, then New England had certainly been spread thin.[17] Before a national audience, Wilson could state his point without irony:

In talking of the New England and of the Southern forces in our life, we have dismissed the Middle States from the reckoning under the impression that they were only a region in which New England and the South shaded off to a middle neutral line lying, no doubt, somewhere in Pennsylvania. As a matter of fact, if we are determined to be partial in our view and to pick out a single set of influences to be traced through the later intricacies of our history, the Middle States have rather more claim to our choice than either New England or the South.[18]

Of course, Wilson's close friend, Turner, was more important than any Inbetweener in the assault on New Englandism, but Turner substituted one regionalism for another. Wilson, though he accepted most of the frontier thesis, never became a Western regionalist. Though Wilson said things that could have been carried further to a Middle States thesis, he stopped. If you must have a regionalism, his tone was, then others have even better claims than New England, but why indulge in regionalism of any kind? It was, in a sense, O'Callaghan all over again. This Middle Atlantic rebuke to regionalism, this negative nationalization has manifested itself recently in the writing of Richard H. Shryock, born in Philadelphia and now Professor of American History at the Univer-

---

[17] "The Puritan," in Ida M. Tarbell, ed., *Selected Literary and Political Papers and Addresses of Woodrow Wilson* (3 vols., New York, 1925-27), I, 105.

[18] "Goldwin Smith's 'Views' On Our Political History," *Forum* (1893), XVI, 496. In another place, Wilson added, "The local history of the Middle States,—New York, New Jersey, and Pennsylvania,—is much more structurally a part of the characteristic life of the nation as a whole than is the history of New England communities or of the several States and regions of the South." "The Proper Perspective of American History," *Forum* (1895), XIX, 544.

sity of Pennsylvania. Discussing "Philadelphia and the Flowering of New England," Professor Shryock argued not that Philadelphia had flowered more but "that Boston once excelled in cultural achievement by the simple device of defining culture in terms of those things in which Boston excelled." [19]

The nationalizing approach of the Inbetweeners brought important results in their handling of the Civil War and Reconstruction. The war had continued to be fought in histories long after Gettysburg, and many of the men who gave up artillery replaced it with something hardly less sectional—the olive-branch. Wilson, throwing aside gun and olive-branch alike, brought New England and Southern traditions together in a larger synthesis. The South was right in law but wrong in history, ran the premise of his book, *Division and Reunion*. The North, on the other hand, was wrong in law but right in history. Proceeding from this premise, Wilson concluded that there was no American nation until after the Civil War.[20] In this way, as a contemporary reviewer put it, Wilson refused "to engage in the old debate upon the ground originally occupied by the disputants, but leads us away to another position, from which both sides of the shield can easily be seen." [21] Little wonder that Wilson's approach became conventional in the rising national historiography.[22]

Meanwhile, Reconstruction was being fitted into the same type of matrix by William A. Dunning, the Plainfield, New Jersey boy who had received most of his higher

---

[19] *The Pennsylvania Magazine of History and Biography* (1940), LXIV, 313.

[20] *Division and Reunion* (New York, 1893), especially pp. 211-12 of the 1899 edition.

[21] Unsigned review of *Division and Reunion,* in *Atlantic Monthly* (1893), LXXII, 275.

[22] See William E. Dodd's discussion of *Division and Reunion,* in *Woodrow Wilson and His Work* (New York, 1920), p. 28.

education at Columbia and was setting up his own historical school at that Middle States university. Dunning had no use for the men who made a " *diabolus ex machina* . . . of the raw head and bloody bones of a slavocracy," but he also showed little interest in reinterpreting Reconstruction as a means of defending or placating the South.[23] Dunning did not even wish to give the South the major share of space in telling the story because to him Reconstruction was a " step in the progress of the American nation. In this aspect the North claims our principal attention." [24] The same national approach permitted the Columbia professor to present the besmirched Andrew Johnson as a man of " integrity of purpose, force of will, and rude intellectual force." [25] Of course, Southern students flocked to Dunning's seminar, as Southerners delighted in Wilson's writings, but these historians had as little use for the blue-baiters as for the gray-baiters. Inbetweeners, they spoke for their region by being deregionalizers.

This Inbetweener thesis correlates with the present trend of American historiography, and suggests a future. With the increasing industrialization of the whole country, the South, the West, and New England no longer have dominant ways of life so distinct from each other. In the mixture of their interests and ideas, Oregon and Alabama, even Maine, resemble the old Middle States more than they resemble themselves seventy-five years ago. As more and more of the states have become Middle States in this economic and cultural sense, conspicuously regional-minded historians have diminished in influence.

[23] The quotation is from " A Generation of American Historiography," in J. G. de Roulhac Hamilton, ed., *Truth in History and other Essays by William A. Dunning* (New York, 1937), p. 156.
[24] Dunning, *Reconstruction, Political and Economic* (New York, 1907), Author's Preface.
[25] *Ibid.*, p. 19.

The steadily rising interest in economic interpretations, urban syntheses, and similar approaches means, among other things, that historians are looking at the country more along horizontal lines of social groupings than along vertical lines of regionalism. Southern Agrarians and some of the Turnerites and New Englanders are disturbed; but John Bach McMaster, we may suspect, would have nodded his approval.